The TEACHING CHURCH

The TEACHING CHURCH

Moving Christian Education to ***Center Stage***

EUGENE C. ROEHLKEPARTAIN

Foreword by Donald L. Griggs

ABINGDON PRESS
Nashville

THE TEACHING CHURCH:
MOVING CHRISTIAN EDUCATION TO CENTER STAGE

Effective Christian Education: A National Study of Protestant Congregations, conducted by Search Institute, on which this book is based, is a landmark study of more than 11,000 adults and youths in six U.S. denominations: Christian Church (Disciples of Christ), Evangelical Lutheran Church in America, Presbyterian Church (U.S.A.), Southern Baptist Convention, United Church of Christ, and United Methodist Church. Major funding for the project was provided by the Lilly Endowment and the participating denominations.

94 95 96 97 98 99 00 01 02 — 10 9 8 7 6 5 4

This book is printed on recycled, acid-free paper.

Library of Congress Cataloging-in-Publication Data

Roehlkepartain, Eugene C., 1962–
The teaching church:moving Christian education to center stage/
Eugene C. Roehlkepartain;foreword by Donald L. Griggs.
p. cm.
Includes bibliographical references
ISBN 0-687-41083-5 (alk. paper)
1. Christian education. I. Title.
BV1471.2.R645 1993
268'.804'0973—dc20 92-41987

MANUFACTURED IN THE UNITED STATES OF AMERICA

To my father,
Dr. Jack Partain,
whose enthusiasm for Christian education
is infectious

Contents

Foreword

Christian Education at a Crossroads

DONALD L. GRIGGS

Christian education for mainline Protestant congregations is at a crossroads. At this moment in history, it is not clear which path churches will choose.

• Will they continue with "business as usual"? Or will they decide to raise Christian education to a higher priority?

• Will they continue to believe that the problems are greater than they can solve with their own limited resources? Or will they become more creative and committed to seeking solutions to their own unique situations?

• Will leaders continue to despair the declining attendance and diminished influence they are experiencing with their present programs? Or will they experiment with new models for Christian education that are relevant to their faith tradition and to the real needs of their people?

• Will churches continue to be satisfied with whatever little time, energy, and money their people are able to give? Or will they challenge their children, youths, and adults with increased expectations of commitment?

• Will Christian education leaders continue the quest for the latest, classiest, most appealing, and attractive program or resource? Or will they reclaim some of the strengths and proven successes of the past that have been abandoned because they were not "modern" enough?

• Will churches continue to identify Christian education primarily as a Sunday program for children? Or will they explore ways to increase the involvement of youths and adults in a through-the-week, lifelong process of learning about and growing in Christian faith?

• Will church leaders continue to be attracted by an "entertainment mode" of programming? Or will they renew their commitment to present the gospel with integrity and substance?

• Will Christian education continue to be seen as separate, with its own programs, staffs, budgets, facilities, and resources? Or will it begin to be seen as an indispensable, integral part of the church's whole ministry?

EMERGING CLUES

Many signs suggest that too many churches will continue down the path of least effort and challenge. On the other hand, there are emerging clues that many church leaders and others involved in educational ministry are challenged by the path that leads to renewal and increased effectiveness in Christian education, and thereby renewal for the whole church.

In a recent three-day period, I received four phone calls from four different cities in the United States. These calls represent conversations I have had in the past several years with many pastors, educators, and church leaders. The calls and conversations are, for me, hints that there is a grassroots ferment in many places. This search for new directions implies that leaders are willing to take the path that will be less certain and require more risk. They are sure that "business as usual" is no longer appropriate. Each phone call was from someone in the midst of rethinking the ministry of Christian education in his or her church.

A pastor asked, "Do you know of any churches that have been successful in their Christian education by doing it at a time of the week other than Sunday morning?" The question was prompted by a recommendation from his church's Christian education committee the week before. It was suggested that the traditional Sunday school be discontinued for six months, so that a task force could evaluate why their program was not as successful as they want it to be and to propose new strategies. In the meantime, the committee plans to include the children as part of the worshiping congregation for the whole service each Sunday. "Do you have any resources or procedures to recommend?" he asked.

Another pastor called with a similar concern: "We are doing a good job of teaching the Bible on Wednesday afternoon in our Logos Program, but we're doing a lousy job of teaching on Sunday morning. We have a surplus of teachers for Wednesday and can hardly persuade anyone to teach on Sunday. How come? Is there something else we can do with the Sunday-school hour that would make it more interesting and effective?"

A director of Christian education called with a question about strategies and resources for teaching the Bible. She said that many adults in her church expressed interest in studying the Bible (also identified as the highest interest of adults in the *Effective Christian Education* study), but when Bible-study classes are offered, only a few people show up. "What's the answer?" she asked.

The fourth call was from a mother of two children whom I had never met; her sister is a friend. She has been a teacher in her church for several years; now she is superintendent of Sunday school. The church is searching for a new director of Christian education, and she is on the committee to write a job description. She expressed great frustration: "We don't want someone to come to our church and do the same old thing. We want someone with energy and imagination who will lead us to find better ways. How do we write a job description for such a person? How can we find someone like that?"

In each instance, the conversation lasted a half-hour or more. Much energy, much passion, much frustration were expressed in each voice. I listened carefully to each person and asked probing questions to get to the heart of the matter.

It was impossible to make specific recommendations without being on the scene to gather more information and perspective. Yet, several specific suggestions were relevant to each situation. I advised that they find others in their church with similar concerns. Spend time with them praying, reading the Bible, reading other resources, discussing what they read, sharing their concerns and visions for Christian education, and charting a course of action.

None of the people who called knew about the Search Institute study, *Effective Christian Education: A National Study of Protestant Congregations.* Needless to say, each one learned about it before we finished our conversation, along with my recommendation to engage in a study of the report, using the available resources (see Selected Resources). I affirmed each person, confirming that they were on the right track by raising such questions. I suggested that they keep their questions in the forefront of their thinking and praying, and keep working toward solutions. Reach for high goals. Be willing to risk rejection or failure, but stay faithful to the shared vision.

KEY THEMES

As I reflect on effective Christian education in a teaching church, I am sure several factors will make a discernible difference in enabling people to mature in faith. All these are confirmed by the *Effective Christian Education* report.

It is not just a matter of education; there must be an emphasis on nurture. Christian education is *more* than learning Bible stories, doctrine, and all else that contributes to one's faith heritage. Effective Christian education involves people of mature faith nurturing others who are growing in faith. Such nurture includes caring relationships, meaningful conversations, working together in a variety of serving activities, sharing faith stories, and being with the larger faith community in workshop and fellowship, as well as in many other activities.

Values in educational strategies from the past must be reclaimed. Our highly technical, computerized, multimedia, fast-everything society tempts church leaders to think that Christian education resources and programs must reflect these contemporary phenomena. Sharing a story in conversation with one person or a small group; involving parents in the Christian nurture of their children; expressing ideas, feelings, beliefs through writing, speaking, constructing, or dramatizing; participating in mission projects to serve others—these strategies are as valid today as they ever were.

Christian educators often have been guilty of emphasizing the latest fad to the point that it becomes worn out. And then they seek the next "new thing," instead of developing a repertoire of teaching strategies that will serve well for a lifetime.

New models of Christian education must be discovered and implemented. On the one hand, we affirm the value of educational strategies from the past. On the other hand, we affirm the need to develop and implement new models. Churches must consider carefully the needs and interests of their people and, at the same time, evaluate whether those needs and interests are being addressed.

Adult Christians shared their faith with the younger generations for eighteen centuries without a Sunday school. Then, for almost two centuries, Sunday school served the people well. However, if the Sunday school is no longer an effective way of nurturing children, youths, and adults, shouldn't we be searching for a structure that will do the job of Christian nurture better?

Christian education must be viewed holistically, not as a separate entity. Every aspect of a church's ministry contains educational implications. Basic principles of teaching and learning include: involving everyone in the process, being sensitive to needs of the participants, having a clear focus on what is to be communicated and accomplished, enabling participants to make connections between the subject matter and their own lives, providing opportunities to give expression to what they think and believe, and motivating them to put into practice what they believe.

These principles are relevant to planning for worship, even though worship should never be seen as an educational event. They are also appropriate considerations for conducting meetings of church groups, organizing a stewardship program, or planning a mission and outreach emphasis.

NEW INTERPRETATION

Many leaders share some of these convictions and want to improve the Christian education ministries in their churches. When they explore the findings found in *Effective Christian Education: A National Study of Protestant Congregations,* many will find corroboration of what they know in their own churches.

The statistical results of this landmark study by Search Institute have been available since the Spring of 1990. Articles have been written, workshops attended, and discussions held that have engaged many church leaders. However, interpretation of the statistics, with reflection upon their implications for educational ministry in particular congregations has not been available to a larger constituency.

That deficiency is now addressed by Eugene Roehlkepartain in this book, *The Teaching Church.* This is not just a how-to book that outlines ways to improve Christian education in a particular church. It includes many, many practical suggestions for various possibilities.

And this is not just a book filled with graphs and charts which present a multitude of statistics. It provides a helpful presentation of significant data gleaned from the study, supported by illustrations from the many people and churches involved.

Neither is this just another book on education theory. Here are revealed many theoretical implications that give us much to explore.

This book provides much that is helpful to church leaders who will invest time and energy in discerning the needs of Christian education and devising ways to respond to those needs.

Acknowledgments

Taking credit for a book such as this is almost dishonest. Most of the work took place before I joined the staff of Search Institute, as the *Effective Christian Education* project team developed survey instruments, surveyed congregations, analyzed data, and interpreted the study results. Without those years of labor by dozens of people on Search Institute staff, on the project advisory committee, and in congregations across the country, this book would not have been possible. I am deeply indebted to them all.

In particular, several colleagues on Search Institute's staff guided, supported, and encouraged me through the process of writing this book. Carolyn H. Eklin's careful evaluations, patient explanations, and unending affirmation made working on this book a pleasure. Thanks also to Dr. Peter L. Benson and Dr. James V. Gambone, who entrusted this important work to me and offered insight, advice, and analysis along the way. Several reviewers enhanced the manuscript with their critiques: Duane Ewers, Charles Logsdon Christopher, Sara P. Little, and Marvin Simmers.

I am also grateful to Jill Reddig and Paul Franklyn of Abingdon Press. Not only have they believed in and advocated for this book, but their clear and precise editorial crafting made me comfortable in turning the manuscript over to them. I knew the book would be better when it left their desks.

Finally, I would like to thank my family—my wife, Jolene, and my son, Micah—who saw less of me than I would have liked during this project. Your love, support, and encouragement kept me going through draft after draft.

All these people made writing this book a learning and growing time for me. I hope that reading it will be learning and growing time for each reader.

Introduction

Churches at Risk?

A Nation at Risk—That was the alarming title of a 1983 government report on public education in the United States. After 18 months of study, the National Commission on Excellence in Education concluded bluntly that public education was being washed away in a "tide of mediocrity."

"For the first time in the history of our country," the report warned, "the education skills of one generation will not surpass, will not equal, will not even approach those of their parents." The report concluded that "our very future as a Nation and a people" is at risk.[1]

The educators went on to list a plethora of problems. Teachers weren't qualified. Academic standards and requirements were almost nonexistent. The nation lagged behind most other industrialized countries.

"If an unfriendly foreign power had attempted to impose on America the mediocre education performance that exists today," the report declared, "we might well have viewed it as an act of war."

The report created a furor around the country. After years of neglect, parents, politicians, and business leaders began to pay attention to schools. By 1988, *Newsweek* reported that the report had "set off a wave of reform not seen since the sputnik era."[2] By that time, all fifty states had adopted some sort of reform. More than a dozen had overhauled their school systems. Many had changed graduation standards, raised teacher requirements, and increased teachers' salaries. And while dramatic improvement wasn't visible on a national level, educators had begun pointing toward individual success stories. The report's conclusions had caught people's attention and motivated them toward positive—often innovative—experimentation and change.

PARALLEL PROBLEMS

In recent decades, many U.S. churches have sensed a similar level of crisis. Since the 1950s, mainline churches have faced declining memberships, increased illiteracy about the Bible and the faith, and a fear that faith was being reduced to a superficial, peripheral part of life for many professing Christians. What was happening to the churches? How real or serious were these problems? What was causing them? What could be done to reverse harmful trends?

In 1986, leaders were asking those kinds of questions. Search Institute interviewers found widespread hand-wringing about mainline churches' general failure to attract young adults and young families, an inactivity in congregational life, loss of members, and a loss of denominational identity.

Furthermore, interviewers also discovered deep concerns about Christian education, including disinterest among adults, high "dropout rates" among teenagers, trouble finding and keeping volunteer leaders, and inability to involve parents in their children's religious education.

In response to these and other issues, Search Institute—a Minneapolis-based nonprofit research organization—began an unprecedented study of Christian education in the United States, titled *Effective Christian Education: A National Study of Protestant Congregations.* Funded by the Lilly Endowment, the study took more than three years and surveyed 11,122 adults, teenagers, pastors, Christian education coordinators, and teachers in 561 congregations, in five mainline denominations (which represent 85% of "mainline Protestantism"), and the Southern Baptist Convention (see Figure 1 for details).[3]

ELUSIVE MEASUREMENTS

From the beginning, the researchers faced a formidable task. How does one measure Christian education's impact? Many church-growth advocates point to increasing numbers as signs of improvement and sliding numbers as symptoms of decline. A church's budgetary health is monitored for signs of irregularity. Others watch for stable ministries, as reflected in pastors' and other leaders' tenure in a congregation.

Though sometimes useful (and the realities they represent important), these criteria seem simplistic at best and theologically suspect at worst. Such numbers simply don't tell the whole story. Indeed, if Jesus' ministry had been judged solely "by the numbers," he certainly would have been deemed a failure.

First, he may have had a following at times. But in the end, he had only eleven true disciples. You could argue that he attracted people initially, but often they didn't stay. His budget wasn't impressive either. Jesus himself said, "The Son of Man has nowhere to lay his head" (Matt.

8:20). And concerning the matter of tenure: Jesus' total ministry lasted only three years—hardly adequate by today's standards. To be sure, some people were very satisfied with his ministry. But others were quite displeased and had him crucified.

Jesus' ministry focused on changing people's lives. He apparently evaluated his ministry in terms of subtle—and therefore difficult to measure—qualities.

In a parallel fashion, researchers tried to develop a new way to measure congregational effectiveness. After interviewing theologians and denominational leaders, they suggested that *the primary goal of congregational life is to nurture in people a vibrant, life-changing faith—the kind of faith that shapes a person's way of being, thinking, and acting.*

Then researchers developed and conducted in-depth surveys that evaluated people's faith maturity and the factors that enhance—or detract from—a growing faith. The resulting data led to four central conclusions, which are at the heart of this book.

1. In general, U.S. Christians don't have mature faith. According to the criteria used in the study, only 32 percent of adults have a mature faith, and most youths (64 percent) have an undeveloped faith. For most people in our churches, faith is dormant and inactive.

2. Christian education is the most important vehicle within congregational life for helping people grow in their faith. Done well, Christian education—in all its many expressions—has more potential for promoting faith than any other area of congregational life. Getting people involved in education is the key to addressing the passive faith found in the study. Richard Robert Osmer puts the challenge strongly in *A Teachable Spirit: Recovering the Teaching Office in the Church:*

> The restoration of a church that can teach with authority . . . may be *the* pressing issue before mainline churches today. . . . The American mainline Protestant churches are at a crossroads. Which path they take may very well rest on whether they can restore the teaching ministry of the church to its rightful place of importance.[4]

3. Despite its potential impact, most congregations don't have effective Christian education. The average congregation has in place only about 46 percent of the factors that make its educational ministries effective. Indeed, most Christian education in congregations revolves around outdated processes, methods, and content. The original research report concluded:

> Christian education in a majority of congregations is a tired enterprise in need of reform. Often out-of-touch with adult and adolescent needs, it experiences increasing difficulty in finding and motivating volunteers, faces general disinterest among its "clients," and employs models and procedures that have changed little over time.[5]

4. Concrete changes in churches can improve educational effectiveness and help people to grow in faith. We don't need to sit and wring our hands helplessly, watching members leave or stagnate. The keys to effective Christian education are within the reach of most congregations. That's what *The Teaching Church* is all about.

WORDS OF CAUTION

Research such as this study can help in at least two important ways. First, it can confirm, with numbers and percentages, things about which we already had hunches. This confirmation can spur us to act on our hunches, addressing the problems at hand.

An equally important function of research is to challenge our preconceptions with new information, insights, and perspectives. It can point to issues we may never have considered. Or it can challenge us to rethink the way we operate. The *Effective Christian Education* study helps a great deal in both areas.

But research isn't the final word. It's not a divinely inspired process without limitations. Several cautions must be kept in mind about this study.

• First, the faith-maturity scale that lies behind the study is not infallible. It's not the final word on what it means to be a mature Christian. It is simply one perspective on faith, based on a set of 38 statements.

• Second, the implications and suggestions that grow out of the study are not a prepackaged kit for building a Christian education program. The study's findings are limited to the questions asked, the people talked to, and the mental acuity of the people who interpreted the results, including myself. The study may have implications that haven't been noticed. It may have flaws that skew results. And particular congregations may face realities and concerns that aren't addressed.

The goal of this book is not to create a nation of McChurches with bland, prepackaged programs and innocuous decor. The goal is to challenge churches to reflect, creatively and intentionally, about their

Christian education. Then, based on a congregation's specific needs and heritage, church leaders can create their own vision of effective Christian education and find a way to make that vision a reality.

In some senses this book is like a specification guide an architect might use. It tells how many rooms, what the rooms will be, and other basic information. The architect would also factor in his or her knowledge of traffic patterns, materials, and so on, in conceptualizing the space. The architect then uses the information to design the building. Within the general guidelines, the architect has a great deal of freedom and flexibility. Similarly, this book describes some of the "raw materals" that are important to effective Christian education. These can be put together in many different ways, depending on the needs of each location.

• Third, this book does not seek to spell out a comprehensive, historical, theoretical, or theological base for Christian education. Numerous other books have adequately and thoroughly addressed this concern. While theological and theoretical issues are alluded to in various contexts, they are not the focus of this effort. Rather, it is hoped that this book will be useful to those who seek to bring various approaches into dialogue with the study's insights.

CREATIVE POSSIBILITIES

When educators began to analyze the report *A Nation at Risk*, most agreed with its findings about the state of education. But many disagreed with its recommendations for change. Others believed alternate methods would be more effective.

So each educator began experimenting and exploring. Special—often controversial—schools were started to explore ways to meet specific needs. New training and administrative processes were developed. Some have worked; some haven't.

Yet, despite the debates, one could argue that the initial report was the catalyst for change and innovation—innovation that the original writers may never have imagined. Essentially, the report made education a top priority for the nation. That alone made the report valuable.

Perhaps *The Teaching Church* can have a similar effect in churches. You may disagree with its details, or you may have other proposals to consider. But if the book causes you to take a hard look at Christian education and begin reforming or renewing your ministry, it has accomplished its purpose.

Figure 1

Project Description

The *Effective Christian Education* study is unprecedented in its size and scope. Here are some details.

• **Participating Denominations**—A nationally representative sample was drawn from a random group of 150 congregations, within each of the following denominations:

Denomination	Number of Participating Congregations
Christian Church (Disciples of Christ)	102
Evangelical Lutheran Church in America	110
Presbyterian Church (U.S.A.)	101
Southern Baptist Convention	68
United Church of Christ	93
United Methodist Church	87

• **People Surveyed**—The study surveyed 11,122 people in 561 randomly chosen congregations, with sampling stratified to ensure representative distribution by church size. The breakdown of five samples is as follows:

Adults (not on church staff or involved in Christian education leadership)	3,567
Adolescents (grades 7-12)	3,121
Teachers	3,466
Pastors	519
Christian education coordinators	499

Sample sizes were weighted to ensure that the data maximally would represent the national denominational populations.

• **Survey of Administration**—In 1988, in-depth surveys were administered in nationally representative congregations, under the supervision of a project director in each congregation. Survey sessions were governed by a set of standardized procedures described in a detailed administration manual. Careful procedures were established to guarantee and preserve confidentiality for each respondent. Survey sessions lasted from one and one-half to two and one-half hours.

• **Site Visits**—In 1989, teams of trained observers visited 52 congregations that were judged to have particular strengths in helping members grow in faith. Twenty-one congregations were gleaned from survey results because of evidence from the surveys that they were particularly effective in nurturing faith. The remaining 23 were racial/ethnic congregations nominated by denominational staff. Stories from these site visits are included throughout this book.

Chapter 1

Moving Christian Education to Center Stage

"Why do we want people to come to church?"

The people around the church basement tables seem puzzled by the question.

"Why do we want people to come to church? Or why *should* they come?" the questioner prods. "Or maybe there aren't any good reasons." That comment shakes out some answers.

"So they'll learn about Jesus," a Sunday school teacher suggests.

"To help them grow in their faith."

"To learn how to serve others in Christ's name."

Now things are rolling! So the questioner keeps pushing: "Why do *we* want people to come to *this* church?"

Silence again.

"Aren't there any other motives . . . honestly?"

"Well," comes a reluctant answer, "we sure could use more pledges to meet budget." People laugh, but they're also nodding their heads.

"It's more than money," someone else protests. "Having committed people makes the church stronger, more stable."

"Yeah, it adds energy to the church when people are excited to be here."

"Besides," says someone near the front, "being part of a church helps them, too. They experience the warmth and support of the faith community."

"So," the leader sums up, "we basically want people to come to church for two reasons. First, to grow in their faith. And second, to become loyal, active parts of the community. Two words: faith and loyalty. That's where we want to go, right?"

Heads nod.

"How do we get there?"

FINDING A PURPOSE

How *do* we get there? How do we help people grow in their faith, while also promoting a sense of commitment to Christ's body, the church? Are faith and loyalty magical, spontaneous characteristics over which the church has little or no influence?

Search Institute's study of six denominations, *Effective Christian Education: A National Study of Protestant Congregations,* discovered that churches can and do significantly influence people's faith and loyalty. By concentrating on the central aim of nurturing faith, congregations also gain commitment. Furthermore, the area of church life that has by far the most influence on faith maturity and growth in faith is Christian education. So if our goal is to nurture faith and loyalty in the congregation, *nothing in church life matters more than Christian education.*

Can such a statement be justified? *Effective Christian Education* reached this conclusion by first evaluating the faith maturity of 11,000 adults and youths. (The process and framework for evaluating faith maturity is explored in chapter 2.) Then researchers analyzed factors in the lives of people who are growing in faith, factors that generally are not present in the lives of those who are not growing. By isolating the unique factors, researchers determined which ones might contribute to a person's faith maturity.[1]

To illustrate, suppose a manufacturer makes two types of ice cream: chocolate chip and rocky road. The rocky road quickly sells out, but the chocolate chip sits on the shelf. The manufacturer begins comparing the two. Both have equal amounts of cream, sugar, salt, milk, and chocolate chips, so those ingredients don't make a difference. Both are in similar packages. But the rocky road also has walnuts, marshmallows, and chocolate syrup. So, the manufacturer concludes, the walnuts, marshmallows, and chocolate syrup must be important ingredients for attracting people. Further tests might help identify which one—or which combination—is most attractive.

Similarly, each person's faith is influenced by a wide range of factors. Researchers examined more than twenty "ingredients"—both within and outside the church—that might influence faith and loyalty. By comparing people who are growing in faith with those who are not, the study found which "ingredients" appear to make a difference and which ones don't. Obviously, the mix is more complex than a batch of ice cream, and connections are more difficult to make. But the interrelationships are strong enough that we can be reasonably sure they are important.

In some ways, the findings aren't all that surprising (see Figure 2). Of all biographical factors, family religiousness has the greatest influence on teenagers' faith maturity. For years, researchers have affirmed parents' influence on their young people's values and beliefs. And it seems logical that lifetime church involvement for adults would significantly influence faith maturity.

What *is* surprising is the power of Christian education in areas of faith and loyalty. Christian education relates consistently to mature faith. That is, people toward the higher end of faith maturity tend to be particularly distinguished by their involvement in Christian education.

Figure 2
Influences on Faith Maturity

What factors have the greatest influence on growth in faith? This chart shows factors with the strongest and weakest relationships to faith for both adults and youths. While these statistical connections don't prove cause and effect, these correlations do suggest areas of the greatest influence. As you can see, the lists are similar for both ages.

	Adults	**Youths**
Strong relationship	• lifetime church involvement • lifetime involvement in effective Christian education	• lifetime family religiousness • lifetime involvement in effective Christian education
Modest relationship	• friends' and spouse religiousness • involvement in a caring church • involvement in nonchurch religious activity • serving others • family religiousness during childhood and youth	• lifetime church involvement • friends' religiousness • involvement in a caring church • involvement in nonchurch religious activity • serving others
Weak relationship	• age • gender • income • education	• age • gender • geographic region
No clear relationship	• geographic region • denomination • congregational size	• income • denomination • congregation size

So while effective Christian education isn't the only thing that matters in church life, it is by far the most influential factor in nourishing faith. Thus, if congregations want to enhance people's faith and loyalty, the best approach is to involve members in effective Christian education.

In the study, and in this book, Christian education is defined broadly as programs and events intentionally offered by a congregation to teach faith to children, teenagers, and adults. These might include Sunday school, church school, Bible studies, confirmation, discipleship training, camping, retreats, workshops, youth ministry, children's and adult choirs, men's and women's auxiliaries, prayer groups, drama groups, vacation Bible (or church) school, new-member classes, and intergenerational or family events.

FOCUS ON NURTURING FAITH

Some may argue that the church has other roles and responsibilities that are more important than nurturing faith. However, to say that congregations' primary aim is to nurture faith is not to say that churches should become self-absorbed and self-serving. Just the opposite. What it suggests is that the congregations should be primarily about the task of "equipping the saints" for ministry. The church structure and institution should empower people for ministry, rather than accomplishing the ministry for them.

Too often, members become passive because little is expected of them. It may be helpful here to imagine what the parable of the sheep and goats might have sounded like if Jesus had intended that people only designate others to serve for them.

> Then the king will say to those on his right hand, "Come, you that are blessed by my Father, inherit the kingdom prepared for you from the foundation of the world; for I was hungry and you sent a donation to your favorite charity, I was thirsty and you sent a missionary to drill wells, I was a stranger and you sent me to a welcoming committee, I was naked and you sent me to a thrift store, I was sick and you sent your pastor to visit me, I was in prison and you sent a chaplain to hold prayer services with me."

Not that charities or missionaries or welcoming committees or thrift stores or pastors or chaplains don't have important roles. Each does serve important needs, and each must be supported. What's important here is the word *sent*. Each of these activities separates individual Christians from ministry and acting on faith. Instead of acting on faith, too many church members leave ministry to others.

The challenge to congregations, then, is to help each member see himself or herself as an active minister—as a representative of Christ in the world. When local churches take seriously this responsibility to nurture each person's faith, the work of the church will be done through and by its members, who are, after all, the church.

HOW ARE WE DOING?

If Christian education does indeed have unparalleled power to nurture faith, how well are churches using that potential? A blunt answer: Not well. By and large, mainline churches don't involve many members in Christian education. Compounding the problem, most Christian education programs don't include basic elements of an effective program. Let's look at each issue separately.

Christian Education Involvement—In most congregations, Christian education includes only a faithful remnant. Christian education involvement plummets after childhood, when 60 percent of children attend Christian education. By adulthood, only an average of 28 percent of churchgoing adults actively participate in Christian education (see Figure 27). As the study's summary report concluded, "If nothing matters more than Christian education, then the weakest link in promoting faith and loyalty occurs here—a failure to draw adolescents and adults into the sphere of Christian education."[2]

The decline isn't steady across the years. The most dramatic drop-off in involvement is between ninth and tenth grades, when we see a 17 percent slide in youth participation (from 52% in grades 7 through 9 to 35% in grades 10 through 12). Thus, churches are losing young people at the very time when they are making major life choices and setting life patterns. And, given the low participation of adults, it's clear that most teenagers will not become active again as adults.

Christian Education Effectiveness—In addition to concern about youth and adult involvement in Christian education, people who do participate in Christian education are not necessarily experiencing effective Christian education. Thus, their involvement doesn't have its potential impact. To reach this conclusion, researchers isolated a variety of factors that tend to be part of effective Christian education programs. These center around three areas:

1. *Youth Education*—Researchers identified 25 factors that make a youth education program effective. They can be grouped into seven categories: teachers, pastor, educational process, educational content, peer involvement, parental involvement, and goals. (These are explored in chapters 7-9.) In an average mainline congregation, only 36 percent of these factors are in place.

2. *Adult Education*—For adults, researchers isolated 17 factors that increase a program's effectiveness. They involve teachers, pastors, educational process, educational content, peer involvement, and goals. (These are also explored in chapters 7-9.) In the average mainline congregation, only 46 percent of the factors are in place.

3. *Educational Foundations*—The third area of effectiveness factors involves administrative and governing procedures in Christian education, which affect all ages. Foundations include teacher training, teacher faith formation, planning, governing board support, pastor's training, evaluation, teacher recognition, and coordinated study, with a total of 18 specific factors. (These are explored in chapters 6 and 7.) On average, congregations succeed in 47 percent of these administrative areas.

Taken together, these findings paint a gloomy portrait of the state of Christian education today. Indeed, few, if any, observers believe that Christian education is thriving. For example, evangelical author Tim Stafford examined Sunday schools in the evangelical world soon after the Search Institute study was first released. He concluded that "practically everyone involved, from curriculum publishers to ordinary Sunday-morning teachers, expresses frustration with [Sunday school at] present and uncertainty about its future. . . . Nearly everyone says it has problems with no solution in sight."[3]

How has Christian education reached its current state? Though this study doesn't answer that historical question, its findings seem consistent with C. Ellis Nelson's analysis in *How Faith Matures.* In reviewing the shape of religious education since Old Testament times, he argues that churches always have developed faith-nurturing strategies that are appropriate for a given social/historical situation. In the New Testament, for example, Christians were a small, persecuted minority, trying to figure out what it meant to be followers of Christ. They used the educational strategies they knew from the synagogue, which involved a community of believers sharing their faith, parents instructing children, and adults seeking to follow God.[4]

However, he writes, our current models of Christian education were essentially developed in the 1700s and 1800s, a time when the entire nation was essentially Protestant. Churches were key influencers of society. Pastors were the natural leaders of both church and society. And homes were agencies of Christian character. Though none of these characteristics are operational today, we basically use the Christian education model developed during those years—Sunday school: "When the Sunday school was developed, it was not a problem but the solution to a problem. The reason it is a problem today is that, although times have changed, the Sunday school as an *agency* of education has not."[5]

Nelson is quick to note that Sunday school, itself, is not a failure. "The failure is the idea that the Sunday school alone—with little help from parents, church, or community—can be an effective agent of Christian education." He explains that in the nineteenth century, Sunday school merely supplemented the religious training that was received through all institutions of a "Christian America," including schools, media, government, and community affairs. For better or worse, those supporting influences are no longer in place. Yet the church has done little to reshape the way it nurtures faith in its members.[6]

Richard Robert Osmer also suggests that the church has forgotten its calling to teach:

> What is missing from mainline Protestantism today is a vital teaching office by which the foundations of Bible and Christian doctrine are taught to members of most congregations. In the absence of such a teaching office, individuals are left to sort out their own understandings of God and the moral life or turn to groups offering absolutes to fill the void they are experiencing.[7]

MYTHS THAT MUDDLE

These and other historical and social factors have led to a number of myths about education in general, and Christian education in particular.[8] These widespread myths show up in congregations, in magazines, in denominational emphases, and in individuals' involvement in Christian education. Five key myths come to mind.

1. "Christian education is for children." This myth is reflected in the downward spiral of involvement in Christian education. While 60 percent of elementary-age children participate in Christian education, the percentage drops to 52 percent for junior-high youths, 35 percent for senior-high youths, and 28 percent for adults.

"In many parts of the United States, Sunday school for adults has died on the vine," writes C. Kirk Hadaway. "It is seen as something for kids. What sort of lesson does that teach our children—that personal prayer and Bible study are childish activities that are not needed by adults?" Some congregations add to the misperception by scheduling worship and Sunday school concurrently for convenience. The net result of this strategy is that children never experience worship, and adults don't have an opportunity to participate in regular Christian education.[9]

This erroneous belief and the accompanying practices are widespread, and may be the most damaging of the myths. Faith changes and grows and evolves throughout our lives. By leaving Christian education programs during early adolescence, we risk not growing beyond a thirteen-year-old's understanding of God, the world, and faith—hardly an adequate basis for a life-shaping adult faith.

In contrast, what is needed is a view of Christian education as a lifelong process. As mentioned earlier, *lifelong* involvement in Christian education is a key to faith maturity in adults. And until parents and other adults participate in Christian education, young people—who are doing everything they can to act like adults—won't participate in Christian education either. The effects are cumulative, either positively or negatively.

2. "A good Christian education program is a big Christian education program." Too often, churches have been seduced by the bigger-is-better mentality. *Everything* needs to grow. And when everything is bigger, then everything will be great. In one way or another, people say, "Once the church is bigger and the Christian education program is larger, *then* we can do effective Christian education. Right now we just don't have enough people or enough money to do much."

The *Effective Christian Education* study looked carefully for correlations between church size, budget, and location, to determine what impact, if any, these factors play in Christian education effectiveness. The study found virtually no differences. People were just as likely to have mature faith in a large urban congregation in Texas as in a small rural congregation in Nebraska. These factors simply aren't significant enhancers or deterrents to growth in faith. The 52 congregations visited by researchers illustrate this truth. Some of the outstanding congregations had 5,000 members and served large, metropolitan communities; others had fewer than 50 members and served rural communities.

This finding encourages and challenges all congregations. Unalterable church demographics are not major obstacles to (or legitimate excuses for!) Christian education effectiveness. Rather, the factors that do make a difference involve dynamics of congregational life—dynamics that can be altered. *Every congregation has the potential of developing a more effective Christian education program*—if it commits itself to the endeavor.

3. "Good teaching means transferring information." This myth is evident in many churches' overdependence on lectures and other forms of one-way communication for learning. In *Contemporary Approaches to Christian Education,* Jack L. Seymour and Donald E. Miller describe it as an "overwhelming and almost customary orientation of many Sunday schools to training and indoctrination."[10]

Sunday schools aren't the only culprits. Adult forums, which have replaced adult Sunday school in many churches, often rely on a slate of outside experts to give presentations on interesting topics. Small Bible-study groups sometimes have leaders who spend the hour reading through the notes they took on their favorite commentary. Indeed, few settings are immune from the tendency for one person to be the expert, while others passively listen.

This myth grows out of a teacher-centered educational approach described by Malcolm Knowles, a pioneer in adult education. In this approach, he writes, "the teacher [has] full responsibility for making all decisions about what will be learned, how it will be learned, when it will be learned, and if it has been learned. It is teacher-directed education, leaving to the learner only the submissive role of following a teacher's instructions."[11]

While this approach may be useful for some types of information and settings, it is generally inadequate in most Christian education contexts. *For Christian education to be effective, it must not only transmit insight and knowledge, but also must allow insight to emerge through students' self-discovery and experience.* From this perspective, "the Christian teacher, in mutuality with the student, will be a guide in the search for meaning and vocation."[12] With this approach in mind, other teaching and learning methods must be explored and implemented (see chapter 10).

4. "Teaching can occur without training." In the national study, only 34 percent of teachers for youths and 44 percent of teachers for adults know educational theory and practice for their age group. Yet only 53 percent of churches provide instruction in effective teaching methods at least once a year.

Apparently, too many churches hand a teacher the curriculum and hope for the best. If teachers know or learn more about teaching, it's from their own initiative or outside experience. That approach might be fine if teachers had an adequate background, but teachers are not always convinced of their own abilities. Of the teachers surveyed, only half evaluated as good or excellent their performance as a teacher; 14 percent evaluated it as fair or poor.

This myth has another side effect as well. Without training and guidance from church leaders, teachers usually are on their own to find, use, and apply resources. Most often, they will rely on those that are readily available or attractively packaged. Some of these resources may be superior; others contain poor educational methods, poor theology, and simplistic discussions of difficult issues. The result is that much misinformation may be communicated through Christian education programs.

Good teaching requires good training. The study confirms that teachers who have training tend to be better teachers. And the result is better Christian education. Until this widespread myth is buried, adequate training is unlikely in many churches. Chapter 7 explores this need.

5. "Christian education is separate from the rest of congregational life." For too many people, Christian education is something that happens between 9:30 and 10:30 on Sunday mornings. When it's over, the church moves on to other, unrelated things. The survey found evidence of this myth when it asked how many times during the last year the church's governing body, during its regular meetings, had thoughtful discussions about Christian education. Only half of the churches said such discussions took place three or more times.

People involved in the *Effective Christian Education* study have repeatedly encountered this myth. It has been difficult to convince many pastors to accept the notion that a study on Christian education is important for their ministry. Whenever a workshop is billed as having a focus on "promoting faith maturity," the event is attended primarily by pastors. But when the event is billed as "effective Christian education," it is attended primarily by Christian education coordinators and teachers. Though both events may contain essentially the same information, Christian education is seen as a specialized part of the church's ministry, not as an encompassing theme.

This myth is harmful not only to Christian education but also to the church and its members. It fragments people's religious experiences, and as a result, they don't see connections between the faith they explore in Sunday school, the faith they confess in worship, and the expressions of faith they make during the week through service and action. Unless we intentionally help people make the connections, they don't see how the potluck dinners, committee meetings, or coffee hours relate to—and even help them to grow in—their faith.

In contrast, Donald L. Griggs and Judy McKay Walther suggest that Christian education should be "a central element of the ministry of every church. . . . It is in and through the educational ministry of the church that men and women and boys and girls are enabled to hear, experience, and put into practice the teachings of Jesus and of the sages, prophets, apostles, and the saints of all generations of the church's heritage."[13]

This perspective is affirmed by C. Ellis Nelson. What is needed, he suggests, is "for mainstream Protestants to consider the *congregation* as the agency of education . . . . Minister and lay leaders of a congregation must resolve to develop the congregation as a community of believers who are seeking God's will for their lives."[14]

When education becomes a center of energy in a congregation, it has the potential to invigorate all of congregational life. Instead of a boring, meaningless administrative necessity, church business meetings can become opportunities for discovering how the church can embody its faith. Social gatherings can become opportunities to embody koinonia. Service projects become central expressions of a living faith. Indeed, an environment in which learning is both valued and expected enhances all aspects of congregational life and brings Christian education to center stage where it needs to be.

Chapter 2

In Search of Faith Maturity

What is faith? Any quick answer to that question is either simplistic, vague, or incomplete. My dictionary lists nine definitions. As definition number three, it offers, "belief in God or in the doctrines or teachings of religion." Definition number five: "a system of religious belief." Hardly adequate.

A small Bible concordance lists more than 60 passages that include the word *faith.* But even that list doesn't include the references to *faithful, faithfulness, faithless,* or *faithlessness.* Furthermore, even combining all the Bible passages that specifically mention the word *faith* wouldn't tell the whole story. Indeed, hundreds of books have been written and thousands of sermons preached on the subject.

Yet, as elusive as the concept of mature faith may be, Christians must grapple with it and its implications. What does it mean to be faithful? What are the implications of our faith? How does faith grow? What does faith look like? Faith also is a key concept to address as Christian educators. What is Christian education, if it doesn't somehow have something to do with faith? And how might we enhance or nurture that faith in the faithful?

At the heart of this book and the study it concerns is the conviction that "the primary aim of congregational life is to nurture—among children, youths, and adults—a vibrant, life-changing faith, the kind of faith that shapes one's way of being, thinking, and acting."[1] This goal makes two important assumptions:

1. *Faith is a way of living, not just adherence to doctrine and dogma.* While faith includes believing, it involves allowing those beliefs to shape one's life, as V. Bailey Gillespie writes in *The Experience of Faith:*

> My claim is that Christian faith is a lived reality with a belief conviction, a trusting relationship, and a love-filled life. . . . Until all of us in the church understand the faith nurturing process that assists

us in experiencing God, until all of us have actually sensed the reality of "calling out" and "calling to" as seen in faith commitment, and until all of us are nurtured to actually live out in the life the radical calling of religion, nothing—insight into truth, doctrinal clarity, magazines, or study guides—will do very much for us.[2]

2. *Faith is life-transforming and has a dramatic, lasting impact on the believer.* Faith involves conversion and sanctification—a change of heart. In his *Treatise Concerning Religious Affections* (1746), Jonathan Edwards wrote: "There never was any thing considerable brought to pass in the heart or life of any man [woman] living, by the things of religion, that had not his [her] heart deeply affected by those things."[3] Such a transformation is a gift from God, not an act of human will. In the words of Ephesians 2:8: "For by grace you have been saved through faith, and this is not your own doing; it is the gift of God."

As explained in chapter 1, the *Effective Christian Education* study found that Christian education has more potential to promote this kind of faith than does any other area of congregational life. To understand the implications of this claim and to focus the agenda for Christian education, we must examine this study's definition of faith maturity.

UNDERSTANDING FAITH MATURITY

Any attempt to synthesize faith into a measurable concept is tricky at best, and treacherous at worst. Any construct inevitably reflects the perspective of those involved. And, inevitably, it cannot account for the nuances and specific emphases of everyone across the theological spectrum.

Perhaps the best-known social-science definition of this century comes from Gordon W. Allport, in his distinction between intrinsic and extrinsic religion. He believes that intrinsic, or mature, religion "regards faith as a supreme value in its own right. It is oriented toward a unification of being, takes seriously the commandment of brotherhood, and strives to transcend all self-centered needs. . . . A religious sentiment of this sort floods the whole life with motivation and meaning. Religion is no longer limited to single segments of self-interest."[4]

More recently, James Fowler's thinking has influenced the understanding of faith and faith development: "Faith has to do with the making, maintenance, and transformation of human meaning. It is a mode of knowing and being. In faith we shape our lives in relation to more or less comprehensive convictions or assumptions about reality. Faith composes a felt sense of the world as having character, pattern, and unity."[5]

For the *Effective Christian Education* study, Search Institute researchers interviewed theologians and denominational leaders, analyzed open-ended surveys of hundreds of adults, and reviewed literature in psychology and religion to help identify and measure mature faith. This information helped focus on eight faith expressions which, *when taken together,* give a well-rounded portrait of a person with faith maturity.[6]

Here are the eight marks of faith maturity, according to this framework. Figure 28 shows percentages of youths and adults who have developed each of these marks.

1. Trusting and Believing—People of mature faith trust in God's saving grace and believe firmly in Jesus' humanity and divinity. This mark of faith builds a bridge to the Christian story and tradition by focusing on the faith community's basic theological affirmations: Jesus' humanity and divinity; God's unconditional love; God as both transcendent and immanent; and the reconciling of human suffering and God's love.

But more than intellectual consent to these theological truths, a person with mature faith experiences God's guidance in daily life; these truths shape one's life. "Christian faith is at least belief," writes Thomas H. Groome, "but it must also be more than belief if it is to be a lived reality."[7] Or, as Dietrich Bonhoeffer stated, "Only he who believes is obedient, and only he who is obedient believes."[8]

While the *Effective Christian Education* concept includes basic theological precepts, it emphasizes practice—acting on one's beliefs, or the "outcomes of faith." As a result, it avoids debates about doctrinal fine points and has been widely used across the theological spectrum. Leaders in denominations as diverse as United Church of Christ, Southern Baptist Convention, Lutheran Church–Missouri Synod, Seventh-day Adventist Church, and the Roman Catholic Church have undertaken studies using this scale.

2. Experiencing the Fruits of Faith—People of mature faith experience a sense of personal well-being, security, and peace that grows out of their faith. It is the "life in all its fullness" that Jesus offers (John 10:10).[9]

Some critics have argued that this mark of faith contradicts the prophetic, uncomfortable side of faith, turning Christianity into a feel-good, narcissistic religion. To be sure, an exclusive focus on this dimension of faith would have that effect. However, as people such as Thomas Merton and Desmond Tutu have shown, this inner peace and security give us the energy and hope to work actively for change without disillusionment. The two sides of faith form a healthy paradox; faith is not mature unless it has both.

3. Integrating Faith and Life—Faith isn't just a Sunday-morning phenomenon. Mature Christians' faith is a filter through which they evaluate everything they see, hear, or think. Faith is integrated into vocational, familial, relational, financial, political, moral, and ethical decisions. In short, faith shapes all aspects of life.

4. Seeking Spiritual Growth—People of mature faith know that faith is a journey. Like any other relationship, a relationship to God through Christ cannot be strong if it is static. So they seek to grow spiritually through study, reflection, prayer, and discussion. And instead of relying on childhood understandings of God and the world, they affirm changes in belief and meaning as they grow in their faith.

5. Nurturing Faith in Community—"The congregation is where we encounter people who know something already of negotiating the Christian life," says Suzanne Johnson. "Our ability to pray, to do justice, and to love mercy develops only if we so keep company that a 'participant' is incorporated into our own consciousness."[10] In community, people witness to their faith and nourish one another. In this context, they support others' faith and share their own faith story. And they experience God through these interpersonal encounters.

6. Holding Life-affirming Values—Life is good and should be affirmed, people of mature faith believe. They are committed to life-affirming values such as racial and gender equality, as well as cultural and religious diversity. They feel a personal sense of responsibility for others' welfare. These values also affect their personal lives. They pursue a healthy lifestyle and affirm the sanctity of creation.

7. Advocating Social Change—The Christian faith is not a passive faith. Mature Christians understand that it involves advocating social and global change to bring about greater social justice, including the reducing of poverty and improving of human welfare. They believe that faith demands global concern and that the church belongs in the public sphere.

8. Acting and Serving—People of mature faith not only advocate social change, but become personally involved in serving, consistently and passionately, through acts of love and justice. They work to protect the environment and devote time and energy to social service, social justice, and peacemaking.[11]

TWO DIMENSIONS OF FAITH

These eight elements also can be collapsed into two "dimensions" of faith, which parallel Matthew 22:34-39. Jesus was asked which Commandment is the greatest. He replied, quoting the Torah: " 'You shall love the Lord your God with all your heart, and with all your soul, and with all your mind.' . . . And a second is like it: 'You shall love your neighbor as yourself.'" In essence, Jesus defined two interdependent themes of a mature Christian faith:

First, a Relationship with God—the *vertical* dimension of faith which symbolizes God reaching "down" to humanity. The study defined this dimension as *a life-transforming relationship to a loving God.* Some ways in which Christians express this part of faith include worshiping God, praying, and studying their Bibles.

Second, a Relationship with Our Neighbors—the *horizontal* dimension of faith. This can be defined as *a consistent devotion to serving others.* Some ways Christians express this part of faith include helping people in need, becoming involved in social issues, and taking care of the environment.

FAITH MATURITY AMONG ADULTS

The national results based on this concept of faith maturity are anything but encouraging. Only a minority of mainline Christian adults show an integrated, life-encompassing faith. In fact, the average churchgoing adult embodies only about 20 of the 38 indicators of faith maturity. Specifically, 36 percent of adults have an undeveloped faith, and only 32 percent have an integrated faith. In between, 10 percent have a vertical faith, and 22 percent have a horizontal faith (see Figure 3).

Viewed from another perspective, two-thirds of adults in the churches have a faith that lacks either a horizontal or vertical dimension, or both. For most, faith is one-dimensional—either a personal piety without any social dimension, or a social activism without any sense of a personal relationship with God. Answers to specific questions in the study give additional insight. For example, in the past year . . .

. . . 78 percent of adults never spent time promoting social justice;

. . . 72 percent never marched, met, or gathered with others to promote social change;

. . . 66 percent never, or rarely, encouraged someone to believe in Jesus Christ; and

. . . 66 percent didn't read their Bibles when alone.

Worksheet 1
Measuring Faith Maturity

In the *Effective Christian Education* study, the eight dimensions of faith maturity were the basis for 38 survey questions. To understand the process, take the following self-test, which is simplified from the faith maturity scale. Read each statement and decide how well it fits you. Write the appropriate number next to the statement. Choose your response from these options:

1 = never true **2 = rarely true** **3 = true once in a while**
4 = sometimes true **5 = often true** **6 = almost always true**
7 = always true

____ 1. Every day I see evidence that God is active in the world.
____ 2. I feel a deep sense of responsibility for reducing pain and suffering in the world.
____ 3. I am spiritually moved by the beauty of God's creation.
____ 4. I care a great deal about reducing poverty in the United States and throughout the world.
____ 5. I devote time to reading and studying the Bible.
____ 6. I do things to help protect the environment.
____ 7. I have a real sense that God is guiding me.
____ 8. I am concerned that our country is not doing enough to help the poor.
____ 9. I like to worship and pray with others.
____ 10. I give significant portions of time and money to help other people.
____ 11. I seek out opportunities to help me grow spiritually.
____ 12. I go out of my way to show love to people I meet.
____ 13. I take time for periods of prayer or meditation.
____ 14. I speak out for equality for women and minorities.
____ 15. I talk with other people about my faith.
____ 16. I think Christians must be about the business of creating international understanding and harmony.
____ 17. My faith helps me to know right from wrong.
____ 18. I try to apply my faith to political and social issues.
____ 19. My faith shapes the way I think and act each and every day.
____ 20. In my free time, I help people who have problems or needs.
____ 21. My life is filled with meaning and purpose.
____ 22. I am active in efforts to promote social justice.
____ 23. As I grow older, my understanding of God changes.
____ 24. I am active in efforts to promote world peace.
____ 25. I know that Jesus Christ is the Son of God who died on a cross and rose again.
____ 26. I help others with their religious questions and struggles.
____ 27. I tend to be accepting of other people.
____ 28. I don't have a hard time accepting myself.
____ 29. I take excellent care of my physical health.
____ 30. I accept people whose religious beliefs are different from mine.
____ 31. I do not feel overwhelmed by all my responsibilities and obligations.
____ 32. I feel God's presence in my relationships with other people.
____ 33. I accept that there can be both a loving God, and so much pain and suffering in the world.
____ 34. I do not believe my salvation depends upon obeying God's rules and Commandments.

____ 35. I am confident that I can overcome any problem or crisis, no matter how serious.
____ 36. My life is committed to Jesus Christ.
____ 37. My life is not filled with stress and anxiety.
____ 38. I want the churches of this nation to become involved in political issues.

The first 24 items were used in developing the horizontal and vertical faith framework. The remaining items were included also as part of the scale for the eight dimensions of mature faith. To identify your "faith type" based on this concept, use this process:

First, add together the sum of the fives, sixes, and sevens you wrote on the *odd*-numbered statements from items 1-23. The result is your *vertical* score.

Now add together the sum of the fives, sixes, and sevens you wrote on the *even*-numbered statements from items 2-24. The result is your *horizontal* score.

Finally, discover your "faith type," using the following key:

1. If both your horizontal and vertical scores are higher than 60, the survey indicates that you have a *mature or integrated faith.* A Christian with an integrated faith experiences both a life-transforming relationship to God and a devotion to serving others.

2. If your horizontal score is greater than 60, but your vertical score is lower than 60, the survey indicates that you have a *horizontal faith.* A Christian with a horizontal faith is devoted to serving others, but lacks a life-transforming relationship to God.

3. If your vertical score is greater than 60, but your horizontal score is lower than 60, the survey indicates that you have a *vertical faith.* A Christian with a vertical faith has a life-transforming relationship to a loving God, but lacks a devotion to serving others.

4. If both your horizontal and vertical scores are below 60, the survey indicates that you have an *undeveloped faith.* Christians with undeveloped faith do not strongly exhibit their faith through either serving others or a life-transforming relationship to God.

What emerges from these statistics is a portrait of mainline adults whose faith is latent or dormant. Even though 63 percent say that faith is a "very important" or "the most important" influence in their lives, it certainly doesn't have the life-changing influence for which we might hope. For most, faith is more a matter of the head than of the heart, hands, and feet.

Particularly noteworthy is that an overwhelming majority of church members appear unmoved by mainline denominations' emphasis on peace and justice issues. Furthermore, this concern isn't strong at the congregational level, either. Only 13 percent of adults say their church places a strong or very strong emphasis on "getting members to work for social justice and peace." Furthermore, 58 percent of adults say they don't even want churches to become involved in political issues.

These results confirm suspicions, but they also raise questions for people who see the centrality of service and justice issues to our faith. How can we find specific ways to get people interested and involved in service and social issues? We'll explore this question in more detail in chapter 10.

Figure 3
Adult Faith Types

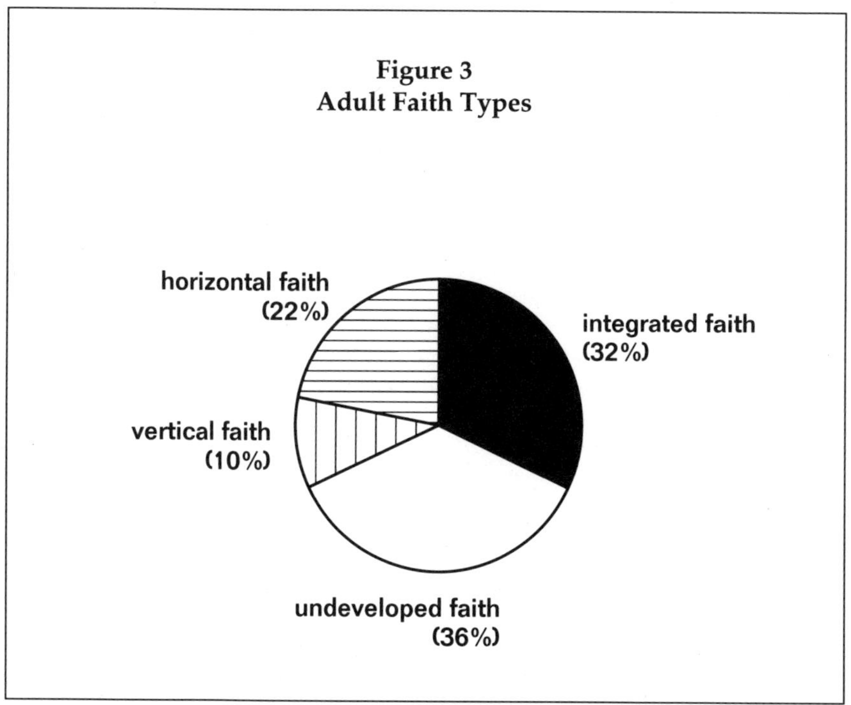

DEMOGRAPHIC DIFFERENCES

Particular problems and areas of strength arise when we compare the results based on a variety of demographic data. Three factors—age, gender, and ethnicity—appear to have a measurable impact on adult faith maturity.

Age—As might be expected, older churchgoing adults are more likely than younger adults to embody faith maturity. While only 16 percent of adults in their twenties have an integrated faith, the percentage climbs to 57 percent of people 70 or older.

Though the age differences may not be surprising, they do raise questions. Since this wasn't a longitudinal study, we don't know whether people's faith will naturally mature as they age, or we are truly seeing a long-term weakening of faith across the generations.

An analysis of the baby-boom generation by David A. Roozen, William McKinney, and Wayne Thompson suggests a more optimistic view. They found that regular worship attendance increased within this cohort from 33.5 percent to 42.8 percent between the early 1970s and 1980s. They attribute 90 percent of the increase to changes in family status (becoming parents) and a "conservative drift" in the population. They also note, however, that most of the return is among those who had never severed ties with the church and that the return does not appear to be as strong as in the previous generation.[12]

The *Effective Christian Education* data may also suggest, in part, a cohort effect, not just a developmental progression. That is, some of the lower levels of faith maturity will likely "travel" with the younger generations, so that in the future, the older populations will exhibit lower faith maturity than the current generation.

This conclusion is suggested by comparing a wide range of faith experiences of various ages of adults. In remembering their past, older adults are more likely to report participating in faith-shaping activities. Thus we dare not relax and assume that people will naturally grow in faith as they age. Such complacency could have disastrous effects in coming decades, if we discover that, in fact, these adults are not maturing in faith. Their influence on their children could, in turn, point to even lower levels of faith among succeeding generations.

Gender—At every age, adult women have a more developed faith than adult men (see Figure 4). While 38 percent of women have an integrated faith, only 21 percent of men do. And men seem to have particular difficulty in the vertical theme—the relationship with God. Seventy-three percent of men have either an undeveloped or horizontal faith, compared to 49 percent of women. It shouldn't come as a surprise, then, that only 21 percent of women (compared to 52 percent of men) say that their spouse is one of the top five positive influences on their faith.

The findings regarding the strength of women's faith are consistent with studies by other researchers. In *The Restructuring of American Religion*, Robert Wuthnow notes that, in national polls, only half as many women (6%) as men (11%) claim not to be religious. Women also are more likely to report attending church, reading the Bible, and thinking about their faith. Furthermore, Wuthnow adds that after analyzing data on education, employment, and income, "Gender differences in religious commitment seem remarkably immune to the changing roles that women have begun to play."[13]

In addition to the basic gender differences, a troubling dip in faith maturity occurs for men in their forties, where half of the men have an undeveloped faith (compared to 33 percent of women), and only 8 percent have an integrated faith (compared to 43 percent of women). While this study can't isolate the reasons for this drop, several factors could be at work.

First, these men may be experiencing mid-life crises, when few elements of life seem "integrated." When the crisis is resolved, their faith could recover as well.

These men—many of whom are climbing to the tops of their careers—could have become so engrossed in their work that other aspects of life have been neglected. Indeed, work may have become an escape from a sense of incompleteness in other areas of life.

Figure 4
Mature Faith Among Men and Women

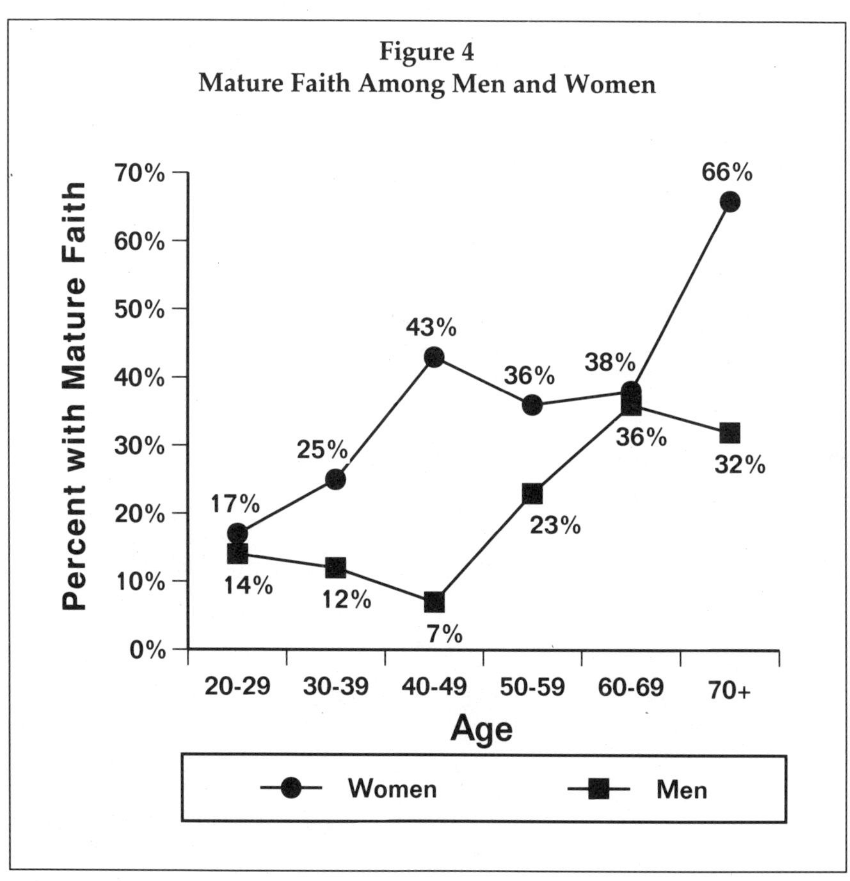

Yet another possibility is that these men are the baby boomers who experienced most dramatically the turbulence of the 1960s. Those formative experiences may have interfered with experiences that promote growth in faith. If such is the case, we can anticipate that this generation of men will not mature toward integrated faith at the same level as other generations.

Ethnicity—It is unfortunate that the study's design could not allow for comparisons among specific ethnic/racial groups. Yet when we compare all minorities to all whites, significant differences emerge that can't be ignored. Among adults, people of color are almost twice as likely as Caucasians to have an integrated faith (57% vs. 31%). Furthermore, while 36 percent of whites have an undeveloped faith, only 13 percent of people of color score in this category.[14]

These findings renew the challenge for predominantly white churches and denominations to listen to the experiences of the racial/ethnic communities, to learn from them, and to take seriously their worship and educational styles.

WHAT MAINLINE ADULTS BELIEVE

The faith maturity scale doesn't measure faith in terms of a particular set of orthodox beliefs. But the survey did ask adults their views on a variety of theological issues. Their responses show a mix of beliefs that crosses the theological spectrum.

God—About 92 percent of adults say they are certain God exists. But they're less sure how to describe God. When asked how God relates to the world, 43 percent chose the statement that "the world is part of God, but God is greater and larger than the world." Only 28 percent believe the more orthodox view that "God transcends the world but is actively involved in the world"—a position held by 74 percent of the pastors.

When asked about God's attributes, mainline adults tend to believe God is forgiving (97%); is loving (96%); accepts them as they are (86%); is aware of everything they think and do (81%); and has a plan for their life (70%). They are much less likely to believe that God is judging (37%); is mysterious (36%); punishes those who do wrong (19%); and decides everything they do (7%). Only 8 percent say they think God should sometimes be referred to as "she."

The Bible—Most mainline adults do not accept the fundamentalist view of scripture. Only 9 percent of those surveyed agreed that the Bible was dictated by God without the writer's influence and that everything in it is true—historically, scientifically, and in matters of faith and practice.[15]

Instead, 54 percent of mainline adults believe the Bible was inspired by God and recorded by writers who interpreted God's message for their time. Thus scripture is true in matters of faith and practice, but may contain some historical and scientific errors. Another 31 percent believe the Bible was written by people who tried their best to describe and interpret their understanding of God and God's activity in the world. The remaining 6 percent believe that the Bible records stories, legends, and myths, or that it contains no more truth than other religious books.

Unorthodox Beliefs—A number of unorthodox beliefs have made inroads into mainline churches. One-third of adults believe that "through meditation and self-discipline I come to know that all spiritual truth and wisdom is within me." Nine percent believe in reincarnation and astrology. And 7 percent believe it's possible to communicate with the dead.[16]

A PORTRAIT OF MATURE CHRISTIANS

What kind of adults do well in the concept of faith maturity proposed by this study? Did the study find, for example, that people with faith maturity have conventional or conservative beliefs on theological and social issues? Is the concept biased against, say, people who have a "searching" faith?

In examining the beliefs of those with faith maturity, these fears appear to be unfounded. People with integrated faith run the gamut of theological and political perspectives. Many appear to be nonconformists and nontraditionalists. They have ups and downs in faith, are social critics, are highly interested in inclusivity, and hold some unorthodox views of faith and the world.

Consider, for example, people's views on several social issues. Sixty-six percent of those with a mature faith say it is always wrong for a company to pay women employees less than men employees for similar work. That figure compares to 53 percent of those with an undeveloped faith, 50 percent of those with a vertical faith, and 72 percent of those with a horizontal faith. Similar findings hold true for several theological issues, some of which are illustrated in Figure 5.

Figure 5
Theological Views of People with High Faith Maturity

This chart compares views of people with mature faith views with the views of people in other faith types.

	Mature Faith	Horizontal Faith	Vertical Faith	Undeveloped Faith
Believe that good Christians have as many questions about faith as they have answers.	75%	77%	74%	71%
Want their church to do more to include the experience, wisdom, and insight of women in its theology, doctrine, and understanding of the Bible.	59%	61%	37%	37%
Want their church to do more to include the experience, wisdom, and insight of minorities in its theology, doctrine, and understanding of the Bible.	57%	69%	38%	32%
Believe Christians should never have any doubts about their faith.	15%	8%	21%	14%
Spent time in the past month promoting social justice (for example, racial equality, women's rights, economic reform), or world peace.	28%	28%	6%	7%
Believe God is a force in the world working to make societies more just and fair for all people (chose "absolutely true").	39%	15%	21%	8%

It should be noted, of course, that people who exhibit faith maturity also can hold traditional conservative views on these and other issues. What is important is that one's particular views on theological or social issues are not determining factors in developing an integrated faith, with a vibrant relationship with God and an ongoing, active concern for the world.

It is also interesting to note that this partial profile of mature Christians is not incompatible with the final stage in James W. Fowler's stages of faith, which he calls universalizing faith: "The movement toward Universalizing faith is marked by . . . the radical decentralization from the self. . . . It means 'knowing' the world through the eyes and experiences of persons, classes, nationalities, and faiths quite different from one's own." At this stage, a person also "owns" the values and concerns of other beings.[17]

FAITH MATURITY AMONG YOUTHS

Not surprisingly, adolescents (grades 7 through 12) generally have lower levels of faith maturity than adults. It would be unrealistic to expect otherwise. Overall, 64 percent of teenagers in mainline churches have an undeveloped faith, twice the rate of adults. Only 11 percent have an integrated faith. (Though this percentage is small, it reveals that faith maturity is at least possible among adolescents.)

Though ups and downs may be normal, the study does give reason for concern about the faith of these young people. As they mature physically, few young people are maturing in their faith. In fact, levels of undeveloped faith stay relatively constant between the seventh and twelfth grades.

Even more troubling, faith maturity in boys actually declines in the ninth and tenth grades. While 66 percent of seventh- and eighth-grade boys have an undeveloped faith, the percentage leaps to 83 percent in the ninth and tenth grades. The decline for girls is less pronounced and tends to occur more in the eleventh and twelfth grades. These gender differences are supported by adults' reports of "crises in faith." Men in their twenties were more likely than women to say they experienced such a crisis at ages 13 to 15, while women were more likely to report a crisis at ages 16 to 18.

Developmental theorist James W. Fowler describes the stage of faith entered by young adolescents as "synthetic-conventional faith." During this stage, he writes, young people begin synthesizing—putting together pieces of their self-concept, their values, their stories. The faith is conventional in that the beliefs are drawn from others in the young person's life. During this time, we expect some ups and downs in faith as young people test limits, experiment, doubt, and question. These realities are natural and healthy parts of "owning" the faith.[18]

The question is, Who will young people be with as they put together the pieces? Will they do their searching and synthesizing within the supportive and nurturing context of the church? Or will they leave the church to look elsewhere for life direction? The possibilities are disturbing when we realize that teenagers and young adults (those who tend to have a "searching" faith) are least likely to say that their church helps them find meaning and purpose in life, or that it helps them with religious questions.

Since this was not a longitudinal study, which tracks individuals across time, it's difficult to say for certain what will happen in the long term. But the danger is that as adults, young people may not return to the church or grow in faith. When asked the likelihood that they would be involved in church at age 21, only 25 percent said there was an "excellent" chance. They seemed more certain that they would be involved later—34 percent thought there was an excellent chance they'd be involved in church by age 40.

Despite being widespread, this decline in involvement appears not to be inevitable. Two denominations—Southern Baptist Convention and the Christian Church (Disciples of Christ)—do not experience the same rapid decline in involvement in Christian education through high school. In fact, about half the youths in these denominations remain active. In the Evangelical Lutheran Church, The United Church of Christ, and The United Methodist Church, the number falls to about a third for grades 10 through 12 (see Figure 27). While keeping every other teenager involved may not be ideal, it suggests that something can be done to prevent many youths from leaving.

QUALITY OF LIFE FOR YOUTHS

Another reason it is vital that congregations reach and keep young people during adolescence is that youths are facing critical issues, challenges, and stresses during this time. The study of congregations identified several areas of concern.[19]

Sadness and Depression—These negative feelings are common among adolescents. Sixty-one percent of mainline teenagers say they felt very sad or depressed ten or more times during the past year. Twenty-one percent felt this way forty or more times. Forty percent say they have even thought of killing themselves.

Depression is most pronounced among ninth- and tenth-grade girls; 73 percent reported feeling sad or depressed at least ten times during the past year. And 26 percent of these girls say they needed help but had no one to turn to.

Alcohol Use—Though the legal drinking age in all states is 21, drinking is common among mainline teenagers. Half of all the teenagers had drunk alcohol with friends in the past year. Forty-seven percent had been to parties where others their age were drinking.

Use increases with age. Among eleventh- and twelfth-graders, 70 percent of boys and 69 percent of girls drank alone or with friends. And 46 percent of girls and 42 percent of boys reported having drunk to the point of intoxication (five drinks or more).

Other Problem Behaviors—Cheating is widespread. Sixty-eight percent of teenagers say they have cheated at least once in the past year. In a 12-month period, 44 percent hit or beat up someone, and 60 percent were in trouble at school. During that same time, 10 percent of church youths used marijuana, and 2 percent used cocaine.

Despite these troubling realities, it also should be noted that youths in churches face these problems at a significantly lower rate than other youths. In fact, Search Institute's study of 47,000 sixth- through twelfth-graders in public schools found that churchgoing youths are less than half as likely to engage in any of eighteen at-risk behaviors as non-churchgoing youths.[20]

HELPFUL RESPONSES

How do we respond to the study's findings on faith maturity among youths and adults? One possibility would be to dismiss the study, perhaps by arguing with details in the faith-maturity concept. While such a debate would be healthy (this concept certainly isn't the final word on faith), it would not address the immediate, real concerns raised by the study.

The study itself offers a more constructive response. It examines the factors that influence the various elements of faith maturity. By identifying those factors, we can strengthen the ones that enhance growth in faith, while simultaneously working to overcome some of the barriers.

Chapter 3

Nurturing Congregational and Denominational Loyalty

"Those Mainline Blues," *Time Magazine* wailed in a 1989 headline. "The central fact about mainline Protestantism in the U.S. today is that it is in deep trouble," the article reported. "This stunning turnabout is apparent in the unprecedented hemorrhaging of memberships in the three major faiths that date from colonial times." The article then described the following declines since 1965, which represented a net loss of 5.2 million members, while the U.S. population grew by 47 million:

- 20 percent decline in The United Church of Christ;
- 25 percent decline in the Presbyterian Church (U.S.A.);
- 18 percent decline in The United Methodist Church;
- 43 percent loss (after a de facto split) for the Christian Church (Disciples of Christ); and
- 28 percent decline in the The Episcopal Church, U.S.A.[1]

Friends, foes, and outsiders have responded to studies and statistics about the declines in mainline denominations with a plethora of predictions, prescriptions, and plans. Many within the denominations wring their hands, wondering how to respond.

"Our mainstream churches are not merely in decline; we who have been assigned responsibility to be leaders are frightened," writes J. Edward Carothers in *The Paralysis of Mainstream Protestant Leadership.* "We are huddled in dismay. We have a paralysis of mind and heart. We are dedicated to our tasks, but we have found that nothing we urge our people to do is curbing the stubborn decline of our membership, our ministry, and our cultural influence."[2]

Other observers, however, have less alarmist responses. C. Kirk Hadaway notes that the mainline denominations are being measured against the 1950s, when the churches had an unprecedented grip on the nation. Neither the declines in the mainline churches nor the increases in the conservative churches are as dramatic as they have been portrayed, he argues.[3]

But the declines certainly merit attention, particularly if the conclusions of Wade Clark Roof and William McKinney are correct. After an in-depth examination of recent religious trends in *American Mainline Religion: It's Changing Shape and Future,* they predict:

> The churches of the Protestant establishment, long in a state of decline, will continue to lose ground both in numbers and in social power and influence. The proportion of the population that is Protestant will continue its gradual decline in the decades to come, and within Protestantism, denominations and revitalization movements will continue their contest for power and influence.[4]

It's clear that something has changed. In a study of religious identification of 130,000 American households by the City University of New York, about 15 percent of those surveyed could only identify themselves as Christian or Protestant, without supplying any denomination ("non-denominational" and "independent" were among the options). Thus a sizable proportion of Americans don't even know how to identify themselves religiously![5]

In initiating the *Effective Christian Education* study, researchers and denominational leaders were particularly concerned about . . .

. . . failure to attract young adults and young families;
. . . inactivity in congregational life;
. . . loss of members; and
. . . loss of denominational identity.

Among the goals of the study were to identify, if possible, some of the reasons for the decline, and to pinpoint Christian education's possible role in revitalizing these denominations. This chapter examines those dynamics.

THE EFFECTS OF LOYALTY

Some critics have responded with disdain to the study's emphasis on loyalty. The focus is self-serving, they say. People shouldn't worry about loyalty; they should worry about promoting faith—regardless of the denomination or congregation. On one level, these critics have a point. Congregations and denominations do have vested, even selfish, interests in making the institutions financially strong, growing, and viable.

But the motivation isn't purely selfish. Loyalty breeds commitment, and commitment breeds involvement. Loyal members become active, vital parts of Christ's body. It's good for them. It's good for the church. Loyalty to both congregation and denomination is a good predictor of congregational health, the study found.

When members are loyal, data analysis shows that the following dynamics tend to occur within the congregation: Members tend to give more; the congregation tends to grow; there tends to be more congregational activity.

So, whether loyalty precedes health, or health precedes loyalty, the two are somehow connected. Fostering one will likely have a positive impact on the other.

LOYALTY AMONG ADULTS

To some extent, the study offers more optimism in its findings on loyalty than on faith maturity. Most adults express commitment to both their congregations and their denominations. Two-thirds of mainline adults have a high denominational loyalty, and three-fourths have a high congregational loyalty. We see this loyalty reflected in several ways.

Sixty-five percent of adults gave $100 or more to their church in the past year. Forty-one percent gave $1,000 or more. While these figures may not solve congregations' budgeting problems, levels of contributions to other organizations pale in comparison. The next-highest giving category was "charities or social service organizations." But only 38 percent of adults gave more that $100, and a mere 4 percent gave more than $1,000.

Eighty-nine percent of adults say their church matters a great deal to them. As a result, 75 percent of adults say they would feel a great sense of loss if they had to change churches. In fact, only 10 percent of adults agree that they would change churches if their own congregation developed major problems in leadership or finance.

People also show relatively strong denominational commitment. When asked if they would seek out a church of the same denomination if they were to move, 85 percent said "probably" or "absolutely." Most (84%) express satisfaction with their denomination.

Despite these signs of strength, the study found reason for concern due to age differences. Loyalty is much "softer" among young and middle-age adults than among older adults. In terms of denominational loyalty, 78 percent of those 60 and older have high loyalty. But the percentage drops to about 58 percent for those younger than 60. A similar pattern holds for congregational loyalty. While 85 percent of those 60

Figure 6
Adult Loyalty by Age

This chart shows the level of congregational and denominational loyalty among adults, on a scale of 1 (low) to 5 (high).

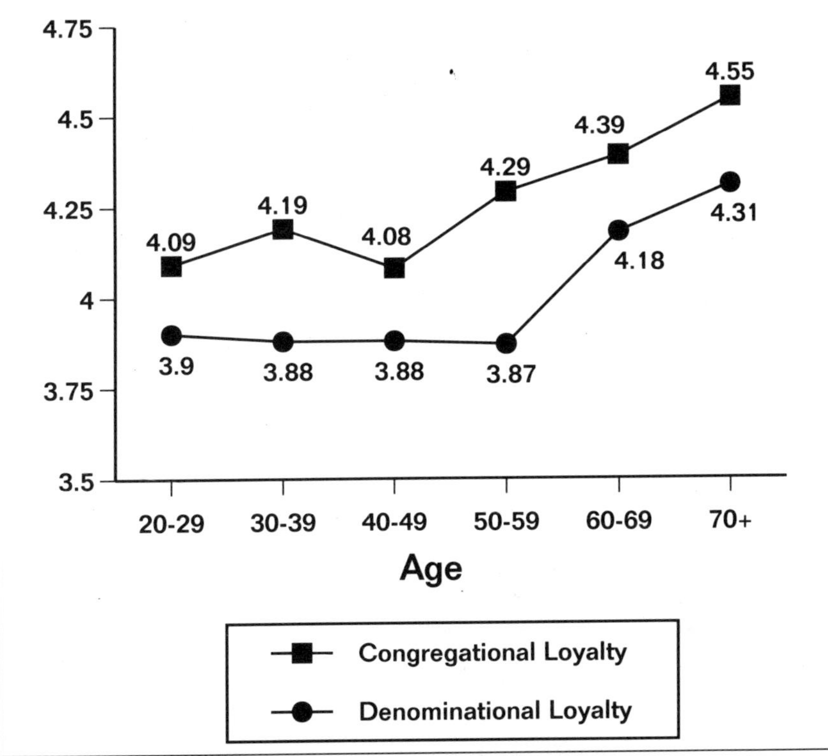

and older have high loyalty, the percentage falls to 73 percent for those 40 to 59, and to 69 percent for those 20 to 39 (see Figure 6).

While loyalty may increase naturally with age, the age differences may also reflect a shift in the way people view the church. In other words, the younger generation may not be as loyal to institutions as previous generations were. Roof and McKinney refer to this dynamic as "the New Volunteerism" brought on by widespread religious and cultural individualism:

> Radically individualistic religion presumes an autonomous believer, one who is on a spiritual journey, on his or her own quest, and often with little involvement in or connection with a particular religious community. . . . Religious belonging for many is no longer viewed as a presumed outgrowth of belief; it has become a matter of taste.[6]

One Presbyterian pastor articulated many people's perception: "[People] feel free to cross denominational lines. They have no particular loyalty. . . . People don't want to make commitments. They are very cautious about commitment. They want to hold on to their personal freedom. . . . People don't want to be told how to live or how to behave."[7]

Because the Search Institute study does not trace patterns across the years, it cannot confirm or deny these trends. Other studies suggest that the decline in loyalty may be accurate. Norvall D. Glenn has analyzed the "no religion" responses to national surveys of Americans between the 1950s and 1980s and found that the older generations tended to have higher levels of religious participation—even when they were young—than more recent generations.[8] These findings indicate that congregations do indeed need to be concerned about weakening loyalty among younger adults, as their lower commitment could seriously undercut future church leadership.

LOYALTY AMONG YOUTHS

As with faith maturity, congregational and denominational loyalty are lower among teenagers. Depending on their age, from 56 to 65 percent of teenagers have high loyalty. Interestingly, levels of congregational and denominational loyalty are almost identical. Some of the same indicators of adult loyalty also hold true for youth.

Though most teenagers don't contribute significantly to *any* organization, they are most likely to give to their church. About 85 percent of mainline teenagers gave money to their church in the past year (69% gave less than $50). The next-highest recipient of teenagers' contributions was also "charities and social service organizations." Only 53 percent of teenagers gave to these groups.

Teenagers are less likely to be saddened by having to change churches, but most (58%) say they would experience a great sense of loss. Like adults, only 10 percent of youths would change churches if leadership or financial problems developed in their church.

Eighty-three percent of teenagers say they are satisfied with their denomination. And 73 percent say they would seek a church of the same denomination if they moved to another city.

How do we evaluate young people's commitment to their congregations and denominations? Without any historical benchmarks against which to measure, we must look elsewhere for clues. Other questions in the study give some insight. For example, we find that young people are less likely than adults to evaluate congregational life favorably. Adolescents are *less likely* than adults to say that . . .

. . . they gain more within the church than outside it;
. . . their congregation feels warm;
. . . they learn a lot in their congregation; and
. . . their congregation expects people to learn and think.

The study also revealed a significant drop in the percentage of young people who say their church helps them find meaning and purpose, or that it helps them with religious questions. While 60 percent of youths 13 to 15 years old say the church helps them most in finding meaning and purpose in life, only 48 percent of youths 16 to 18 make this claim. Similarly, 59 percent of those from 13 to 15 say the church helps them most with religious questions; the percentage drops to 44 percent among the older youths.

In some senses, these changes are subtle, given the life upheavals adolescents experience. But they do raise concern about the memories about church these young people carry with them into adulthood. If these formative church experiences aren't positive, will these young people turn to the church when they become adults?

INCREASING LOYALTY

With the potential long-term problems in loyalty among younger adults as well as youths, what can congregations do to increase loyalty? A simple answer would be: Nurture faith. Churches that do the same things they would do to foster faith maturity will likely discover that loyalty also is growing—as if by accident. The data lead to five observations that can help set a congregation's agenda, if it is particularly concerned with increasing congregational and denominational loyalty among youths and adults.

1. Essentially the same factors of congregational life that have a positive impact on faith maturity also nourish loyalty: effective Christian education; a thinking climate; a warm climate; spiritually uplifting worship; members experiencing the care and concern of other members; and service to others.

2. As is the case with faith maturity, participation in effective Christian education has the greatest impact on congregational and denominational loyalty among both youths and adults.

3. A thinking climate is more important than a warm climate for denominational loyalty. Yet, for congregational loyalty, a warm climate

is more influential than a thinking climate. (Of course, both climates are influential; the difference is a matter of degree.)

4. Among specific factors in effective education, the addressing of common adolescent developmental needs appears to be particularly important for nourishing both kinds of loyalty. These needs include self-concept, friendship, and finding purpose in life. (Chapter 8 examines these content issues in detail.)

5. Christian education programs that emphasize denominational theology, history, and tradition have a small but significant impact upon denominational loyalty (though these emphases have little impact on faith maturity).

HOPEFUL DIRECTIONS

As we noted at the beginning of the chapter, mainline churches are deeply concerned about declining loyalty and involvement, and various pundits have suggested various cures. Sometimes the suggested cures involve major surgery—taking out a major part of the denomination's heritage and theology (usually the emphasis on social issues). At other times, the cures focus on relatively superficial changes, such as worship style or facilities.

The findings of this study suggest a third alternative: Focus energy on the development of more effective Christian education programs in local churches. By educating people in their faith and heritage, and by providing a congregational climate that promotes faith growth, mainline churches will make headway in reversing the continuing declines in loyalty.

Chapter 4

Promoting Faith Through Congregational Life

I'll admit it—I'm not a baseball fan. I don't understand what's fun about sitting on hard bleachers, miles from home plate, watching tiny people running to catch a ball you can hardly see. Besides, in most cases, it's easy to find out everything that happened during a game by watching the evening news.

Obviously, baseball fans disagree vehemently. They recount the great plays and great players and great years. They remember statistics and records and rankings. But most of all, they extol the atmosphere—the roar of the crowd, the crack of the bat, the pungent smell of peanuts and popcorn, the unique taste of ballpark franks.

When pressed, they often admit that they don't go only to watch the ins and outs of the game itself. "It's such a great feeling just to be in the stadium with the crowd and the atmosphere," they testify. "There's nothing like it!" That's probably why there was such a furor about adding lights to Wrigley Field in Chicago; it changed the game's culture.

The culture of a baseball game is vital to the interest and enthusiasm of fans. Similarly, a congregation's culture or ethos is vital to the nurture of faith. The way people think about themselves, the way they interact among themselves and with newcomers, their vision of what the church is and ought to be—all these are important influences on growth in faith.

It is no surprise, then, that the study of Christian education also highlights the importance of the congregational context for effective Christian education and the promotion of faith maturity. Indeed, a Christian education program will be less effective if the congregation's whole ethos or climate does not also help promote faith among the members.

As mentioned in chapter 1, the *Effective Christian Education* study found that Christian education has the greatest potential for promoting faith in youths and adults. Yet the study also found that five other elements in congregational life play important roles. The more each factor is present in a congregation, the greater the faith maturity among members. This chapter looks briefly at each of these factors, summarized in Figure 7. (For congregational emphases, see Figure 29.)

Figure 7
Faith-enhancing Traits of Congregations

Faith maturity—as well as denominational and congregational loyalty—are strongly related to the characteristics of a congregation. The research indicates that the more each of the following characteristics is present, the stronger the faith and loyalty of both adults and youths. The size of each circle indicates its relative importance as compared to the other factors.

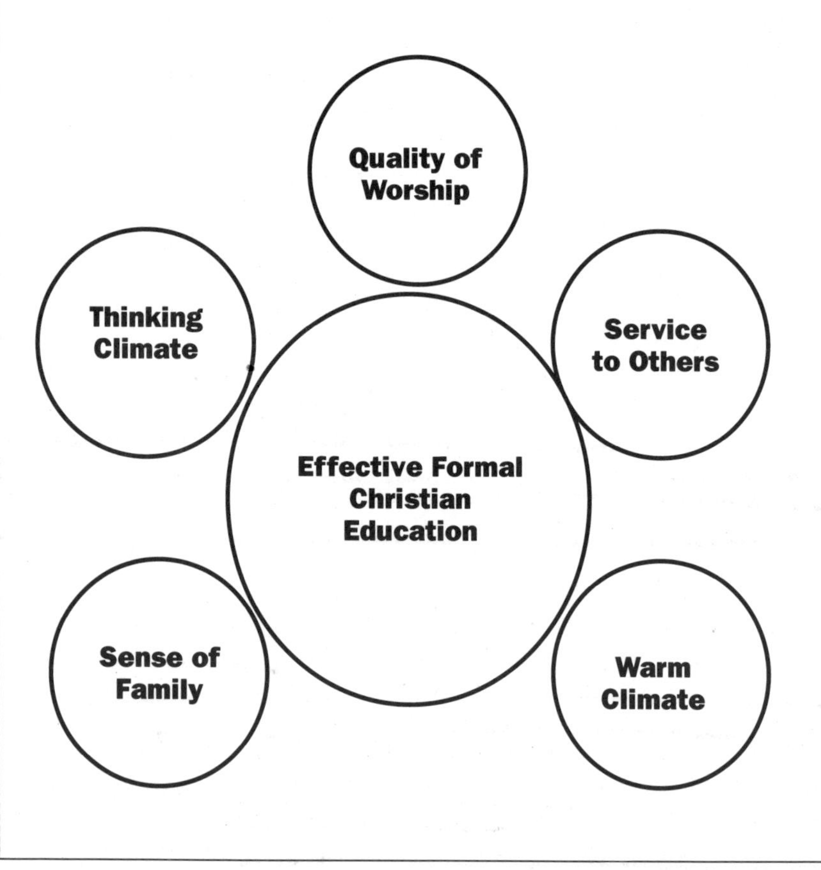

A WARM CLIMATE

A California church in the heart of high-tech Silicon Valley ministers in a community with some of the most highly educated, highest-paid people in the nation. The community also has high divorce and remarriage rates, high mortgage payments, and high spouse-abuse rates. In this context, the church provides an extended family for these people who had moved West for jobs. The church provides a haven away from the competitiveness and pretenses of the other part of their lives. One member said the church provides a "chance to listen to what God is saying, in a neat, wonderful cocoon with the church family."

This congregation illustrates the discovery made by the researchers when they visited the 52 congregations with strengths in promoting faith: The congregation's warm climate. Virtually all these effective congregations, even the large ones, described themselves as a "family." They were warm and welcoming—not only toward friends, but also toward visitors.

Of the five factors described in this chapter, a warm climate has the greatest influence upon a person's loyalty to the congregation. (Christian education—the largest circle and greatest influence—is explored in depth in subsequent chapters.) People want to feel comfortable, welcome, and at home in church. Indeed, a warm, accepting climate can compensate for other problems. "Church friendships appear to bind churchgoers to their church, even in the face of dissatisfaction with other areas of church life," writes Daniel Olson, who studied social networks, commitment, and church growth.[1]

According to members' perceptions, most mainline congregations do fairly well in promoting a warm climate for adults. Almost three-fourths of adults say their church is both warm and friendly. Among youths, 63 percent say their church is warm, while 85 percent say it's friendly.

Church members tend to feel slightly less enthusiastic when asked how welcome their congregation makes strangers feel. Only 63 percent of adults and 69 percent of teenagers make such a claim. Similarly, youths are more likely than adults to say that their church accepts people who are different.

How can congregations create or enhance a warm climate—one that will provide.an appropriate context for enhancing faith? It doesn't come without effort. "A fellowship does not simply learn to love . . . by accidentally bumping into each other," Daniel G. Bagby writes in *The Church: The Power to Help and to Hurt*. "A commitment to learn to care, and specific ways in which the fellowship can learn to take initiative toward one another, are essential."[2] Several clues for creating a warm climate arise from the study.

Make everyone feel included. Some churches that say they are families are slow to accept in-laws! Their families are not only tight-knit, but closed-knit. For a church truly to provide a warm climate without being incestuous, it must be open and accepting of all.[3]

It's important to note that active church members may have perspectives on church climate that are different from those on the fringe. We analyzed responses from active and inactive members and found significant differences.[4] While 43 percent of active adults say their church feels warm, only 12 percent of inactive adults do. A similar difference occurs between those who say their church accepts people who are different (43% of actives vs. 15% of inactives). This finding suggests that active members should not rely merely on their own experiences in judging church climate.

Help members develop strong interpersonal skills. Many church members may want to be more welcoming toward others, but they don't know how. By teaching people to show warmth, to listen and express care, churches can nourish within members the characteristics necessary for a church climate to be warm, accepting, and open.

Based on interests of both adults and teenagers, such training would be well-received. Seventy-four percent of adults said they would be "interested" or "very interested" in "improving my skills at showing love and concern." Moreover, 69 percent expressed similar interest in "making more friends at church." Among teenagers, the top interest was "knowing how to make friends and be a friend," with 75 percent of teenagers expressing interest.

Make visitors feel welcome. "It is not easy to walk into a strange church," state Roy M. Oswald and Speed B. Leas in *The Inviting Church: A Study of New Member Assimilation.* "One does not feel welcomed if he or she is left alone, unattended, feeling lost and helpless." Yet those writers report that 42 percent of visitors to the congregations they studied said they had never been identified as newcomers.[5]

But it's possible to be too pushy, according to a Barna Research Group survey of unchurched Americans. Visitors like to be noticed, but they don't want to be made the object of undue attention. The two worst things a church can do, the survey indicated, are to identify visitors during worship and have them wear name tags. And visitors did not like receiving a house call within a week of visiting the church. On the other hand, visitors did like the following . . .

. . . receiving information about the church from ushers;

. . . getting a thank-you letter or phone call from the pastor the week after the visit;

. . . being personally greeted by individual church members after the service.[6]

Assimilate new members into church life. When one interviewer asked a high-school girl about the best thing that had happened to her at her church, she responded, "Being accepted the first time I came to youth group." The interviewer pressed to see whether the girl's experience was unusual. "Of course not," a boy replied, "that's the way this congregation is."

Daniel Bagby writes about visiting a family that was leaving his church to join another one in the community. When he asked how the church had failed them, they replied, "We tried very hard to belong here; no one seemed to care enough to include us. Everyone seemed to have his or her own group and to be quite satisfied with keeping their circles of friendship just like they were. No one seemed to care whether we were around or not."[7]

Welcoming people into the fellowship of a local church can be a challenge. Some people want only minimal commitment. Others want to dive into leadership almost immediately. Yet all need to develop a network of support where they feel wanted and needed. Without this network, people are likely to drop out or change churches when a problem arises—either in the church or in their personal lives.

A THINKING CLIMATE

When people come to church, do they shut off their brains? Are they spoon-fed simple answers to tough questions? Can people come and just sit passively? Or are they challenged to think about faith in new ways? Unless the latter is true, it's likely that people will stagnate in their faith.

Though our faith is not merely a rational faith, it is not merely an emotional faith, either. It is a faith that demands that we love God with "all your heart and with all your soul, and with all your mind" (Matt. 22:37). It is a faith that involves both our feelings and our intellect.

A "thinking climate" through the whole congregation is invaluable in helping people grow in their faith, as well as their loyalty. It rivals warmth in terms of impact. Churches with thinking climates expect people to devote time to thought and study. They expect members to grow and learn and think for themselves. They encourage people to ask tough questions about themselves, their world, and God.

Churches are less likely to have a thinking climate than to be warm and friendly. Though 61 percent of adults say they learn a lot at church, only 46 percent say their church challenges their thinking. Only 40 percent say their church challenges them to ask questions. Furthermore, only 36 percent of adults say that "most members want to be challenged to think about religious issues and ideas." Teenagers are just as unlikely as adults to experience a thinking climate at church. Only 42 percent say their church challenges their thinking, and 45 percent say their church encourages questions (see Figure 30).

Congregations with thinking climates stretch their members' minds. The California church mentioned earlier emphasizes wrestling with controversial issues. Among the issues that have arisen there in recent years are whether to baptize children of nonmembers, whether to allow children to participate in communion, whether to let an AIDS support group use the church facility, and whether to welcome members regardless of sexual orientation.

Each of these policy matters became an opportunity to think about faith and its implications. For each issue, a task force was formed to develop a proposed policy statement. Then the proposal would be discussed in various settings, where many people could express themselves and find a common ground. As one member put it: "We resolve things by study, not by emotions."

Congregations do not create thinking climates by initiating new programs. Rather, a thinking climate must be part of the fabric of everything in congregational life. Evaluating—and then adjusting—the climate within your own congregation can begin by struggling with a series of questions.

Are questions encouraged or discouraged? When someone asks a question about faith, is that person affirmed or discounted? Is it safe to ask a question—any question—without being considered an unbeliever? One church member in Minnesota told that he was not afraid to ask questions or to express doubts. The result was "growth in safety," he said.

How does the congregation deal with diverse opinions? American journalist Walter Lippmann once declared: "When all think alike, no one thinks much." By giving people a safe place to express diverse opinions, churches stimulate thinking for everyone. By stifling diverse opinions as unorthodox, or by mandating beliefs, churches discourage thoughtfulness.

Are members challenged to examine their faith in their everyday lives? Is faith merely an intellectual exercise? Or does it challenge people to grow and change? Do people think about the implications of their faith on their families, work, recreation, finances, and other areas of life? Or are those issues "too personal" to bring up in church? "The unexamined life is not worth living," warned Plato in his *Apology*. A thinking climate provides a context for that examination.

Are people given answers, or are they led to discover answers? A small Korean congregation in Illinois models a teaching style that takes seriously each person's ability to grapple with faith issues. The goal of the children's education program is to help children analyze questions and come to their own conclusions. By giving young people the skills to think about their faith and to discern truth, the church hopes young people will learn to recognize values in the secular world that conflict with the Christian faith.

UPLIFTING WORSHIP

Worship services are the heart of congregational life in most churches. In these experiences, the whole body comes together to celebrate God's love and respond with praise and adoration. From a theological and historical perspective, the preeminence of worship is appropriate. But the question for us is, Does worship also promote faith?

Based on the *Effective Christian Education* study, the answer is yes, provided the worship is "spiritually uplifting." To be sure, worship is not as strong an influence on growth in faith as Christian education. But it is certainly a significant factor, as C. Ellis Nelson affirms: "Worship . . . with its prayers, music, scripture, sermon, and sacraments, stimulates, instructs, and guides the minds of believers. The content of worship—particularly the sermon—and informal conversations of members define an approved style of life."[8]

It is important to keep this potential influence in mind when we consider the number of people whose only regular church involvement is through worship services. According to a Barna Research Group report, 38 percent of Americans attend worship on a typical Sunday, but only 16 percent attend Sunday school.[9] This would mean that for about 22 percent of Americans, the only church experience during an average week is Sunday-morning worship. These worship-only attenders probably will not grow rapidly in their faith, but worship can and does have a positive influence.

In evaluating their own worship services, adults generally believe that their churches provide spiritually uplifting worship services.

Seventy percent say the worship experiences are good or excellent. Though the survey did not ask teenagers the same question, another question indicates that their evaluation wouldn't be as positive. When the study asked people to choose from a list of 28 factors the five most positive influences on their faith, only 14 percent of youths included worship on their list, while 29 percent of adults mentioned worship.

While some mainline churches don't include children in the worship service, most do. In fact, 79 percent of churches include church-school children in the entire service, while in another 19 percent of churches, they attend part of the service. Only 2 percent do not have opportunities for children to attend worship.

Each person has a different perspective on what makes worship spiritually uplifting. Even the congregations chosen as exemplary in promoting faith use a variety of worship styles, from the traditional Lutheran or Catholic liturgy to the informal, seemingly unstructured Quaker services, to spirited African American Baptist or Pentecostal services. Due to these differences, it would be impossible to suggest specific, useful avenues for enhancing worship.

One helpful perspective on worship is found in Kennon L. Callahan's *Twelve Keys to an Effective Church.* He suggests five factors that "contribute to corporate, dynamic worship," which are presented here to promote discussion:[10]

The warmth and winsomeness of the service and the congregation. This factor relates obviously to the warm climate, discussed earlier.

The dynamic and inspiration of the worship. Callahan estimates that 40 percent of the typical worship service consists of music. He suggests that a solid music program mixes planning and spontaneity, balance and variety, quality and depth.

The character and quality of preaching. Good sermons, Callahan suggests, have three characteristics. They are easy to follow and they make sense. They involve the humor, struggle, and drama of the text and of contemporary life. And they share something that is helpful and hopeful in the midst of the pain, suffering, and injustice in this present world.

The power and movement of the liturgy. Instead of a series of disconnected elements, an effective liturgy is like a drama in which one element builds on the other with power, rhythm, movement, and direction.

The seating range of the sanctuary. A sanctuary needs to be comfortably filled for worship to be most uplifting.

RECEIVING CARE

When someone misses a Sunday because of illness, does anyone notice? When someone experiences difficulty in the family or on the job, do other church members express concern and encouragement?

Members of caring churches feel that others in the congregation care about them, particularly in times of crisis or difficulty. In contrast, a significant reason people drop out of church is that they fail to receive that care during a time of crisis. In *What Can We Do About Church Dropouts?* C. Kirk Hadaway describes those people who leave because "the people there just don't care." No one came to see them when they were hospitalized or when a family member died. And so they feel estranged and angry.[11]

Thus it is disturbing that a significant portion of adults do not feel they receive care from their congregations. Only 57 percent say they often experience the love, care, and support of other adults. Young people feel even less support; only 32 percent say adults in the church often care about them, and just 38 percent say their peers often care about them. How can a caring climate be nourished? Consider these avenues:

Christian Education—Christian education can play a crucial role in developing a sense of care, since it often provides opportunities for person-to-person interaction. Taking time to show concern during Sunday school and other educational contexts could be significant in helping people grow in their faith and loyalty to the congregation.

The caring climate will, in turn, enhance the education. In his handbook *Do You Care? Compassion in the Sunday School,* Duane A. Ewers advises: "Learning is enhanced when persons are surrounded by love, warmth, acceptance, and compassion. . . . In a 'congregation of care,' persons will risk sharing their ideas, insights, creative expressions, and feelings when they know such sharing, so important for learning, will be treated 'care-fully.'"[12]

Many congregations develop their Sunday schools as centers of care. These small groups of people meet weekly to study and build relationships. If someone is missing, a class member is responsible for follow-up. If a class member is sick, hospitalized, or has other needs, the class rallies together to meet the need, and to make the rest of the congregation aware of that need. When a majority of a congregation is connected to formal Christian education, this approach naturally provides care to most members.

Small Groups—A California church has a weekly attendance of more than 1,500. Yet even with its size, creating a caring environment is a key goal. "Caring is what we hope to get across," several teachers said. The congregation does this through small groups for all ages, where individuals can be affirmed and supported. The church sees itself as a collection of smaller congregations, each with its own staff person as its primary minister.

Shepherding Programs—Several congregations in the study have instituted various kinds of shepherding programs through which the church stays in touch with people and their needs. One widely used model is derived from Stephen's Ministries, described in Kenneth C. Haugk's *Christian Caregiving—A Way of Life.*[13]

Special Needs—Because of the difficult problems many people face, programs to address special needs can be important ways to show care. One Arkansas church has a "Survivors Class" for children whose parents are divorcing. It starts when there is a need and continues until the children feel ready to disband. Young people who have been through the group before provide leadership.

SERVICE TO OTHERS

In addition to being at the heart of the gospel, our study found that providing regular service opportunities helps members grow in their faith: "The experience of serving others, through acts of mercy, compassion, or the promotion of social justice, is an important influence on the deepening of faith. . . . Some of the best religious education occurs in these moments of giving, of connection, of bonding to others."[14] These service opportunities include . . .

. . . helping people in the community;
. . . helping the poor;
. . . doing community service; and
. . . becoming involved in peacemaking and social justice initiatives.

Despite its importance, only 43 percent of adults say their congregation does a good job of involving them in community service. Indeed, only about half of youths and adults say their church emphasizes "reaching out to the poor and hungry," and only one in four says his or her church emphasizes "involving members in helping people in your town or city." Finally, the lowest emphasis in the list of 22 possibilities was "getting members to work for social justice and peace." Only 12 percent of adults and 21 percent of youths say their church has this emphasis.

Complicating the problem is that people express little interest in getting involved in service and justice. Only 36 percent of adults say they would be interested in community service projects, and only 20 percent express interest in social-justice activities.

Given these statistics, how can congregations persuade members to become involved in service and justice issues? Some might respond that we should simply ignore these issues, focusing instead on issues about which people are interested. With this market-driven approach, churches would respond only to the expressed needs of the "constituents." As popular as such an approach has become in some circles, it neglects our calling as Christians to be servants, and truncates a central theme in scripture.

Others might suggest that churches must first nurture faith in the protected environment of the Christian community, and only later begin outreach. Yet, few churches apparently ever move to the outreach part. Furthermore, serving others also nurtures faith in important ways—ways that cannot be simulated in the protected confines of the church.

Rather than ignoring or postponing service in our congregations, we need to discover specific, creative ways to build both interest and involvement in service. "If the church is to take seriously God's redemptive activity in the world," says Suzanne Johnson, "then the church will help its members find where that activity is going on and assist them in participating in it."[15]

Several congregations visited by researchers have placed service at the heart of their ministries. Each has found its members growing in faith through these efforts. Below are several "entry points" for service ministry.

Build on congregational identity. When most people think of service-oriented churches, a particular image comes to mind: the prophetic, liberal, activist church—what Carl S. Dudley and Sally A. Johnson describe as "the crusader church." Yet these researchers contend that many different kinds of churches can be quite effective in social ministry—as long as that ministry grows out of the congregation's own identity. Rather than being a barrier to social ministry, congregational identity can become an asset:

> Each self-image has special, irreplaceable gifts that these congregations can alone offer to others through social ministry, gifts that make them stronger and richer in the act of giving:
> The survivors can cope where other styles would collapse.
> The crusaders can raise issues where others might let them slide.

The pillars can legitimate change where others might ignore it.
The pilgrims can embrace diversity where others might deny it.
The servants can care for individuals who might otherwise be lost.[16]

Raise awareness. Congregations with active service ministries are also active in raising the issues of poverty and justice in sermons, Christian education, and other areas of church life. Particularly if this consciousness-raising is done in creative ways, it can pique people's interest and concern.

Build on individual members' concerns. One small-town church member in Indiana became concerned about homeless people in Indianapolis, so he began going to the city every Sunday afternoon to distribute food and blankets. This initial effort turned into a congregation-wide ministry known as The Shepherds. Listening for, affirming, and supporting such "callings" can become the impetus for important ministries.

Create opportunities for service. I once taught a young adult Sunday school class in which we discussed Christian responsibility to serve those in need. One class member was almost in tears as she expressed her frustration: "I want to do something," she said, "but I don't know what. I don't know where to go. I don't know where to start."

It's easy to point to members' low involvement in service as the problem. But do congregations offer real opportunities for people to become involved? Though few members may be interested in service, providing initial low-risk and low-commitment entry points can be the spark to light up involvement. And once a few people are involved, others soon will follow.

Link with other churches and organizations. An Illinois church offers a residential shelter from domestic violence, a crisis hotline, legal assistance, a treatment group for male abusers, a preschool, a clothing room, and a community organization for low-income residents. How does one church do all this? Not alone. It is part of a network supported by 34 congregations in the area. By working with other churches, this congregation has expanded its services and broadened its opportunities for service—far beyond what it could do alone.

Research by Joseph B. Tamney and Steven D. Johnson on forming ecumenical social ministries suggests some useful "talking points" for evaluating cooperative ministries. The researchers contacted churches in an Indiana community to evaluate their interest in a variety of cooperative ventures. They found broad support across liberal/conservative lines for efforts to lessen drug abuse, teenage pregnancy, and family abuse.

Excluding the very conservative Protestant pastors would broaden the support to include issues such as providing food for the poor, providing clothing and housing for the poor, and lessening racial discrimination. Similarly, campaigning against pornography gains broad support, except among the most liberal clergy.[17]

Work with the youth. Adolescents (particularly younger ones) tend to be more eager to be involved in service projects. Capitalize on their interest, and make their service visible in the congregation. Chapter 10 focuses on creating service opportunities for both youths and adults.

EVALUATING YOUR OWN CONGREGATION

Many of the factors addressed in this chapter are intangibles. They deal with atmosphere, feelings, and priorities which are difficult to name, but you intuitively know when they are in place and when they are missing. The "Congregational Life Worksheet" (Worksheet 2) allows you to evaluate your congregation in light of the information in this chapter. The following questions may also be useful to consider:

1. What was your own experience as a first-time visitor in your congregation? From that perspective, which factors in this section seemed strong and weak? Has your perception changed?
2. Do you think others in your congregation would have totally different impressions of these categories? If so, what factors contribute to the differences?
3. Which of these factors is strongest in your congregation? What can you do to celebrate that strength?
4. What weakness in your congregation disturbs you most? How might you or an appropriate person in your congregation begin to address the problem?
5. What first steps need to be taken to begin addressing weak areas? How can that process be started? Who will be responsible for implementing change?
6. What long-range issues need to be addressed? How might you start the process of evaluation and change?

Worksheet 2
Congregational Life Evaluation

Use this worksheet to evaluate your congregation, based on the five factors in congregational life described in this chapter. Read each statement, then select a number that best represents how well your congregation does in this area, for both adults and youths. Use the following numbers:

1 = rarely true
2 = sometimes true
3 = often true
4 = very often true

Area of Congregational Life	Your Church (Adults)	Your Church (Youths)
Thinking Climate		
Our congregation challenges members' thinking.	______	______
Our congregation encourages members to ask questions.	______	______
Warm Climate		
Our congregation feels warm.	______	______
Our congregation is friendly and welcoming.	______	______
Caring Church		
Adults experience the love, care and support of other people in the church.	______	______
Young people feel that other youths in the church care about them.	______	______
Young people feel adults in the church care about them.	______	______
Service to Others		
Our church involves members in helping people in the community.	______	______
Our church encourages members to provide help, care, and support to others in the church.	______	______
Worship		
Our church has spiritually uplifting worship services.	______	______

EFFECT ON CHRISTIAN EDUCATION

None of the five areas of congregational life described in this chapter—warm climate, thinking climate, a sense of care, uplifting worship, and opportunities for service—has to do specifically with Christian education as it is often narrowly defined. Yet each is vital. And each creates a climate in which Christian education can either flourish or flounder.

Education can take place in many different settings, not just traditional classrooms. In the words of Clark M. Williamson and Ronald J. Allen, churches need to become "teaching communities" or "neighborhood theological seminaries": "We propose that the congregation is first a neighborhood theological seminary whose primary purpose is to help its members relate the Christian tradition appropriately, intelligibly, and morally to the contemporary world situation and vise versa." They go on to describe how worship, administration, pastoral care, missions, and other areas of congregational life can serve a valuable educational role in the lives of members.[18]

Consider the impact on Christian education when a congregation truly encourages thinking and questioning. Or imagine the interaction that can develop in a warm, caring group. By making the effort to examine and reinvigorate these factors, churches can develop an effective Christian education ministry that builds on all aspects of congregational life.

Chapter 5

How Churches Shape Their Educational Ministries

Paging through most magazines for church leaders leaves the strong impression that every church needs to launch a new ministry every month. There's always a challenge to start a new program to meet a new need. Usually the article explains how "attendance nearly doubled" as a result of some innovative program.

Some church leaders read the articles and start effective ministries. But most simply turn the page, saying, "Nice idea, but . . . ." They feel they already are doing as much as—or more than—they can realistically do.

The good news growing out of the *Effective Christian Education* study is that churches don't necessarily need more programs to be effective. The study found no correlation between numerous programs and effective Christian education. Both churches with numerous programs and those with few programs have the potential of being effective in Christian education. As the research report concluded: "Program quantity . . . does not appear to matter in any systematic way."[1]

The difference comes in how effectively churches carry out the programs they do have. The report continues: "Effective Christian education can be transmitted through a small number of programs and events, as long as, in combination, they have effective leadership, process, and content. Accordingly, what matters is how things are done rather than numbers or range of programs."[2] Thus, the study's insights can be applied to large and small churches, and rural, urban, and suburban churches, each of which must minister out of its own setting and resources.

Before examining the dynamics of effective Christian education, it is helpful to gather some "baseline data" on Christian education's current shape. Where does education take place? What programs do churches actually operate? How are these programs organized? This material, then, is *descriptive*, not *prescriptive*. It shows how churches organize their Christian education ministries, not necessarily the most effective ways to organize them. However, it does generate new thinking about more effective ways.

CHILDREN'S EDUCATION

Because of the difficulties of doing in-depth survey research with children, the *Effective Christian Education* study did not include children younger than seventh grade in the survey. However, it did ask adults and leaders to describe and evaluate their congregations' children's education programs.

In general, children's programs focus on traditional activities, such as Sunday school, vacation Bible school, children's sermons and children's choir. More innovative programs, such as youth groups for upper-elementary children, church-related day care, and after-school programs, occur in relatively few churches (see Figure 8).

Most people believe their churches make a positive difference in the lives of children. Eighty-five percent of Christian education coordinators and the same percentage of adults call their church's children's program "good" to "outstanding." Yet the opinions are qualified. Only the following percentage of each group rated their children's programs "excellent" or "outstanding" (on a 7-point scale): adults: 29 percent; Christian education coordinators: 22 percent; youths: 22 percent; teachers: 19 percent; pastors: 11 percent.

Figure 8
Children's Programs

According to Christian education coordinators, here are the percentages of mainline churches that offered each of the following children's education programs in the past year:

Sunday or church school, kindergarten: 99%
Sunday or church school, grades 1 through 6: 99%
Sunday or church school, pre-kindergarten: 98%
Vacation Bible school: 90%
Children's sermons during worship services: 78%
Children's choir: 74%
Church-related nursery school: 48%
Youth group for grades 5 and/or 6: 31%
Church-related day care: 19%
Church-related after-school programs: 13%

The study asked church leaders to assess and describe their children's program in more detail. The leaders identify a variety of strengths, weaknesses, and emphases.

Strengths—According to Christian education coordinators, the strongest aspect of their children's programs involves atmosphere. Eighty-two percent say it is "very true" that the children's classes and events feel warm and inviting. Not surprisingly, 74 percent say the children enjoy the program. Sixty-one percent also believe their children's program promotes growth in religious faith and conviction.

Weaknesses—Weaknesses in children's programming tend to focus more on the educational process and content. Only 45 percent of coordinators believe their program is innovative and creative. About half (51%) think the program challenges children to think. And 53 percent believe the program addresses children's needs and interests. Finally, just 48 percent of coordinators say that adults in their congregations place high priority on Christian education for children.

Emphases—One emphasis stands above all others in children's ministry: teaching Bible stories. Eighty-nine percent of Christian education coordinators say it is a strong emphasis, and this seems entirely appropriate, given children's developmental abilities and needs. Developing Bible knowledge is a distant second at 67 percent. Relatively few mainline churches (20%) emphasize Bible memorization for children.

Though much weaker, a second area of emphasis involves decision-making and values. About 58 percent of churches place a strong emphasis on teaching moral values. Similarly, 54 percent emphasize learning to apply faith to everyday life. Four out of ten churches emphasize teaching moral decision-making.

Perhaps one reason children enjoy Christian education classes is that they allow children to build friendships. Half of all programs (49%) strongly emphasize fellowship or social interaction. Such interaction must be primarily with the children's own age group, since only 21 percent of churches emphasize intergenerational interaction.

Theological issues rank fairly low in order of emphasis. Only 15 percent of churches emphasize theological reflection on human experience. About the same percentage (13%) emphasize denominational theology, tradition, and history. Understanding and appreciating religious symbols ranks high in just 29 percent of churches, and only 6 percent emphasize an awareness and understanding of other faith traditions.

Though educators emphasize the need for nurturing positive social values and commitments at an early age, few churches do. Thirty-eight percent report providing opportunities for children to help other people, and still fewer emphasize the following social values: multicultural awareness and understanding: 15 percent; peacemaking: 14 percent; global awareness and understanding: 12 percent; discussion of local or national issues: 4 percent.

Finally, disturbingly few churches emphasize working with parents of children. Only 21 percent of churches emphasize involving parents in program decisions and planning, and just 5 percent emphasize informing parents of students' progress. Furthermore, churches do little to support parents of children. Just 8 percent have a strong emphasis on providing classes on effective parenting or communication, and only 7 percent emphasize providing classes to help parents learn how to promote faith in their children.

Teachers—Teachers in children's education tend to have a lower faith maturity than teachers of youths and adults. Only 32 percent of children's program teachers show a mature faith. Chapter 7 focuses more on teacher characteristics and needs.

YOUTH EDUCATION

As indicated in chapter 1, declines in Christian education are dramatic in high school. The strengths, weaknesses, and emphases reported by Christian education coordinators are symptomatic of the declining involvement—and may speak to some of the causes.

We see some of the symptoms when looking at the most common programs in churches (see Figure 9). The top two programs—seventh- to ninth-grade Sunday school and confirmation programs—apply only to young adolescents. Fourteen percent fewer churches provide Sunday school for high-school youths than for junior-high youths.

Strengths—Like children's education, the strongest areas of youth education, as reported by adult leaders, involve atmosphere. Sixty-three percent of coordinators say it is "very true" that youths enjoy the program, and 61 percent say youth classes and events feel warm and inviting. In comparison to children's education, though, these percentages are significantly lower.

Another area of relative strength involves young people's intellectual development. Fifty-six percent of coordinators say their programs

Figure 9
Youth Programs

According to Christian education coordinators, here are the percentage of mainline churches that offered each of the following youth-education programs in the past year:

Sunday or church school, grades 7 through 9: 92%
Confirmation program for young adolescents: 85%
Camping for youth: 84%
Sunday or church school, grades 10 through 12: 78%
High school youth group*: 77%
Junior high/middle school youth group: 70%**
Community service projects for youths: 57%
Youth choir: 47%
Travel seminars for youths: 42%
Weekly opportunity to study the Bible (other than Sunday school): 37%
Weekly opportunity for mission education: 12%

**Grades 9–12, or 10–12*
***Grades 7–8, 7–9, or 6–8*

challenge youth to think, and 55 percent say their program promotes growth in religious faith and conviction. (Youths report similar strengths. Sixty-two percent say it is true or very true that their church challenges them to think.)

Weaknesses—Fewer than half of Christian education coordinators (48%) say their program addresses youths' needs and interests. Furthermore, only 35 percent say their programs are innovative and creative. Part of the problem may be that youth ministry is not a priority. Only 44 percent of coordinators say adults in their congregation place high priority on youth Christian education.

Emphases—Many churches seem to have bought the idea that youth ministry is "fun and games." The strongest emphasis is on providing fellowship or social interaction, with 70 percent of coordinators saying this is a strong emphasis.

While fewer than half the coordinators say their churches meet youth needs, learning how to apply faith to everyday life is a strong emphasis in 66 percent of churches. Similarly, 64 percent emphasize teaching moral values, and 60 percent emphasize teaching moral decision-making. Only about half as many (36%) emphasize theological reflection on human experience.

Though Bible stories rank highest in children's education, the biblical emphasis declines for junior and senior high. Fifty percent say their church strongly emphasizes developing Bible knowledge. Only 39 percent emphasize teaching Bible stories. And just 9 percent emphasize Bible memorization for youths.

Though youth education programs place more emphasis on social values than do children's programs, these remain relatively weak emphases. About 39 percent of churches emphasize providing youths with opportunities for helping other people. But only 22 percent emphasize peacemaking, and 20 percent emphasize discussion of local or national issues. Multicultural awareness and understanding are emphasized in 18 percent of churches, and 16 percent of churches emphasize global awareness and understanding.

In the same way children's programs place little emphasis on family, youth programs don't make these connections a high priority, either. A quarter of coordinators (26%) say their churches have a strong emphasis on involving parents in program decisions and planning. Eight percent emphasize informing parents of students' progress. Classes for parents on effective parenting or communication are relatively rare, with only 9 percent of churches emphasizing them. Similarly, only 6 percent emphasize providing classes to help parents learn how to promote the faith of their children.

Teachers—Fewer than half of youth teachers (40%) have a mature faith. While this percentage is higher than for teachers of children, it remains significantly lower than for adult education teachers.

Challenges—Keeping young people involved in the church and growing in their faith is a vital challenge facing the church. Not only do young people have much to offer now, but their involvement as teenagers can have a significant impact on their later involvement. When adults were asked about their earliest faith commitments, few in the mainline denominations identified a single, identifiable moment of conversion. Rather, many indicated that their faith had grown gradually over time, often since early childhood.

Thus churches would do well to provide young people an atmosphere in the congregation where faith is taken seriously and growth is encouraged, expected, and elicited. These early explorations of faith are vital to a lifetime commitment.

ADULT EDUCATION

Only about three in ten mainline adults participate in Christian education programs. Yet, as Figure 10 shows, churches provide myriad educational programs for adults. Furthermore, Christian education coordinators identify numerous strengths in their adult programs.

Strengths—As with other ages, the strongest areas of adult education involve classes that feel warm and inviting (75%). Similarly, 72 percent of coordinators say adults enjoy the program. Coordinators also believe their programs promote growth in religious faith and conviction of adults (64%) and challenge adults to think (62%). Likewise, 56 percent say programs address adults' needs and interests.

Figure 10
Adult Programs

According to Christian education coordinators, here are the percentage of mainline churches that offered each of the following adult education programs in the past year:*

Women's group or women's auxiliary: 94%
Adult choir: 93%
Sunday or church school or adult education classes: 89%
Missions projects: 78%
Informal Bible studies for adults: 73%
Intergenerational events: 73%
Membership classes for adults: 69%
Community service projects: 65%
Formal, long-term, in-depth Bible study: 61%
Prayer groups: 60%
Religious plays or dramas: 55%
Men's group or men's auxiliary: 53%
Retreats for adults: 53%
Camping for adults: 50%
Missions conferences: 47%
Support groups for adults with special needs: 42%
Lectures, speeches, or workshops on social or moral issues: 41%
Discussions or seminars for parents: 37%
Discussions or seminars for young adults: 33%
Seminary or college-based extension courses for laity: 18%
Training in language or reading skills: 6%
Job or vocational sessions or programs: 1%

**Some of these programs may include other ages.*

Weaknesses—Despite these perceived strengths, only 39 percent of coordinators say that adults in the congregation place a high priority on adult Christian education. Furthermore, only 33 percent say the adult program is innovative and creative.

Emphases—Christian education coordinators indicate that emphases in adult education vary more than in education for youths and children. Each of the following is a strong emphasis, according to coordinators: learning how to apply faith to everyday life: 75 percent; developing Bible knowledge: 74 percent; providing fellowship or social interaction: 71 percent; theological reflection on human experience: 61 percent.

Among adults, the emphasis shifts considerably to values and decision-making, away from basic Bible knowledge. Forty-five percent of coordinators report a strong emphasis on teaching moral values, and 44 percent report an emphasis on teaching moral decision-making. In contrast, 39 percent emphasize teaching Bible stories, and 9 percent emphasize Bible memorization for adults.

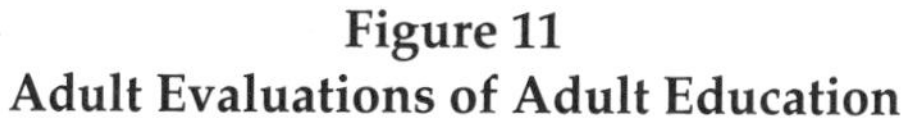

Figure 11
Adult Evaluations of Adult Education

The study asked adults to evaluate Christian education in their church. Here are the percentages of adults who say each characteristic of their church's educational program is "true" or "very true."

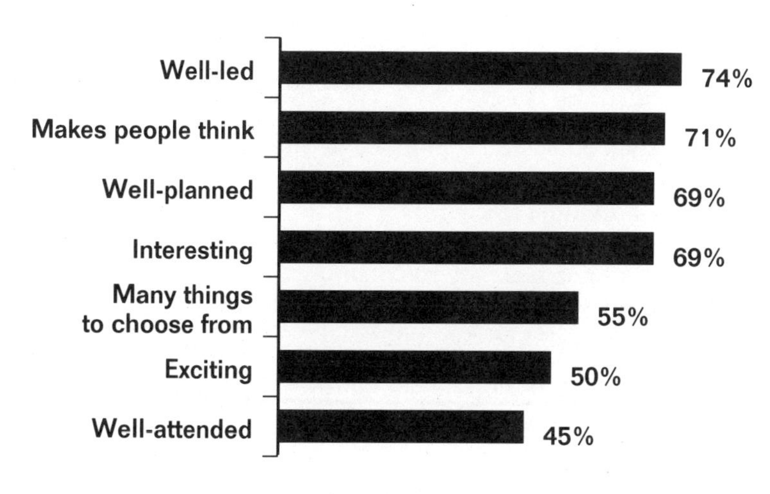

hasis on social values and issues is stronger than it was for d youth, though it still is not strong. Half of all churches asize providing opportunities for giving help to other people. Only 36 percent emphasize discussion of local or national issues, and 31 percent emphasize global awareness and understanding. Peacemaking is emphasized by 29 percent of churches, while 24 percent emphasize multicultural awareness and understanding.

Denominational and theological issues also rise in emphasis for adults. A third (32%) of coordinators say their adult education program has a strong emphasis on denominational theology, tradition, and history. One out of four (26%) emphasize understanding and appreciation of religious symbols, and 42 percent emphasize the appreciation of religious music. Finally, 22 percent emphasize awareness and understanding of other faith traditions.

Teachers—Among teachers of all ages, adult education teachers are most likely to exhibit faith maturity. Fifty-five percent have a mature faith. Since adult teachers tend to be between ages 50 and 70, this higher level of faith maturity is not surprising, given the younger teachers for younger ages.

CURRICULUM

Central to most churches' Christian educational programming is their choice of curriculum. This material guides both the content and the process for teachers in the classroom. Most churches recognize its importance by allocating significant portions of their education budgets to curriculum. The responsibility for choosing curriculum varies among congregations. Most commonly, the Christian education committee decides, but variations abound:

Christian-education committee decides: 35%
Teachers meet together to decide: 18%
Each individual teacher: 14%
Director of Christian education: 13%
The pastor or associate pastor: 9%
Superintendent of Sunday school or church school: 8%
Curriculum review committee: 3%

In general, Christian education coordinators seem satisfied with their curriculum. Eighty percent say that quality children's curriculum resources are available; 73 percent say quality resources are available for youths; and 75 percent say quality resources are available for adults. Furthermore, only 7 percent say that lack of quality resources is a major or somewhat major problem in their Christian education program.

If usage indicates satisfaction, churches are most satisfied with their denominational curriculum for children, but less satisfied with resources for youths and adults. Exclusive use of denominational resources plunges from 60 percent in sixth grade to 38 percent for grades nine through twelve.

In place of exclusively denominational resources, many churches turn to various combinations to meet the needs of youth and adult education (see Figure 31). For adults, congregations are almost as likely to use combinations as they are to use exclusively denominational resources. Interesting denominational differences also arise, with Southern Baptist congregations being almost twice as likely as any other denomination to use exclusively denominational material for their adult Bible study (see Figure 32).

About 27 percent of mainline churches say they never use nondenominational materials. When the other 73 percent look beyond their own denomination for curriculum, what sources do they turn to? Apparently they turn to a wide variety of sources, since the highest response to that question was "other." Among specific publishers, David C. Cook is the most common source, with 31 percent of mainline churches ordering from this publisher. Other sources include: Standard: 12 percent; Winston-Harper & Row: 9 percent; Scripture Press: 8 percent; Gospel Light: 7 percent.

The survey also asked which adult Bible-study programs churches use. Most (71%) do not use any. The most common programs are *The Bethel Series* and *Disciple*, each of which is used by 8 percent of churches in the study. *Search Weekly Bible Studies* is used by 7 percent; *The Kerygma Program*, *Word & Witness*, and *Trinity Bible Studies* are each used by 3 percent; and *Crossways!* is used by 2 percent of mainline churches.[3]

This trend toward diverse curriculum use in congregations may not reflect a simple dissatisfaction with denominational resources, but may be a sign of the larger phenomenon of churches turning to special-interest organizations for resources. Of the broader phenomenon, Robert Wuthnow suggests:

> To the huge denominational bureaucracies that were erected earlier in the century have now been added dozens and dozens of highly institutionalized organizations oriented to special-interest groups within denominations, to coordinating the complex relations

among denominations, and to filling crevices with religious activities that denominations have not provided.[4]

Wuthnow provocatively argues, however, that these new groups and structures may have had a positive influence on religious commitment in America:

> In a complex, highly diverse, highly specialized society such as the United States . . . special-purpose groups constitute a valuable way of sustaining religious commitment. People can participate in these organizations for limited periods of time. When their interests change, or when a more pressing need emerges, they can switch to a different organization.[5]

His contention deserves thought and discussion among church and denominational leaders as it relates to curriculum development.

Furthermore, the diverse interests and learning styles of youths and adults may consciously or unconsciously influence curriculum choices. Since children are grouped by age, while adults are often grouped by interest, use of diverse curriculum may be natural and inevitable. However, before assuming the best, congregations and denominations need to evaluate carefully the reasons for the trends.

In spite of the widespread acceptance of available curriculum, questions need to be raised as to whether it is truly effective. Satisfaction does not necessarily indicate effectiveness. For example, does the curriculum emphasize the elements of content and process that are vital to helping people grow in faith? Do they provide adequate guidance for teachers, who often are not familiar with educational theory and practice? Is the material accessible to children, youths, and adults who may have little biblical or theological background, or who may read only at third- or fourth-grade level? Chapters 6 and 7 give insights and suggestions that will be useful in evaluating curriculum choices in light of effectiveness, rather than of comfort and tradition. Worksheets 7 and 8 contain checklists based on the study for evaluating youth and adult curriculum.

FACILITIES AND EQUIPMENT

Many churches believe that facilities are the key to growth and effectiveness. They undertake renovations, building campaigns, and equipment purchases they believe will revolutionize their program.

However, state-of-the-art facilities and equipment do not guarantee growth or effectiveness. In fact, the national study found no link between quality of facilities and educational effectiveness. With this caveat in mind, let's look briefly at three issues concerning Christian education facilities:

Space—A little more than half of all mainline churches believe their Christian education space is adequate. Sixty percent say their youth space is adequate; 56 percent say their children's space is adequate; and 53 percent say adult education space is adequate.

Multimedia Resources—Once again, about half the churches have quality multimedia resources available. Fifty-one percent of Christian education coordinators say they have quality resources for children and adults; 49 percent say they have such resources available for youth education.

Library or Resource Center—Churches are less likely to have a quality Christian education library or resource center. Only 37 percent of coordinators say they have such a center for children's education. Thirty-five percent say they have one for youths, and 39 percent say they have one for adults.

PROBLEMS AND FRUSTRATIONS

How do Christian educators feel about their overall Christian education program? One way to assess this is to ask about the common problems they encounter. Figure 12 indicates issues with which they struggle. Two general issues rise to the top.

Time—It is no surprise that several of the top problems (including the top three) involve schedules and busyness. Like every other institution, churches are caught by the fast-paced culture in which we live. It affects not only leadership, but students. Churches must discover ways to reach people, even with their busy schedules.

At the same time, busyness may be less problematic than we sometimes think. We know, for example, that youths who tend to be involved in more outside activities also tend to be more (not less) active in church activities.[6] Thus the problem may not be dealing with the busy people, but discovering ways to reach out and include those people who may not be really busy with anything.

Figure 12
Common Problems in Christian Education

Here are the percentages of Christian-education coordinators who say that each issue is a "major" or "somewhat major" problem in promoting Christian education in their congregation.

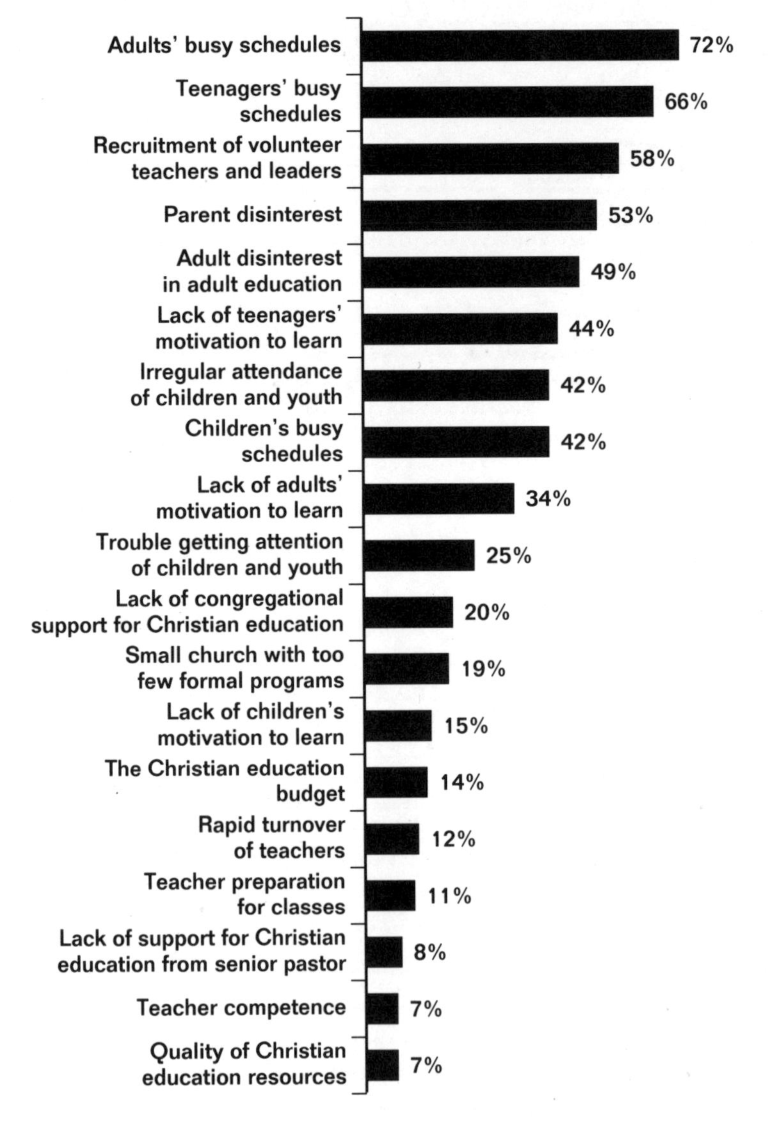

Disinterest—Apathy and lack of motivation may be partly a result of the time pressure as well. People have so many options competing for attention and time and involvement and commitment. Too often, church becomes one of the many choices in the cafeteria of commitments. This disinterest may also reflect the relatively low faith maturity among both youths and adults. As we noted in chapter 3, commitment is higher among people who have a mature faith.

NEW TASTES

Throughout this chapter, we've noted that people are largely satisfied with their congregations' Christian-education programs. Yet, as noted in the first chapter, Christian education is generally ineffective in promoting faith and loyalty among its participants. The question becomes, then, How to move beyond a comfortable status to an effective vision for Christian education? We may be like children who eat decorated sugar cookies at Christmas because they are pretty, when the real delicacies are the pies and cakes and truffles!

Perhaps we are satisfied because we have never tasted or experienced more effective Christian education. The chapters that follow give a taste of how programs can be more effective in promoting faith maturity, beginning with the process and content of effective Christian education.

Chapter 6

Managing an Effective Christian Education Program

Every time I serve on my church's Christian education committee, I feel I might as well have joined the volunteer fire department.

A one-alarm fire involved something like deciding what color to paint the nursery before the regional meeting at the church in two weeks.

A three-alarm fire involved choosing and ordering curriculum for the next quarter (usually four weeks away). How much? Where from? How will we pay for it?

Then there were the five-alarm fires: The junior-high teacher is moving out of town. Who can we get to fill her place? We can't find anyone to teach young adults. What should we do?

I don't believe these committees are exceptions to widespread practice. Most Christian education committees have major and diverse responsibilities—from choosing the curriculum to finding teachers to decorating the foyer to planning picnics. Leaders often feel overworked and fragmented, as dozens of programs and activities demand attention and work. As a result, these committees can lose sight of their focus, as they consume their energy worrying about chalk, chairs, and crackers.

Pastor Norman R. DePuy of Newton Centre, Massachusetts, argues that too many churches treat organization as an end rather than a means:

> [These churches] are a bit like the old paddle-wheel steamboat whose boiler capacity would allow it either to move its wheels or blow its whistle, but not to do both at the same time. If "moving the wheels" is growing in grace, theological understanding and biblical knowledge, then committees are too often merely "blowing the whistle," while the church remains at a standstill.[1]

How do churches switch from "blowing the whistle" to "moving the wheels"? They do it with administration, or management. Some church leaders chafe when they hear those words. They sound so secular! These leaders rightly worry that the negative values and priorities of some businesses could invade the church and undercut its theological calling.

Furthermore, many pastors and other church leaders don't see the connections between management and ministry. "Unfortunately, many pastors resist administrative work," writes Susanne Johnson. "They are tempted to think of it as a series of distractions from the real stuff of ministry. To them, it is nothing but meetings, mailings, charts, reports, budgets, busywork. Or administration is associated with crass business practices unrelated to the mission of the church."[2]

Instead of rejecting the "business" approaches out-of-hand, it seems more useful to reinterpret them and their insights in the church context. Johnson notes that administration always has been at the heart of ministry and service. And DePuy suggests that "all church administration is pastoral." He explains: "Poor administration means hurting and slighting people—to say nothing of poor stewardship of people's time, energy, and intelligence."[3]

Part of creating an effective Christian education program that helps people grow in faith involves creating an administrative foundation for the educational ministry. The *Effective Christian Education* study identified eight key elements of this administrative foundation. The study found that the following eight elements are vital for building and maintaining strong educational ministries: planning; coordination of study; evaluation; teacher training; teacher faith formation; teacher recognition; governing body support; and pastor's training.

This chapter examines the first three elements, which focus on program planning and development. Chapter 7 focuses on leadership issues.

PLANNING

Some people are good at "following their noses." When they're driving, their intuition tells them in which direction to turn, how far to go, and so forth. The rest of us use maps . . . or we drive aimlessly.

I suppose some people could carry out Christian education intuitively. They might know just the right issues to address and themes to emphasize. But the rest of us need maps to tell us where to go and how to get there. Otherwise, we wander aimlessly.

Many programs apparently wander. In evaluating their congregations' Christian education programs, many Christian education coordinators do not think their programs are very well-planned or administered. Only

55 percent say their adult education programs are well-planned and administered. Similarly, 54 percent believe their children's programs are well-planned and administered. But the figure drops to 46 percent for youth programs.

Christian education coordinators are more likely to say that the annual educational budgets are carefully planned. Sixty percent say their children and adult education budgets are carefully planned, while 55 percent make this claim for their youth budgets.

Setting a Direction—A common way to overcome the wandering is by establishing a planning process. The "road maps" used in many planning/administrative models focus on an organization's purpose, goals, and objectives:

- The purpose or vision is inherent in a church or ministry's nature. It answers the basic questions: Why does this church exist? Why do we have a Christian education program? Our study defined a primary purpose of Christian education as nurturing a vibrant, life-changing faith. A congregation's own mission statement for Christian education might be more specific, depending upon how it perceives its calling.
- Goals ask how a church might live out its purpose within a specific context. Thus, many congregations can have the same purpose without sharing the same goals. William E. Hull explains the difference: "Purposes ask *essential* questions about *being*, while goals ask *existential* questions about becoming."[4] So it's not enough to say that we always have Christian education; each year we need a renewed vision that fits within the church's overall mission.

More than half the churches in the study have mission statements for different age groups. Based on responses from Christian education coordinators, 58 percent of churches have mission statements for Christian education for children; 55 percent have mission statements for Christian education for youths; and 53 percent have mission statements for Christian education for adults.

- Unlike goals, which are long-range and general, objectives are short-range and specific. "They break up what may be the task of a decade—or even a lifetime—into manageable units of time," Hull writes, "charting how to get from where we are to where we want to be."[5]

While most churches have mission statements, most don't have learning objectives. Only 41 percent of Christian education coordinators say their church has stated learning objectives for children. Similarly, just 38 percent have them for youths, and 34 percent for adults.

Each of these three planning elements (purpose, goals, and objectives) should be guided by a variety of input. Hull suggests three types of input that should guide congregational planning.[6] The suggestions apply well to Christian education.

1. *Norms*—"Just as the navigator needs fixed stars," Hull writes, "so church leaders must have abiding norms from the Bible, church history, and theology in order to determine what God has done, is doing and yet intends to do through his people." This input requires constant study and dialogue about what it means to be the people of God.

2. *Data*—Using data in a local church "aids communication in the church and provides a needed balance to the intense subjectivity that characterizes much spiritual activity," Hull suggests. Data can include "hard" data (attendance and contribution records, demographics, etc.) and "soft" data (opinions, preferences, values, etc.). Hull believes hard data should be tracked continually, while soft data should be gathered less often—through interviews, informal conversations, and focus groups.

3. *Experience*—Too many churches rely solely on experience for planning. The result can be deceptive, for it tends to limit historical perspective, focusing too heavily on the latest trend. It also tends to blunt self-criticism. At the same time, it is valuable in order to reflect on and evaluate planning and implementation subjectively.

Discussing the Direction—The *Effective Christian Education* study also found that teachers in effective education programs tend to meet at least annually to discuss goals and objectives. Furthermore, teachers in these churches spend a full day each year on coordination and planning. This planning grows out of defined purpose, goals, and objectives. It helps the congregation in many ways:

- The objectives provide the groundwork for making choices and setting priorities—selecting curriculum, planning events, and implementing ideas.
- When all suggestions for programs and events are evaluated in light of the goals and objectives, Christian education leaders do not feel quite so pulled in many directions.
- Meeting together to establish goals and objectives creates a shared vision among teachers. Because the vision is theirs, they are more likely to be committed to it.
- Meeting together for a full day to coordinate and plan also allows teachers to share resources, ideas, and questions. They learn and grow from one another. And they develop a spirit of camaraderie that can sustain them through the inevitable slumps in teaching.

Teachers do discuss goals and objectives in most churches (79%). Yet only 18 percent of congregations ask teachers to meet together for a full day, at least annually, to plan and coordinate. Interestingly, only 45 percent of teachers say they would be interested or very interested in having more discussion about Christian education goals and methods.

Focusing the Plan—In addition to general, overall goals, and objectives for Christian education, it's important to establish specific mission statements, goals, and objectives within each area of education. What are you trying to accomplish in youth education? What are your goals with adults?

It's easy to capture what can happen in adult classes, for example, when Christian education programs don't have mission statements: "We've finished Genesis. Who'd like to do Exodus now? How many would rather try a New Testament book? Any ideas?" Spontaneity is fine; but, taken alone, it's ineffective in promoting growth in faith. A more effective approach might be a three-step process:

1. Spend time thoughtfully developing a mission statement that presents the overall goals of education for each age group.
2. Plan a coherent sequence of studies aimed in an agreed-on, articulated direction which leads to more mature faith and addresses the needs and interests of participants.
3. Think through specific learning objectives for each course of study, which tie to the more general mission statement. These objectives should include specific learning outcomes for each unit of study through the year. It would generally be desirable with youths and adults to include participants in this stage—and in the entire process.

MODELS FOR CHRISTIAN EDUCATION

One way to think about purpose, goals, and objectives is to consider the basic paradigms used by churches in developing their Christian education program. *Contemporary Approaches to Christian Education,* edited by Jack L. Seymour and Donald E. Miller, outlines the following five basic approaches.[7]

Religious Instruction—Outlined by Sara P. Little, this model builds on three central categories or concepts. First, it emphasizes thinking and understanding the gospel and its implications. Second, it focuses on deciding—confronting the problems that confront us and translating the decision-making into action. Third, it includes believing—"a believing that is informed by pursuit of the question Why? and that is held with both 'openness and conviction.'"[8]

Faith Community—Charles R. Foster advocates the community of faith as the guiding image for Christian education. This approach emphasizes formation in the community through rituals, traditions, symbols, and patterns of living that are normative in the particular faith community.

Spiritual Development—This model focuses on developmental models of faith, as presented by Donald E. Miller. The education focuses on nurturing the natural unfolding of faith and on helping people use life experiences and crises as opportunities to grow in faith.

Liberation—In this model, advocated by Allen J. Moore, emphasis is on analyzing and understanding the political, social, and cultural context of human life. It helps learners understand how social systems cause oppression and injustice, then urges action and reflection based on that understanding.

Interpretation—This approach emphasizes the Christian story along with personal experience, according to its proponents, Jack L. Seymour and Carol A. Wehrheim. Learners are encouraged to discover the interrelationships among Christian traditions, God's activity in the world, and personal experience. Teachers serve as guides to help learners interpret their experiences in light of the Christian story.

These five approaches were presented to pastors, Christian education coordinators, and teachers, who were asked to point out the approach emphasized in their congregation for different age levels.

Overall, the religious instruction model predominates, with about four out of ten congregations primarily emphasizing this model. About one in four emphasize the spiritual development model. However, the other models are used in many congregations, particularly among adults. The least-emphasized model is the liberation model, with just over one percent of churches primarily emphasizing this approach (see Figure 13).

These five approaches suggest some ways churches can develop their Christian education goals and objectives. And a congregation that emphasizes the religious instruction approach would likely shape its programs in significantly different ways from a church that emphasizes spiritual development or interpretation. The differences highlight the need for intentional planning, so that the mission and goals are clear. Then specific objectives, strategies, and programs can be developed based on the selected model.

Figure 13
Approaches to Christian Education

Christian education coordinators were presented with five approaches to Christian education. Here are the percentages who say their congregation put "moderate" or "strong" emphasis on each approach in different levels.

Educational Approach	Used with Grades 1–6	Used with Grades 7–12	Used with Adults
Religious instruction	72%	60%	61%
Spiritual development	43%	47%	59%
Interpretation	33%	40%	46%
Faith community	33%	31%	34%
Liberation	6%	9%	17%

The survey also asked pastors, teachers, and Christian education coordinators which of the approaches they wish their church emphasized more. Here are their responses:

Educational Approach	Pastors	Teachers	Coordinators
Spiritual development	30%	34%	35%
Faith community	19%	10%	12%
Interpretation	14%	15%	13%
Religious instruction	10%	17%	16%
Liberation	12%	6%	6%
None	16%	18%	18%

Of course, each approach has justification and benefits, and elements of several would generally be blended in a particular congregation. The key, however, is not the specific approach taken, but whether it is intentionally developed and implemented.

PARENTAL INVOLVEMENT

One of my most painful church experiences occurred in a church in which parents blamed the church's youth program for family problems and for the teenagers dropping out. The youth leaders responded that the parents didn't care enough to support the program. Battle lines were drawn, and the whole church became embroiled in a bitter conflict. Several families left the church angry, and two church staff members resigned under pressure. As often happens, the remaining young people were caught in the middle, scarring their memory of the church for their lifetime.

Many issues, agendas, and problems were involved in this particular incident, many of them unrelated to the youth program. Yet the incident illustrates the importance in children's and youth education of building a team with the parents, so that they are "on board," with their input, support, and leadership.

Not surprisingly, the *Effective Christian Education* study found that parental involvement in program decisions and planning has a measurable impact on a youth education program. Similar connections would likely be found for children's education as well. However, only 26 percent of churches involve parents in youth education planning. And only 21 percent involve parents in children's education planning.

Though the specifics are quite different from Christian education, it's interesting to note the similarities between increasing the parental involvement in both Christian education and public education. An important study by the Carnegie Council on Adolescent Development, *Turning Points: Preparing American Youth for the 21st Century,* examines the dynamics of education for young adolescents. Among its many recommendations was an emphasis on "re-engaging families in the education of young adolescents."

The report argues that many parents believe "they should increasingly disengage from their young adolescents. In the belief that adolescents should be independent, parents come to view involvement in their child's education as unnecessary." Yet, the report continues, "While young adolescents need greater autonomy . . . they neither need nor desire a complete break with parents and other family members."[9]

Due to the family's importance in nurturing a young person's faith, churches must begin to find creative ways to work with parents and involve parents in program leadership. Three general strategies might be employed, as adapted from the Carnegie report:

- Give parents meaningful roles in Christian education decisions, planning, and structure. Their feelings of ownership in the program not only will reduce complaints but will open doors for communication and sharing.
- Keep parents informed through word of mouth, newsletters, and other means. Send letters to parents about special events. Call them to report on their children's progress. One youth leader sends affirming postcards to her group members, knowing parents probably will get the mail first and see the positive comments.

- Offer opportunities for parents to support the learning process. This might involve take-home discussion starters for parents and teenagers to do together. These informal learning experiences can have significant impact. Chapter 10 focuses on nurturing faith in the family.

COORDINATION OF STUDY

Informal discussions play an important role in promoting faith maturity. The challenge for congregations is to find innovative ways to prompt these conversations among friends and family members.

Though used by only 16 percent of churches, one method that appears to be effective is the coordination of study among all ages. This way, everyone in the congregation is studying the same issues or Bible passages simultaneously. Such coordination provides a common basis for conversation among generations and between parents and children. Several approaches are possible for coordinated study:

Intergenerational Experiences—While recognizing the need for age-specific learning, some churches also see the importance of intergenerational contact. For special occasions (such as Advent) or for special series (hunger or the environment), they bring together people of all ages for activities, discussion, and exploration. In this setting, each generation learns from the other, and community forms within the congregation.[10]

Self-designed Learning—Coordinated learning is possible through the careful selection of compatible curriculum for each age group. Thus while children and youths might study getting along with parents, adults might focus on parenting issues.

Uniform Lessons—Using the Uniform Lessons Series—which is followed by many denominations and independent curriculum publishers—throughout the congregation, everyone studies the same Bible passages, though the specific life issues would vary for each age or interest group.

Lectionary Curriculum—Some curriculum publishers have developed resources that follow the common lectionary, used in worship by most liturgical churches. In this way, people not only study coordinated material, but the learning is reinforced through worship and preaching.

Coordinated Planning—Though the results might not be as integrated, coordinated planning among teachers and other leaders can be effective in building bridges across generations. Teachers might, for example, meet monthly to consider special themes, teaching methods, and concerns.

EVALUATION

Many churches are uncomfortable with the idea of evaluating people and programs in Christian education. How can we evaluate volunteers, they ask, when we're just lucky to have someone to teach the class? How do we evaluate programs without offending the teachers?

These misgivings result in less-than-adequate evaluation in churches. According to Dennis H. Dirks: "Evaluation, if done at all, frequently is haphazard or half-hearted at best. Often decisions are left to guesswork or are based on little more than personal feeling. Success or failure is often determined by dubious measures such as increase in attendance or numbers of activities, or even attention to the latest educational fads."[11]

Yet businesses, schools, and many volunteer organizations have discovered the value of evaluation—not to "grill" people, but to discover areas of strength and areas that need to be strengthened. In fact, research in public schools has found that teacher morale actually increases when evaluation is constructive and regular.

People actually like constructive feedback. They want to learn and grow. And they tend to be more committed to something when they know they are valued. Fifty percent of teachers expressed interest in "learning how to evaluate my work as a Christian educator." Yet despite its value, only 21 percent of congregations evaluate teachers at least annually. (For more on teacher evaluation, see chapter 7.)

The *Effective Christian Education* study discovered that churches are much more likely to evaluate programs than people. About eight out of ten churches evaluate children's, youth, and adult educational programs at least annually. Each program should be evaluated in light of the established purpose, goals, and objectives. Throughout this book are evaluation tools that deal with specific areas of Christian education and church life, including the evaluation in Worksheet 3 at the end of this chapter.

One key to evaluation and planning is assessment of the needs and interests of children, youths, and adults in the congregation. Knowing what topics and concerns appeal can be an important key to increasing involvement. It also provides insights into the makeup of the congregation. Congregations are most likely to evaluate youth needs (59%) and adult needs (57%), and less likely to evaluate children's needs (42%).

Assessing needs is important for Christian education for several reasons. First, if the gospel is indeed to touch people's lives, we must identify places where they need to hear the gospel. Second, assessing needs helps planners step back and refocus programs. This process gives clues to the time when particular emphases or programs may no longer be needed. Finally, assessing needs opens doors for unique ministries that can impact people's lives in significant ways.

Congregations can evaluate needs in a variety of ways. Several surveys are available to evaluate the needs of congregations, as well as the needs of specific audiences such as families or youth.[12] Needs also can be evaluated by noting the major transitions people in the congregation go through. These can include moves, deaths in the family, divorce, loss of employment, birth in the family, marriage. Each of these transition times raises a new set of needs to which the church can respond.

ASSESSING YOUR CHURCH

Planning, parental involvement, coordination, and evaluation provide valuable starting points for Christian education planners in local congregations. Instead of rushing to put out the latest fires, the elements in this chapter can provide a focus and center of energy for significant restructuring.

Think about your own congregation, using the "Assessing Administrative Foundations" worksheet (Worksheet 3) as a guide. Think about the following questions:

- Which of the foundational factors is strongest in your congregation? What can you do to celebrate that strength and ensure that it remains strong?
- What weakness disturbs you most? How might you or an appropriate person begin to address the problem?
- What basic data about your congregation are available regarding educational participation, needs, and views of church life? Who will take responsibility for gathering this data? How will it be gathered?

MANAGEMENT AS MINISTRY

Most people in ministry think of administration as a headache to endure, something that takes us away from "real ministry." Administration takes up considerable portions of time. How do we deal with it?

Worksheet 3
Assessing Administrative Foundations

Use this worksheet to evaluate which administrative foundations are in place in your congregation. Use the following scale:

1 = very weak
2 = okay, but not great
3 = pretty good
4 = excellent

Characteristic	U.S. Churches*	Your Church
Planning		
Teachers meet to discuss goals and objectives at least annually.	79%	______
Teachers meet to coordinate and plan for one full day annually.	18%	______
Parental Involvement		
Youth program involves parents in program decisions and planning.	26%	______
Coordination of Study		
Christian education is coordinated so that all ages study the same material simultaneously.	16%	______
Evaluation		
Teachers are evaluated annually.	21%	______
Children's programs are evaluated annually.	80%	______
Youth programs are evaluated annually.	81%	______
Adult programs are evaluated annually.	76%	______
Children's needs and interests are studied annually.	42%	______
Youth needs and interests are studied annually.	59%	______
Adult needs and interests are studied annually.	57%	______
Goals		
There is a clear mission statement for adult education.	53%	______
There are clear learning objectives for adults.	38%	______
There is a clear mission statement for youth education.	55%	______
There are clear learning objectives for youths.	38%	______

**Based on responses from the five mainline denominations in the* Effective Christian Education *study.*

Gaylord Noyce, professor of practical theology at Yale Divinity School, suggests that a primary reason people in ministry become frustrated with administration is that they see no meaning in it. Yet administration is integral to organizing and working with people. Thus it lies at the heart of ministry. Noyce suggests:

> Once we recognize that administration is simply a part of the job of ministering to a faith community, we can then see it not as an unhappy chore that intrudes on the real work of ministry, but as something integral to our calling. We may not necessarily enjoy it or be expert at it, but by acknowledging its importance within the total life of ministry, we can find it a meaningful pursuit.[13]

With that thought in mind, we turn now to leadership characteristics for an effective foundation for effective Christian education.

Chapter 7

Leaders Who Make a Difference

The pastor of a Presbyterian church in Pennsylvania knows the value and importance of education. He arrives early to greet people as they arrive for Sunday school and speaks to each person by name. He often visits the children's classes and teaches an adult class.

• • •

After eleven years, the Sunday school superintendent at a Lutheran congregation in Maryland continues to show his energy and enthusiasm. "I visit classes every week," he explains. "Once a year I meet with each class, and once with each teacher."

• • •

Christian education committee members at a United Methodist congregation in California actively support the Christian education efforts of the congregation. Each committee member adopts a Sunday school class each year for support and dialogue.

• • •

A group of adults in a Baptist church in North Carolina was becoming disenchanted with Sunday school, when a teacher began to lead the group through a critical evaluation of curriculum choices and what the class wanted to learn. As a result, classes are lively and stimulating, and each participant has taken an active role in discovering effective ways to grow in faith through the middle-adult years.

• • •

These four examples illustrate some of the ways leadership plays a vital role in effective Christian education. Whether ordained or lay, leaders set the pace and direction of Christian education. Little constructive learning will happen if the leadership is not committed and involved.

But when church leaders do become committed, a program can become energetic and effective.

The *Effective Christian Education* study confirms this vital role of leaders; it found that effective programs have the following leadership qualities (among others) in place:

- Teachers are high in faith maturity.
- Teachers know educational theory and practice for their age level.
- The pastor is committed to and involved in Christian education.
- The pastor understands educational theory and practice.
- The church's governing body strongly supports Christian education.

In a similar manner, Kennon L. Callahan, author of *Twelve Keys to an Effective Church,* suggests that strong leadership resources are one of the keys to an effective church: "Strong leadership generates enormous power and momentum to advance a congregation forward. That power is neither dictatorial nor authoritarian, neither oppressive nor domineering."[1] He goes on to suggest that leadership may in fact be the key to initiating the other eleven keys he identifies.

To understand the implications of, and the need for, strong leadership in Christian education, we must look in more detail at the skills and abilities needed for effective leadership in different roles.

EFFECTIVE TEACHERS

Teachers are like the narrow neck of an hourglass: Everything passes through them. When they are effective, learning flows freely and steadily. But when they are ill-equipped, learning can be clogged up or only trickle through ineffectively.

The reality of this statement comes into focus when we look at public schools for comparison. Teachers have been at the center of the nation's call for education reform. Though their expectations are often unrealistic in reform agendas, teachers are inevitably involved in suggested solutions. As Ernest Boyer, president of the Carnegie Endowment for the Advancement of Education, says: "Whatever is wrong with America's public schools cannot be fixed without the help of those inside the classroom."[2]

Though the dynamics and issues are quite different, a similar statement could be made about Christian education teachers. No matter how well other leaders in the congregation know educational theory and practice, or have developed in their own faith, the Christian faith won't be adequately communicated without effective teachers.

Here, *teachers* doesn't mean just Sunday school teachers. People who lead Bible studies, youth groups, workshops, drama groups, men and

women's auxiliaries, and other educational programs are also teachers. Others who see education as an outcome of their ministry would be considered teachers, too, though they may never call themselves that. Anyone who fulfills such roles has a tremendous effect on educational effectiveness throughout a congregation, and is certainly a teacher.

The Search Institute study identified three characteristics that make the most significant difference in teacher effectiveness:

1. *Effective teachers have high faith maturity.* It shouldn't be surprising that a teacher's own faith maturity has a positive influence on Christian education. Yet in our haste to find somebody—anybody!—to teach junior high, we apparently neglect this key characteristic.

Overall, only 39 percent of teachers have an integrated faith. And while 55 percent of adult-class teachers have an integrated faith, only 40 percent of youth-class teachers and 32 percent of children's teachers do. Since faith maturity is relatively uncommon among younger adults, this imbalance likely reflects a widespread misperception that one must be

Figure 14
Teacher Register

Average age of all Christian education teachers: 39
Average age of adult Christian education teachers: 50
Average age of youth Christian education teachers: 36
Average age of children's Christian education teachers: 36
Percentage of teachers who have taught in their present church less than three years: 30
Percentage of teachers who spend less than an hour each week preparing for class: 66
Percentage of teachers who don't prepare at all: 4
Percentage of teachers who teach kindergarten and/or preschool Sunday school: 20
Percentage of teachers who teach grades 1 through 6 Sunday school: 39
Percentage of teachers who teach grades 7 through 12 Sunday school: 16
Percentage of teachers who teach adult Sunday school: 19
Percentage of K-6 teachers who are women: 91
Percentage of youth teachers who are women: 59
Percentage of adult teachers who are women: 50
Percentage of teachers who think their teaching is good or excellent: 50
Percentage of teachers who think their teaching is poor: 1

young to relate to the young. In reality, we would do well to discover ways to pair the young with the old, which often has a positive impact on both age groups.

2. *Effective teachers know educational theory and practice for the age group they teach.* Effective adult teachers know how to teach adults. Effective youth teachers know how to teach youths. And effective children's teachers know how to teach children. It seems logical.

Yet only 44 percent of churches have teachers of adults who adequately know educational theory and practice. Even worse, only 34 percent of youth-education teachers know the theory and practice of what they do. And only 29 percent of children's teachers do.

3. *Effective teachers care about their students.* In the study, this factor was most important for young people, and not as important for adult education—at least in terms of promoting faith maturity. In general, youth teachers do well in showing care. Seventy-nine percent of the young people report that their "teachers and adult leaders care about me."

Though two of these three factors are relatively undeveloped in most congregations, the blame doesn't lie solely with teachers. Often they are recruited under duress. And often they have little background or experience that would give them the knowledge and skills needed for effective teaching (see Figure 15). Understandably, then, the *Effective Christian Education* study identified several factors that can enhance teacher effectiveness and, in turn, Christian education effectiveness.

Training and Equipping—Most Christian education teachers are not professional educators. For their living, they sweep floors or sell real estate or design computers or manage companies or work in a factory or work at home. Whatever they know about teaching likely comes from their own experience as a teacher or student. So, in some ways, it is remarkable that about 40 percent of teachers *do* claim to know educational theory and practice!

Instead of blaming teachers for their shortcomings, churches need to begin training teachers—equipping them for this ministry to which they have been called. This training is essential to Christian education effectiveness. Yet, according to Christian education coordinators, only 57 percent of congregations provide leadership training for Christian education volunteers.

In his booklet *How to Prevent Lay Leader Burnout,* Roy Oswald argues that training is an essential element of working with volunteers:

> The function of training is not only to equip people with skills. Through training, they gain understanding of the demands of the task. Even more important, training is a way of offering support.

Figure 15
Teacher Strengths and Weaknesses

Christian education coordinators were asked to assess their teachers or leaders who serve each age group. Here are the percentages of coordinators who say each characteristic is "very true" of their teachers.

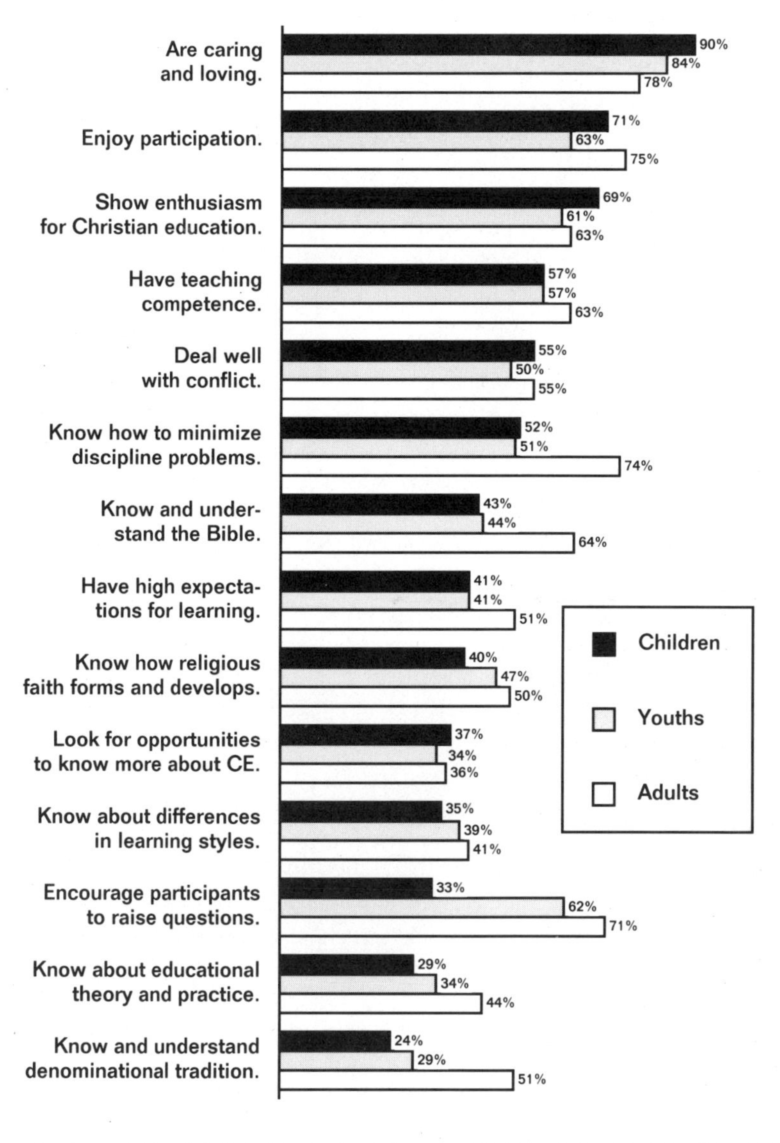

> People are brought into the leadership group to discuss aspects of their new role, and to know that at least someone cares about how they carry out the task.[3]

Training takes place in many ways, both formal and informal. The national survey identified three key types of training that increase educational effectiveness:

1. In-service Training—About 78 percent of churches provide in-service training at least annually. That statistic indicates there are good opportunities in many congregations to help teachers grow in their knowledge, while also providing encouragement and support.

In-service training itself can take many forms. Some churches use the opportunity to talk about teaching methods, developmental abilities, and curriculum choices. Others hold workshops, inviting an expert to share practical ideas with teachers. Many publishers provide videos and other training tools which may be utilized in workshop settings.

These teacher-training events are most often the responsibility of the pastor or Christian education coordinator. Among pastors, 24 percent say they have responsibility for leading teacher-training events, and 28 percent of Christian education coordinators say they have this responsibility.

One key to the effectiveness of such training is to use the same effective learning methods that you would hope teachers would use in their classrooms. Nothing takes the power out of a workshop on experiential learning more than a lecture on the subject![4]

2. Instruction in Teaching Methods—While most churches have in-service training, many seem not to spend any time learning teaching methods. Only half the churches (53 percent) offer instruction in teaching methods. Chapters 8 and 9 on educational process and content give clues to the appropriate emphases in teacher training. Also see Figure 33 for a list of topics that teachers of different age levels say they *want* to learn more about.

3. Instruction in Theology and Tradition—The study found that instruction in denominational theology and tradition has a small but significant impact on people's loyalty to the denomination. Yet only 21 percent of youth programs and 32 percent of adult programs include this emphasis. By showing teachers creative ways to connect denominational tradition and history to life experiences, people become part of—and committed to—that denomination's story.

Also, Mentoring—Though it wasn't addressed in the empirical findings of the *Effective Christian Education* project, visits to effective congregations confirm the benefit of mentoring for teacher training. This less formal approach not only teaches skills but builds a natural support network.

Often, congregations pair experienced teachers with inexperienced teachers in a team-teaching approach. Each teacher learns from the other, and each feels supported. And neither has the burden of sole responsibility for the class.

But mentoring doesn't necessarily require team teaching. Donald L. Griggs and Judy McKay Walther tell about teachers who team up with someone outside the church. One new fifth-grade Sunday school teacher contacted a friend who taught fifth grade in the public school. Not only was the public-school teacher flattered to be asked for advice, but was able to inform the Sunday school teacher about the abilities, needs, and interests of children.[5]

Faith Formation—Few churches provide opportunities for teachers' faith formation—despite the fact that fewer than half the teachers show integrated faith. Only 8 percent of churches provide occasions for teachers to get together three or more times a year for spiritual renewal and growth.

It's difficult to overestimate the value of opportunities for faith formation for teachers. Not only do these opportunities make them more effective in passing on the faith, they also decrease many of the problems often associated with church volunteers, including burnout. "Burnout is far less likely to occur when people feel they are being renewed and refreshed spiritually," Roy Oswald writes. "In fact, by definition, a deep and rich spiritual life is incompatible with burnout."[6] Opportunities for spiritual growth and renewal can take many forms. Churches can . . .

. . . offer times of spiritual reflection and study during training and planning sessions;

. . . plan teacher retreats that focus on renewal and affirmation rather than planning and learning;

. . . hold special teacher prayer breakfasts or gatherings;

. . . encourage teachers to use personal spiritual disciplines of prayer, Bible study, journaling, and so forth;

. . . challenge teachers to be involved in social and justice ministries.

Supervision and Evaluation—As mentioned in chapter 6, many churches are uncomfortable with any sort of evaluation—particularly evaluations of people's performance. As a result, only 21 percent of teachers are evaluated annually. Unfortunately, our fear of "hurting their feelings" often leaves teachers feeling unguided. Roy Oswald makes the case well:

> Supervision is something we don't seem to carry out very well in church systems. Once people are trained and functioning in a role,

> they often get confused and discouraged. At times they make mistakes and need help, and may lose confidence. They need someone to check on them from time to time, to talk with them about their work. Supervision is simply another way of saying, "We care about what happens to you in this role."[7]

Central to this supervision process is regular evaluation. In a booklet titled *What Works: Research About Teaching and Learning,* the U.S. Department of Education compiled elements of teacher supervision that "strengthen instruction and improve teacher morale."[8] Adapted to a Christian education context, the list provides helpful starting points for teacher/leader evaluation:

> Evaluator and teacher should agree on the specific skills and practices that characterize effective teaching. This naturally takes the form of a job description.
>
> Evaluator should frequently observe teacher to see whether the teacher is using these skills and practices.
>
> Evaluator and teacher should meet to discuss evaluator's impressions.
>
> Evaluator and teacher should agree on areas for improvement.
>
> Evaluator and teacher should work together to construct a specific plan for improvement.

Of course, sometimes we must confront problems or deal with an ill-equipped teacher. Though uncomfortable, it is far better to deal with the problem than to ignore it. In *Clergy and Laity Burnout,* William H. Willimon advises:

> Under the guise of graciousness, patience, or tolerance, we often allow people to remain in positions they are unqualified [for] or uninterested in holding. When we do this, we not only fail to affirm and minister to the people who deserve good Christian education . . . but we also miss opportunities to help some fellow Christian struggle with his or her true vocation . . . . By ignoring the problem, we are ignoring the person.[9]

Recognition—Each year, Willimon sends appreciation letters to leaders in his congregation, identifying specific ways each person has contributed to the church. "At each church where I have done this," he writes, "I have been amazed by how many people tell me that they have never received thanks, in the form of a note or anything else, for their work at the church."[10]

Without teachers and other volunteer leaders, formal Christian education would not exist in congregations. But despite their importance, teachers often feel unappreciated in their ministry. In a study of leaders in seven congregations, Roy Oswald found that only 57 percent of leaders believed they were well-appreciated for their efforts. Of the remaining 43 percent, 15 percent said they did not feel appreciated. Furthermore, about 27 percent of those surveyed said their church could be enhanced if they were made to feel more appreciated.[11]

By elevating the teacher's role in the congregation, we affirm the effort and care that teachers put in their ministry. In the process, we also elevate the place of Christian education and increase its effectiveness.

The *Effective Christian Education* study did not explore in depth the many types of affirmation and recognition that may increase educational effectiveness. It did find, though, that simply recognizing teachers in a worship service once a year—which 87 percent of congregations do—has a positive impact. Other possibilities might include:

- Write letters to teachers to express appreciation for their work.
- Purchase an appropriate gift for the teacher. I once participated in an in-depth Bible study in which the leader (a layperson) had spent almost all his spare time for several years preparing for the study group. By collecting just a few dollars from each participant, we were able to buy the leader a complete set of New Testament commentaries, which he had always checked out of the church library. That gift gave him energy to keep teaching another year!
- Publish a profile of a teacher in each church newsletter. Include quotes from class members that affirm the person's ministry.
- Honor teachers at an all-church banquet or picnic.
- Encourage classes to throw parties in honor of their teachers.

Recruitment and Commitment—In many churches, teacher recruitment is a perennial, irritating problem. When asked to identify the biggest problems in Christian education, about 58 percent of coordinators said recruitment is a "major" or "somewhat major" problem. Instead of teaching because they feel called to ministry, many people end up teaching because they were cajoled until they gave in to pressure. The result is anything but effective teaching.

Marlene Wilson, in *How to Mobilize Church Volunteers,* writes that many churches use "Buffalo Bill" recruitment methods: "That means riding into a herd of buffalo and, as they scatter, looking for the stray that lags behind because it is not fast or cunning enough to get away—and lassoing it." The result, she argues, is that we often end up with "volunteers" who aren't enthusiastic about their assignment and lack the skills or personality needed to do the job well.[12]

Numerous helpful books that focus on recruiting and nurturing volunteers are available, so there is no need to repeat their insights here. It should be noted, however, that Search Institute's visits to effective congregations suggest that recruitment becomes less and less difficult as congregations develop effective systems for training, supporting, and recognizing teachers. In fact, some of the effective congregations actually have waiting lists of volunteers! In these churches, teaching is a privilege, not a drudgery. Furthermore, these churches have less trouble with teacher dropout and burnout, because teachers are equipped for the tasks they have been given.

CHRISTIAN EDUCATION COORDINATORS

In most congregations, a Christian education coordinator is responsible for overseeing the total Christian education program. Though the *Effective Christian Education* study did not identify any specific characteristics of a coordinator that are central to effective Christian education, several characteristics are implicit throughout the study—in terms of teacher selection, curriculum choice, teacher training, and program administration.

Since each of these specific issues is dealt with elsewhere in this book, we will briefly look at the people who coordinate Christian education and their ministry.[13]

Faith Maturity—On average, Christian education coordinators tend to have higher faith maturity than other adults and teachers, but lower than pastors. Overall, 47 percent of coordinators exhibit faith maturity.

Loyalty—Loyalty to their denomination is not significantly different for Christian education coordinators than for other adults. On a scale of one to five, the average coordinator scores 3.94, compared to 3.90 for teachers and 4.00 for other adults. However, congregational loyalty is particularly high among coordinators. On the same scale, the average score for coordinators is 4.39. Of course, congregational loyalty is higher among teachers and other adults as well, with both scoring an average of 4.26.

Responsibilities—The title *Christian education coordinator* does not come with a neatly defined set of responsibilities. Based on responses to the survey, coordinators are involved in a myriad of responsibilities, from teaching prekindergarten Sunday school to leading a youth choir to leading teacher training events. Common responsibilities include . . .

. . . teaching vacation Bible school: 35 percent;
. . . organizing and planning adult-education events, other than on Sunday mornings: 34 percent;
. . . leading teacher-training events: 28 percent;
. . . leading Bible studies for adults: 26 percent;
. . . teaching Sunday school for adults: 22 percent;
. . . coordinating social-service projects for children: 16 percent;
. . . leading workshops or retreats for adults: 16 percent.

The study also found that different people fill the coordinator's role. Among those who answered the question, 35 percent chair their Christian education committee, 38 percent are the Sunday school superintendents, 43 percent are directors of Christian education, and others fill other roles. (Obviously, many fill more than one role!)

Whatever their title, Christian education coordinators give many hours to the church. About 59 percent say they volunteer six or more hours per month at their church. In addition, 45 percent say they spend six or more hours each month attending church programs other than worship services. These dedicated, involved leaders contribute significantly to the church's education program through their leadership and influence.

SUPPORT FROM THE CHURCH'S GOVERNING BODY

In chapter 1, we noted that one of the problems in Christian education is that it is seen as separate from other areas of church life. "The typical experience has been that education is segmented from the total life of the church into a church-school-and-fellowship program," write Jack. L. Seymour and Donald E. Miller. "Such a separation of education and ministry ignores crucial tasks in the life of the congregation."[14]

Due to Christian education's impact on faith maturity, all church leaders need to pay attention to its dynamics and needs. And they need to recognize and facilitate learning and growth through all areas of congregational life. For this to happen, church leaders must be involved in and knowledgeable about the church's educational ministry.

Overall, six in ten Christian education coordinators say their church council or governing body is "very interested" in Christian education for each age group. Interest is slightly higher for children's and youth education (61%) as compared to adult education (58%).

One way to build commitment to Christian education is for the church's governing body to discuss seriously the goals, needs, and struggles of the education program. Half of the governing bodies in congregations (49%) have serious discussions about Christian education at least three times a year. By increasing this number, Christian education can gain visibility and support (including financial support) within the congregation. And as this support grows, Christian education will take center stage.

PASTORS AS TEACHERS

The pastor is a key influence on a congregation. Judy McKay Walther remembers when, years earlier, she had been a Sunday school teacher. One Sunday the pastor visited her class, and the next day, the pastor called to compliment her on the fine job she was doing. "From that moment on," she says, "I knew God had called me to be in the classroom."[15]

However, too many pastors don't see that their role as pastor includes the responsibility of being "pastor-teacher," as Wesner Fallaw described it.[16] Dr. David Schuller, a consultant with the Association of Theological Schools, suggests that seminaries focus on the pastor's role as counselor or preacher or change agent. "None of them [pastors] comes out with the sense of being a teacher." He calls on churches and seminaries "to begin to hold up again . . . the role of teacher."[17]

Many current observers share Schuller's concern and emphasis. In *A Teachable Spirit: Recovering the Teaching Office in the Church,* Richard Robert Osmer notes that pastors stand at the intersection of three "centers of teaching authority in the church"—the congregation, the denomination, and the seminary:

> Because of their education and special relationship to the denomination, [pastors] are uniquely qualified to facilitate dialogue between various centers of teaching authority in the church. Their seminary education and ongoing participation in continuing education events put them in a position of being able to mediate the findings of scholarly research and writing to congregations. Similarly, they often are the persons in their congregations most knowledgeable of denominational policies, programs, and teachings. In short, they occupy a critical position amid the three centers of teaching authority.[18]

The pastor's role as teacher is vital for another reason as well—to equip the laity for ministry. Janet F. Fishburn writes: "The present division of labor in the church, and the way leaders are recruited to maintain existing programs and organizations, implies that only clergy are *really* in ministry, as if only pastors really have gifts for ministry." She goes on to suggest that "the time is ripe for new styles of pastoral leadership that will invite all Christians to enjoy their own valid ministries." This, she believes, can be achieved through education in which the pastor equips people with the vision, skills, and understanding that will translate into effective lay ministry.[19]

From the national study, there emerge three central themes that point to a more positive role for the pastor in Christian education.

1. Support and Commitment—For Christian education to become a congregational priority, it must become a priority of the pastor, who often sets the tone and direction of the congregation. As Daniel Buttry states, "The pastor is the person most pivotal in a church's life. For better or worse, the pastor has the greatest potential for influencing individuals and the group psyche of the entire congregation."[20]

Most pastors are committed to Christian education. Among the churches surveyed, 75 percent show a deep commitment to Christian education for adults; 73 percent show such a commitment for youth education; and 74 percent are deeply committed to children's education. About the same percentage is enthusiastic about Christian education for each age group.

Furthermore, Christian education leaders do not see lack of pastoral support as a major problem in Christian education. Seventy-six percent of coordinators say it is "no problem," and 74 percent of teachers had the same response.

2. Involvement—One of the interesting analogies that grows out of the *Effective Christian Education* study involves the characteristics of pastors in relationship to the characteristics of school principals. Though obvious differences emerge out of the unique roles and responsibilities of each, numerous analogies are evident.

For example, studies in public education have found that a principal's involvement in the school and knowledge of education are vital for the school's health. A similar pattern holds in congregations. Pastors who are knowledgeable and involved in Christian education have a positive influence on the shape and effectiveness of Christian education.

With this analogy in mind, consider the following excerpt from a U.S. Department of Education report titled *What Works: Research About Teaching and Learning:*

> Effective principals have a vision of what a good school is and systematically strive to bring that vision to life in their schools. . . .

> Effective principals visibly and actively support learning. . . . Effective principals also build morale in their teachers . . . . They try to develop community support for the school, its faculty, and its goals.[21]

This vision of active, involved school principals is not unlike the need for pastors who are active and involved in Christian education. Yet despite expressions of commitment, direct involvement is much lower. Only about 62 percent of pastors are involved in adult education. Furthermore, only 51 percent of pastors are involved in youth education, and 42 percent in children's education.

At the same time, pastors do seem to care about children and youths. Teachers were asked if their pastors knew the names of most children and youths in the church. Even though it is difficult to do in large congregations, about 43 percent said it was "very true," and 32 percent said "quite true" that their pastors knew the names of most children and youths. Only 5 percent said it was not true.

Pastoral involvement and support can take many forms—leading a youth or adult Bible study, going on retreats, including youth examples in sermons, advocating for resources for Christian education programs, and much more. The point is that pastors see education as central to their ministry, not as a tangent or nuisance. However the pastor chooses to be involved in Christian education, it can have a significant impact.

3. Training—The pastor's education and training in Christian education also provides a foundation for effective ministry. Yet the study found that most pastors are lacking in that area. Only 28 percent of pastors took four or more seminary classes in education. And only 40 percent have taken related continuing education during the past three years.

Part of the problem with education training may be the strained relationship between theology and education in most seminaries. Schools of theology scoff at the schools of religious education, and vise versa. As a result, pastors who focus their education on theology rarely have experience or expertise in educational methods and theory.

In *Empowering Disciples: Adult Education in the Church,* Canadian educator William R. Adamson describes the problem: "In some situations, the departments of education, worship, and pastoral care were looked upon by biblical and theological professors as dealing with 'techniques' and not with the real business of theology. A departmental elitism prevailed. Later, new trends in pastoral counseling or social action overshadowed the task of teaching."[22]

Figure 16
Pastor Preferences

The *Effective Christian Education* study asked pastors how they like doing Christian education with different ages. The first column shows the percentages of pastors who say they like working with each age "quite a bit" or "a great deal." The second column shows the percentages of pastors who spend three or more hours each month working with each age group.

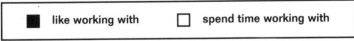

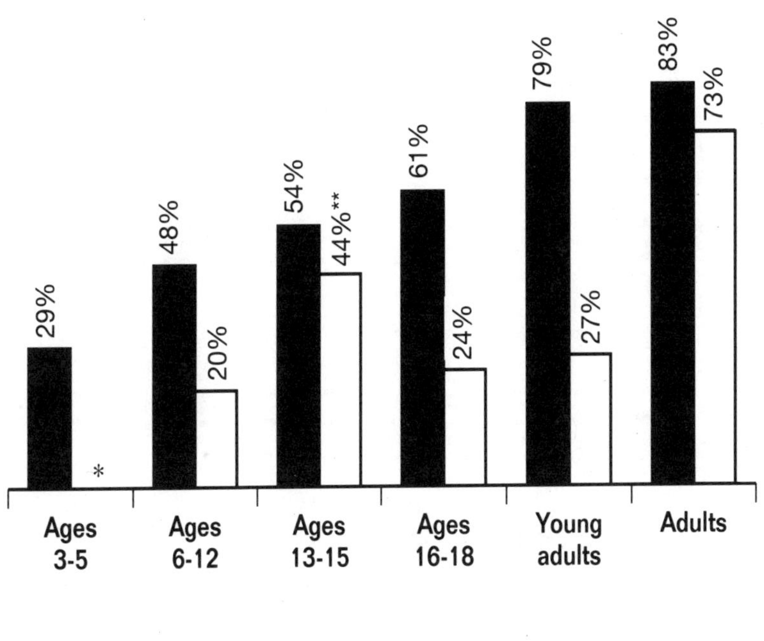

The figure for the percentage of pastors who work with this age group is not available.

***This figure is likely influenced by the pastor's involvement in confirmation for this age group, in some denominations.*

Such a dichotomy not only hurts the church in its educational efforts, but it hurts theological education as well. Some observers see (or hope to see) the relationship changing. In their second book, *Theological Approaches to Christian Education*—which directly addresses the tensions in detail—Seymour and Miller state:

> A fundamental reassessment of religious education seems to be occurring in theological studies. Christian education is no longer seen as merely a technical and applied practical area within the theological encyclopedia. Rather, it is recognized that it has to do with the basic questions of meaning of the Christian faith, the meaning of theological education, and the role of the church in the education of the public.[23]

Some pastors may argue that pastors already have enough—too much—to do without adding another responsibility. And their feelings are valid. However, what if renewing the pastor's role as teacher actually focuses energy, rather than dissipating it? What if teaching people the central truths of the gospel eases the tensions between the pulpit and the pew?

By helping members discover the vital roots of faith, engaging them in theological reflection, and guiding them to apply their faith to their own lives, pastors will likely find that people begin ministering to one another and to the world in ways that ease the burdens that pastors now feel they bear in trying to do the church's work alone.

CHRISTIAN EDUCATORS' INFLUENCE

Though Christian education leaders might appear to have little influence on the pastor, they can promote pastoral effectiveness in Christian education in several ways:

- Urge the pastor to participate in relevant continuing education opportunities. Many denominations and ecumenical organizations provide opportunities for pastors.
- Ensure that the church's budget includes designated funds—over and above salary—for continuing education.
- Support a pastor who feels called to continue formal education while serving in the church.
- Be an advocate in times of transition for a new pastor with training in educational theory and practice.

Worksheet 4
Leadership Evaluation

Use this worksheet to evaluate how well your leadership team embodies the characteristics uncovered in the study to enhance Christian education. If you discover that few of the characteristics are in place, there is no reason to panic. Most of the characteristics can be dealt with through training, recruitment, and intentional effort. The key is to be honest about the deficiencies, so that you can develop strategies to address the weakest areas.

Evaluate each characteristic of your congregation using this scale:

1 = Very weak	**3 = Pretty good**
2 = Okay, but not great	**4 = Excellent**

	U.S. Churches*	Your Church
Adult Education Teachers		
Are high in mature faith.	55%	____
Know educational theory and methods for adults.	44%	____
Youth Education Teachers		
Are high in faith maturity.[24]	40%	____
Care about students.	79%	____
Know educational theory and methods related to youth.	34%	____
Teacher Faith Formation		
Teachers gather for spiritual renewal three or more times annually.	8%	____
Teacher Training		
Teachers receive in-service training at least annually.	78%	____
Teachers receive instruction in effective teaching methods at least annually.	53%	____
Teachers receive instruction in denominational theology and tradition at least annually.	21%	____
Teacher Recognition		
Teachers are named and recognized during worship.	87%	____
Pastor		
Is highly committed to the education program for youths.	73%	____
Devotes significant hours to the youth program.	51%	____
Knows educational theory and practice related to Christian education of adults.	80%	____
Is highly committed to the adult education program.	75%	____
Devotes significant hours to the adult program.	62%	____
Knows educational theory and practice for adults.	83%	____

Pastor's Training		
The pastor took four or more seminary courses in Christian education.	28%	____
The pastor has taken three or more days of continuing education over the past three years.	40%	____
Governing Body Support		
The congregation's governing body has thoughtful discussions about Christian education three or more times annually.	49%	____

**Based on congregations in the five mainline denominations that were part of the* Effective Christian Education *study.*

RETHINKING LEADERSHIP

Underlying much of this discussion of leadership is a reconceptualization of what it means to be a leader. Too often, we equate leaders with experts. We expect them to have all the knowledge, to make all the decisions, to take all the responsibility, to do all the work. If something is wrong, we blame the pastor or the Christian education director or the Sunday school superintendent or the committee chairperson or . . . .

For leaders to be truly effective in Christian education, however, we need to rethink the meaning of leadership. Do facilitators for adult education really need to be experts on every subject? Must a pastor always be the one to lead theological or biblical discussions? What *is* the leader's role?

Recent insights from thinkers such as Robert Greenleaf and Jackson W. Carroll help reframe the issue.[25] In his important work *As One with Authority: Reflective Leadership in Ministry*, Carroll describes the core tasks of leaders. All three tie to Christian education.

Meaning Interpretation—In all aspects of their work, Carroll suggests, pastors are about the business of "assisting the congregation and its members to reflect on and interpret their life, individually and corporately, in light of God's purpose in Jesus Christ."[26] This task involves helping members find meaning in the crises, joys, and dilemmas of life. At its heart, this role is educational, whether it happens in a classroom or by a hospital bed.

Community Formation—The second task involves building a vital Christian community, where people are accepted and have a sense of belonging to the body of Christ. This task not only is essential to creating a warm climate, but is essential to maintaining Christian identity, and also is closely related to meaning interpretation. "Telling the gospel story helps to define the character and contours of Christian community," Carroll notes. "Participation in a community that offers fellowship, expresses caring and support, and seeks justice in relationships of its members is an eloquent example in action of the meaning of the gospel story."[27]

Empowering Public Ministry—The aim here is to empower "members, individually and collectively, to live as the people of God in the world." While this function is often an outgrowth of the other two, it warrants separate emphasis. "Emphasizing the task of supporting public ministry focuses attention on the life of the people of God in the world as the primary arena for ministry."[28] Such an emphasis parallels the basis of the *Effective Christian Education* study, which begins with the premise that the central function of the church is to nurture faith in its members.

To some extent, most pastors already fulfill these functions (however unintentionally) through a variety of specific tasks: leading worship, doing pastoral care, administering programs, teaching classes. The challenge here is to make these functions central and intentional to the pastor's role. When that happens, we can be sure that a pastor will truly be a teacher—whether or not he or she teaches a class on Sunday morning.

FEUDING PARTS

One of my favorite descriptions of the church is Paul's comparison of the church to Christ's body in I Corinthians 12. I can't help thinking that Paul must have chuckled when he wrote the passage.

Imagine a Sesame Street-like argument between a head and a toe and an eye and a nose and an arm and a leg, as each tries vainly to prove its importance over the others. Then I can see Ernie or Big Bird arriving on the battle scene to remind each part that . . .

> an eye is an eye,
> a toe is a toe,
> and we need them both,
> to go where we go.

Though the jingle is trite and simplistic, we in the church need to be reminded of the simple truth of the metaphor of Christ's body. In Christian education, each person needs to discover a role or calling.

Unfortunately, most Christian lay people do not have a sense of calling, or vocation, according to Jackie McMakin, who specializes in helping lay leaders discover such a sense: "People are asked all too often to do jobs for which they have no sense of calling, no training, and, often, no gifts: the round peg in the square hole phenomenon."[29]

As Christian educators seeking to nourish and develop leadership, it is important that we not become so infatuated with teacher training and other techniques that we forget the heart of leadership in the church: A response to God's call to serve. Only when we remember this calling will Christian education be truly effective.

Chapter 8

What Should We Study?

Willow Creek Community Church in Barrington, Illinois, is a widely admired model for the church-growth movement. Three times a year, 500 pastors converge on the church to study how the congregation grew from 150 to 12,000 in its first 14 years. The key to the growth, it is said, is that Willow Creek is one of the few churches in the nation shaped by a targeted "customer" survey. "We decided to defer to the customer, except where it conflicted with scripture," explains pastor Bill Hybels.[1]

Before the church even began, the pastor and three friends spent six weeks on a door-to-door survey. Then they designed a church specifically to meet those needs and complaints. For example, the church doesn't take offerings because the number-one complaint was that "the church is always bugging me for money." Instead of a traditional church structure, the building is more like a convention center, with theater-like seats. Instead of a pulpit and vestments, Hybels preaches behind a Plexiglas lectern, wearing fashionable business suits.

While some people applaud churches like Willow Creek for their methods, others criticize them for placing more value on marketing than on the gospel. It is the gospel that should guide our ministries, critics say, not marketing surveys. By responding only to what people say they want, we risk watering down the gospel.

A similar debate rages in Christian education. To oversimplify, on one side are the proponents of strictly needs-based and interest-based education. Take a poll, then study whatever people say they want to study. If an issue falls to the bottom of the list, ignore it, because people aren't interested.

On the other extreme are those who say that scripture or God's revelation should dictate exactly what people teach and learn. To be true to the gospel, they insist, you must systematically study major themes in scripture or theology. Only people who are faithful will learn and grow.

Somewhere between the two extremes is a helpful balance—a balance that takes seriously both words: *Christian* and *education*. It is a balance that Jesus modeled in the Gospels. Wherever he went, he taught and preached. He responded to people's everyday needs, and he used everyday life experiences as occasions for profound theological insight and teaching.

For Jesus, faith and life were not disconnected realities; they were interrelated. Indeed, such truth is at the heart of the Incarnation—"The Word became flesh and lived among us, and we have seen his glory" (John 1:14).

As Christian educators, our goal is similar: to so nourish God's Word in the lives of learners that it will come alive. This goal demands both a clear understanding of that Word and thoughtful responsiveness to the learner. To say that one precedes the other begs the question; the two must be in dialogue for true Christian education to occur.

In analyzing faith maturity and Christian education, the *Effective Christian Education* study found that a healthy mix of response to needs and theological insight is indeed most effective in promoting faith in both adults and youths. As the original summary report stated, "Effective content . . . blends biblical knowledge and insight with significant engagement in the major life issues each age group faces."[2]

Let's look, then, at the major content issues uncovered by the study of Christian education for both youths and adults.[3] Chapter 9 will then examine some processes and approaches that are effective in conveying this content.

YOUTH CONTENT EMPHASES

A youth leader in a small community believes firmly that young people should participate in planning their own youth ministries. So she went to the planning meeting for the coming fall, intending to let the youths outline their own themes, based on what they wanted to study. She expected them to become excited about topics such as "making friends" and "feeling good about myself." She was surprised when the young people shared their specific concerns and interests:

"What do I say to a friend who has gotten pregnant?"

"Let's talk about skinheads."

"There have been all these suicides around. What can we do about them as Christians?"

"Should I drive friends home when they've gotten drunk at a party?"

"How do Christians deal with AIDS?"

Though the topics and concerns would vary considerably among churches and in different years, the incident illustrates a truth about teenagers that we sometimes forget: They really *aren't* children any more. It's not enough to entertain them when they come to church. Today's teenagers face myriad struggles, problems, and tough choices. Church-going teenagers face the same troubling issues as unchurched youth: drugs, drinking, depression, sexual activity, delinquency.

Furthermore, young people struggle to understand the Christian faith as they develop new thinking capacities. In his *Five Cries of Youth,* Merton P. Strommen tells how a teenage girl mused about the universe and her place in it:

> Sometimes it's kind of scary just to be alive in the middle of all that. I wish I could be as sure as other kids seem to be about where they are and about what's right, and about God really being close by and helping when you have a mess in your life to work out: I'm not there yet, where I can be sure about God. I would like to be, but I'm not.[4]

Churches need to recognize the realities that teenagers face every day. And they must help young people struggle with their faith and apply it to the world in which they live. The *Effective Christian Education* study identified eight key content focuses for youth Christian education, which, when present, help young people grow in their faith.

The Bible—Group Publishing, an interdenominational youth ministry publisher, once polled readers of its now-defunct *Teenage*-magazine to determine their perceptions of the Bible. Some of the responses illustrate the situation with most Christian teenagers today. Many said they didn't read the Bible because they didn't know how. "I sometimes don't understand it, so I stop," said a 13-year-old. Another added, "I don't read it on a regular basis because I'm confused."

Even more revealing were their answers when asked about their favorite book of the Bible: "I like Genesis because it's the first book." "I like the Psalms because it's in the middle of the Bible." "I like Exodus because of all the plagues." "I've only gone as far as Exodus." "I like Daniel. Because it's my name!"[5]

Teenagers clearly don't know or understand the Bible, which is so central to the faith. The Search Institute study found that two out of three rarely read their Bibles when they are alone. Indeed, 36 percent say they never read it; another 31 percent say they read it less than once a month. Only 14 percent read it at least once a week.

Helping young people grow in faith demands that they become familiar with the Bible and its significance. Churches need to help youths see that the Bible isn't an old, complicated, irrelevant, boring book. They also need to help young people begin to understand what the Bible is and how Christians interpret it. Unless young people begin to develop a more adult, sophisticated understanding of scripture than they had as children, they are likely to dismiss the book as archaic.

Religion professors often testify to this problem. Students are shocked—and their faith shaken—when these professors suggest some of the basic conclusions, methods, and insights of modern biblical scholarship (such as views of inspiration and the interpretation of Genesis 1 through 11 or the miracles of Jesus) in introductory Bible courses. Such experiences raise questions about whether churches challenge young people to grow beyond a simplistic understanding of the Bible before they leave high school. (See Figure 34 for the percentage of youths—as well as adults and pastors—who hold various views of inspiration.)

At the same time, young people say they want to learn about the Bible. Sixty-four percent are interested or very interested in learning more about the Bible and its meaning for their lives. Most young people see teaching the Bible as a strong or very strong emphasis in their churches. About 69 percent express this opinion. Furthermore, 66 percent say their churches do a good or excellent job of helping them learn about the Bible and its meaning for their lives.

How do we interpret the dichotomy between teenagers' actual Bible knowledge and practice, and their assessment of the church's efforts? Several possibilities are evident. First, just because youths say their churches' Bible-study programs are strong doesn't mean they actually participate in them. Another possibility is that young people see the programs as strong, but the programs do not, in fact, have a lasting or significant impact on young people's lives. Both possibilities can be addressed by building bridges between the text and teenagers' lives, and by using more effective educational processes.

Core Theological Concepts—Young people need to understand basic concepts about God, Jesus Christ, and the Bible. This understanding becomes the center of energy for their developing faith, as they grasp their relationship to a loving God and their responsibility to the world.

Of all the emphases suggested by the study as important, this one is strongest in most congregations (see Figure 17). Seventy-four percent of mainline churches do well in this area. Of course, it is not enough for young people (or anyone else, for that matter) simply to learn to parrot basic theological concepts, just as it does little good for them to quote scripture without understanding it. They must understand and appropriate those beliefs.

Figure 17
Teaching Youths Core Theological Concepts

Young people were asked to evaluate how well their church does at teaching a variety of basic Christian beliefs. Here are the percentages of teenagers who say their churches do "good" or "excellent" jobs with each core theological belief.

Helping learn who God is: 79%
Helping know and love Jesus Christ: 75%
Helping learn what the church believes about God, Jesus, and the Bible: 74%
Helping experience God's love and forgiveness: 68%
Helping learn about the Bible and its meaning for life: 66%

Numerous theological questions arise during adolescence, and churches that allow teenagers to struggle with those questions will help their young people grow in their faith. By dismissing their questions or responding with simplistic answers, we risk pushing teenagers elsewhere to find answers they can accept.

At the same time, our educational efforts will do little good if young people are bored and stop coming, or if the approach has little impact on their lives. Thus—as with Bible study—building bridges to teenagers' lives and using effective educational processes are the key to teaching core theological concepts.

Friendship—As they go through adolescence, young people naturally break away from their parents to depend more and more upon their peers. Though necessary for a sense of identity, this transition is stressful for both parents and young people. It's little wonder, then, that knowing how to make friends and how to be a friend was the top interest of youths in the survey. Three out of four teenagers say they would be interested or very interested in learning more about this topic (see Figure 18).

Lest this topic seem somewhat trivial in relation to other key content areas for youth education, it's important to remember the tough friendship issues that kids face. Consider, for example, the expressions of loneliness in the following statistics:

- Sixty-one percent of churchgoing teenagers say they have felt very sad or depressed ten times or more in the past year.
- Forty percent have thought about committing suicide.
- Sixty-seven percent have felt as if no one loved them at least once in the past year.

- Fifty-four percent say they have needed help in the past year, but had no one to turn to.

Furthermore, many friends of Christian teenagers are not very religious. Seventeen percent of teenagers say their three or four best friends are not religious at all, and 70 percent say their friends are somewhat religious. The study also asked teenagers that if they invited five of their best friends to a party, how many of those friends would be from the church. Thirty percent said none, and only 13 percent said four or five.

In addition to building life skills and helping young people cope with their feelings, developing friendship skills also benefits the church as the the teenagers become more warm and caring. Their friendship skills become a key to promoting faith maturity in one another and thus make a significant difference in their youth ministry.

According to 65 percent of teenagers, most churches are effective in helping young people deal with friendship issues. This effectiveness may accurately reflect congregational priorities. In the late 1970s, researchers at the Boys Town Center for the Study of Youth Development, at Catholic University, conducted a survey of six denominations to determine what outcomes parents and educators want from religious education in high school. They found that the top priorities focused on creating a healthy self-esteem and on emphasizing that young people set examples of Christian behavior among their friends and associates.[6]

Figure 18
Tantalizing Topics for Teens

What are teenagers most interested in learning about at church? Here are the top ten areas about which teenagers say they are "interested" or "very interested" in learning, according to the survey, out of 34 possibilities.

1. Knowing how to make friends and be a friend: 75%
2. Learning to know and love Jesus: 71%
3. Learning more about who God is: 70%
4. Learning to love life more: 69%
5. Recognizing right and wrong, making decisions: 68%
6. Gaining a sense of purpose in life: 65%
7. Learning to like myself more: 65%
8. Learning about the Bible and its meaning for my life: 64%
9. Experiencing God's love and forgiveness: 64%
10. Developing more compassion for other people: 61%

Human Sexuality—In 1968, the National Council of Churches' Commission on Marriage and Family, the Synagogue Council of America Committee on Family, and the United States Catholic Conference Family Life Bureau issued the following statement:

> The sexual attitudes of children develop as part of their general social attitudes. . . . When the family and society view sex as loving and fulfilling, rather than prurient and exploitative, then both the social and sexual attitudes of children benefit. A healthful approach to sexual relations, willingness and ability to impart sexual information in a manner proportionate to the child's stage of development—these are among the elements which foster healthy sexual attitudes and behaviors in the young.[7]

Though more than two decades old, that statement rings true today. And it continues to call congregations to focus on this significant concern and problem area among children and youths. By the time they're high-school seniors, 37 percent of churchgoing females and 23 percent of churchgoing males have had sex, according to the *Effective Christian Education* study. Furthermore, by grades 11 and 12, 23 percent of females and 10 percent of males have had sexual intercourse six or more times. Though these figures are lower than the national averages, they are still alarming.[8]

Furthermore, other studies have found strong links between early sexual activity and other at-risk behaviors. A study by psychologist Gary Ingersoll of Indiana University, originally reported in the journal *Pediatrics*, found that . . .

. . . girls who are sexually experienced by age 16 are five times more likely to be suspended from school, and ten times more likely to have used marijuana than those who have never had sex;

. . . boys who are sexually experienced by age 16 are six times more likely to have used alcohol, five times more likely to have used marijuana, and ten times more likely to have been in a car with a drug-using driver; and

. . . girls who are sexually active are six times more likely to have tried to commit suicide, while girls with no sexual experience have significantly higher self-esteem. (There were no apparent connections between sexual activity and suicide or self-esteem for boys.)[9]

Despite the long-term dangers associated with sexual activity among teenagers, few churches adequately address sexuality or sexual values. Only 27 percent of mainline congregations deal adequately with sexuality issues in their Christian education programs. Indeed, 59 percent of young people say that in the church, they've talked about sex for less than five hours in their lifetime.[10]

Substance Abuse—Though drugs are a pervasive and troubling factor in youth culture, few churches help young people by addressing chemical use. In fact, of all the content areas found important for effective Christian education, this one is least likely to occur. Only 20 percent of churches effectively address issues of alcohol and other drugs.[11]

Though churches may not address drug- and alcohol-related problems in their midst, the problems are there, nonetheless, particularly alcohol use. Churchgoing teenagers report the following:

- Almost half of churchgoing 11th and 12th graders (42 percent of boys and 46 percent of girls) have been drunk in the past year. Overall, 28 percent of young people have been drunk.
- Half of all teenagers have drunk alcohol in the past year, when they were by themselves or with friends. Among 11th and 12th graders, the figure jumps to about 70 percent.
- Forty-seven percent of church youths have been to a party in the past year where kids their age were drinking.
- Ten percent of churchgoing youths have used marijuana in the past year, and 2 percent have used cocaine. Among 11th and 12th graders, 15 percent of boys and 22 percent of girls have used marijuana, and 3 percent of girls and 2 percent of boys have used cocaine.

Helping youths resist the pressures and temptations to use drugs will require more than "Just Say No" bumper stickers. It will involve raising awareness of the problems and realities, addressing the values and self-esteem issues that are related to most at-risk behaviors, dealing with family issues that often contribute to addiction, and addressing community norms which say that use of alcohol (and even illicit drugs) is acceptable for youth. Though Christian educators presently do little in this area, the potential impact is significant.[12]

Values and Moral Decision-making—Teenagers need guidance in shaping their values and making moral decisions. A Girl Scout survey of more than 5,000 children and adolescents found that nearly half of all junior and senior high students (45%) decide what is true based on their own experience. Twenty percent turn to parents, and 16 percent rely on the teachings of scripture. Others look to science (3%), church leaders (2%), and the media (2%).[13]

The *Effective Christian Education* study asked about sources for moral guidance slightly differently and received slightly different results.

When given four choices, churchgoing teenagers say the church gives them the most help with moral questions (53%). Next, 27 percent say they get the most help from their own private religious experiences, such as prayer and meditation. Nineteen percent choose religious groups or events outside the church, while only 2 percent choose religious television and radio.

It's clear that churches have great potential in helping young people sort through the difficult values and moral choices they face daily. The Girl Scout survey concluded that "the more frequently [children and youths] attend religious services, or for those for whom religion is very important, the less likely they will be willing to cheat, lie or steal, drink alcohol underage, or be libertarian in their decisions about sexual behaviors."[14]

In fact, about six out of ten churches have effectively incorporated this emphasis in their youth education. About 64 percent of Christian educators say teaching teenagers moral values is a strong emphasis; 60 percent say teaching moral decision-making is a strong emphasis. In general, about half of churchgoing teenagers report similar strengths in their congregations:

Fifty-eight percent say their church does a good or excellent job of helping them make decisions about right and wrong.

Forty-nine percent say their church does a good or excellent job of helping them learn to apply their faith to decisions.

Fifty-seven percent say their church does a good or excellent job of helping them learn to resist the pressure to do wrong.

Concern for Others—"Compassion is the sometimes fatal capacity of feeling what it's like to live inside somebody else's skin," Frederick Buechner writes. "It is the knowledge that there can never really be any peace and joy for me until there is peace and joy finally for you too."[15]

As Christian educators, we need to teach young people (and the rest of us!) that kind of Christian concern for others. Earlier in this chapter, we noted a variety of signs of isolation and depression in youths that point to the need for friendship skills. The same factors point to the need for developing caring attitudes and skills.

Two out of three churches (66%) do a good or excellent job of helping youths develop concern for others. Yet young people do not always embody the care that churches seek to nourish. Only 37 percent say they often or always go out of their way to show love to people they meet.

Nourishing caring skills can have broad implications for the church and youth education. As young people learn how to care, others will be attracted to their warm fellowship. This care can also turn outward to the poor and disenfranchised of the world. In *Five Cries of Youth,* Merton P. Strommen's research has found that socially concerned and involved youth tend to show humanitarian concern for others.[16]

Developing caring skills requires more than Bible studies on hospitality (though they may be an important part of the mix). It requires helping youths learn interpersonal skills, develop sensitivities, overcome fears, and perceive needs. And it requires a sense of self-care and self-respect that enables youths to reach out to others.

Peer counseling or peer ministry has become a widely used—and effective—model for developing caring skills in young people. One helpful resource in this area is *Training Teenagers for Peer Ministry* by Barbara B. Varenhorst, which includes 14 sessions to help teenagers develop caring skills.[17]

Another helpful way to develop concern is the small-group model explained by Walt Marcum in *Sharing Groups in Youth Ministry.* Marcum suggests forming sharing groups, through which young people can not only learn to care for others, but also receive support and nurture from others. His approach and structure has broad application and implication for youth education in helping young people develop concern for others.[18]

Finally, direct service to others in the congregation and community is an important vehicle for developing empathy and caring skills, particularly when youths have opportunities to process and internalize the experience. This approach overlaps with the next important youth content area.

Responsibility for Poverty and Hunger—The biblical and theological mandate for Christians to take responsibility for poverty and hunger is clear. The faith-maturity scale developed for this study includes advocating social change (including poverty), and acting and serving on behalf of others, as two marks of faith.

Yet, like other social issues, most churches and youths place little emphasis on this Christian responsibility for the poor. Indeed, only 30 percent of youths report spending more than ten hours at church *in their lifetime* learning about or doing something about people who are poor and hungry. The good news is that young people do express concern about, and interest in, helping people in poverty. The challenge for churches is to nourish those concerns in light of young people's faith. Chapter 10 suggests ways to address hunger and other social issues with youths and adults.

ADULT CONTENT EMPHASES

Just as the key content emphases for youth education involve both "theological" and "life" issues, effective adult education also blends these emphases. The study found four key content areas for effective adult Christian education.

Biblical Knowledge and Understanding—Most churches do relatively well in helping adults know and understand the Bible. Seventy-four percent of churches include this emphasis in their adult education—almost twice the percentage of the second-highest content emphasis. Furthermore, 66 percent of adults say their churches do a good or excellent job of teaching people about the Bible.

The question becomes, What happens to that knowledge and understanding? Consider the results of a Gallup survey of U. S. adults titled *The Role of the Bible in American Society*. The survey found that more than half of all adults read the Bible at least monthly. Yet just over one-third can name the four Gospels. This figure represents a decline from a 1982 survey, when 42 percent could name all four Gospels.[19]

Canadian Christian educator William R. Adamson believes that much of the problem with Bible study is that adults are confused about how to interpret the Bible and make sense of it in our contemporary world:

> Those raised in the Church may be familiar with many of the Bible stories, yet realize there are many contradictions and issues which have not been satisfactorily explained for them. They have bits and pieces of information but are not sure how the Bible originated, how it fits together, how it applies to contemporary living. People who were raised outside of the Church see the Bible as some kind of sacred talisman, but do not comprehend much about it. They may flip it open, try to read it, but without background or assistance it may seem like a rather futile undertaking.[20]

The good news is that adults want to learn more about the Bible. In the list of interests, understanding the Bible rose to the top, with 77 percent saying they are interested in learning more. Furthermore, most churchgoing adults have the intellectual capacity and academic background to use commentaries, handbooks, and other resources to deepen their understanding of scripture. Chapter 9 explores several processes that can make group Bible study more effective with adults.

Figure 19
Top Ten Interests of Adults

Here are the top ten areas about which adults say they are "interested" or "very interested" in studying, learning more about, or being involved in, according to the survey (out of 26 possibilities).

1. The Bible: 77%
2. Developing a personal relationship with Jesus: 75%
3. Improving skills at showing love and concern: 74%
4. Learning how to be a good spouse or parent: 74%
5. Applying my faith to daily living: 73%
6. Making more friends at church: 69%
7. Learning how Christians make moral decisions: 68%
8. Getting help with my spiritual journey: 62%
9. Having greater sense of community at church: 62%
10. Helping members who are experiencing hardship: 59%

Moral Decision-making—If we want people to apply their faith to everyday issues, we need to give them practice in a "laboratory" setting. "I am convinced," writes William E. Diehl, "that our laity desperately need help in connecting their Sunday faith to their Monday world. Bible study and church doctrine are of no help in the weekday world if lay people are unable to make the connections."[21]

The church may be one of the few places where adults can feel safe enough to ask aloud the moral and ethical questions that arise out of their daily lives at home, at work, at play, and in the community. How do I balance my responsibilities to family and employer? What do I do when an employer asks me to compromise my integrity? How can I treat my employees justly? What is my responsibility as a Christian in my neighborhood, community, nation, and world?

Though adults face a myriad of life choices and stresses, fewer than half of all congregations (44%) adequately emphasize moral decision-making in adult education. When asked how well their churches do at helping members apply their faith to daily living, 63 percent of adults say "good" or "excellent." Similarly, 56 percent say their churches do a good or excellent job at teaching members about Christian perspectives on moral questions. Finally, 59 percent of adults say their church is the greatest influence on helping them answer moral questions.

At the same time, other research shows that people find relatively little church support or guidance about their work. A study by the Chicago-based Center for Ethics and Corporate Policy studied members from 158 middle-class congregations in the metro-Chicago area. Most people report that work and faith are "very" or "somewhat" integrated for them, and considerably more say that religion and its teachings are very important to their work lives. Yet 10 percent or fewer of the respondents say they "frequently" or "always" discuss work concerns with friends in the congregation, the clergy, or congregational support groups. Furthermore, these respondents generally indicate that congregational programs, study materials, pastoral care, and support from lay members are generally not very helpful in work decisions.[22]

Christian education efforts should encourage people to discuss relevant moral questions, listen to one anothers' insights, and work through the questions in light of scripture and church tradition. Several thinkers refer to this as "reinterpreting" the faith. And this isn't simply a need in our time. Clark M. Williamson and Ronald J. Allen suggest that, because ours is a living, dynamic faith, the church has been confronted with the task of reinterpreting that faith throughout history.

> At every point in our historical life the community of faith, as well as the individual Christian, is faced with a hermeneutical task: We have to interpret this new situation in the light of the tradition in order to understand it and to incorporate it into this *living* tradition. . . . We must reinterpret the tradition if it is to incorporate new developments and to be credible in the face of them.[23]

This dialogue between faith and life can occur in many ways. It can take place in Sunday school classes where the experiences and concerns of adults are taken seriously. It can occur in special study groups that examine current issues and concerns in light of the faith tradition. It can occur in sermons that challenge parishioners to think of the gospel's implications for particular work-related issues.

On a more formal, congregational level, C. Ellis Nelson suggests that congregations form "central" study groups, in which "a group of adult members [including the pastor] develop spiritual power by relating Christian beliefs to their life situations and sharing their understanding and convictions with the whole congregation." He describes this as "congregational practical theology" in relation to critical faith issues in which the whole congregation has a stake.[24]

Another way to help adults with moral decision-making on a personal level is to examine life stresses and changes. These times represent "teachable moments," times when adults are struggling with questions, stresses, and choices (see Figure 20). Research by Stan L. Albrecht and Marie Cornwall suggests that, in general, positive life events have a positive effect on religious beliefs, while negative events tend to weaken religious

Figure 20
Life Stresses and Changes Among Adults

Listed here are common stressful situations experienced by adults in the past two or three years, according to their survey responses.

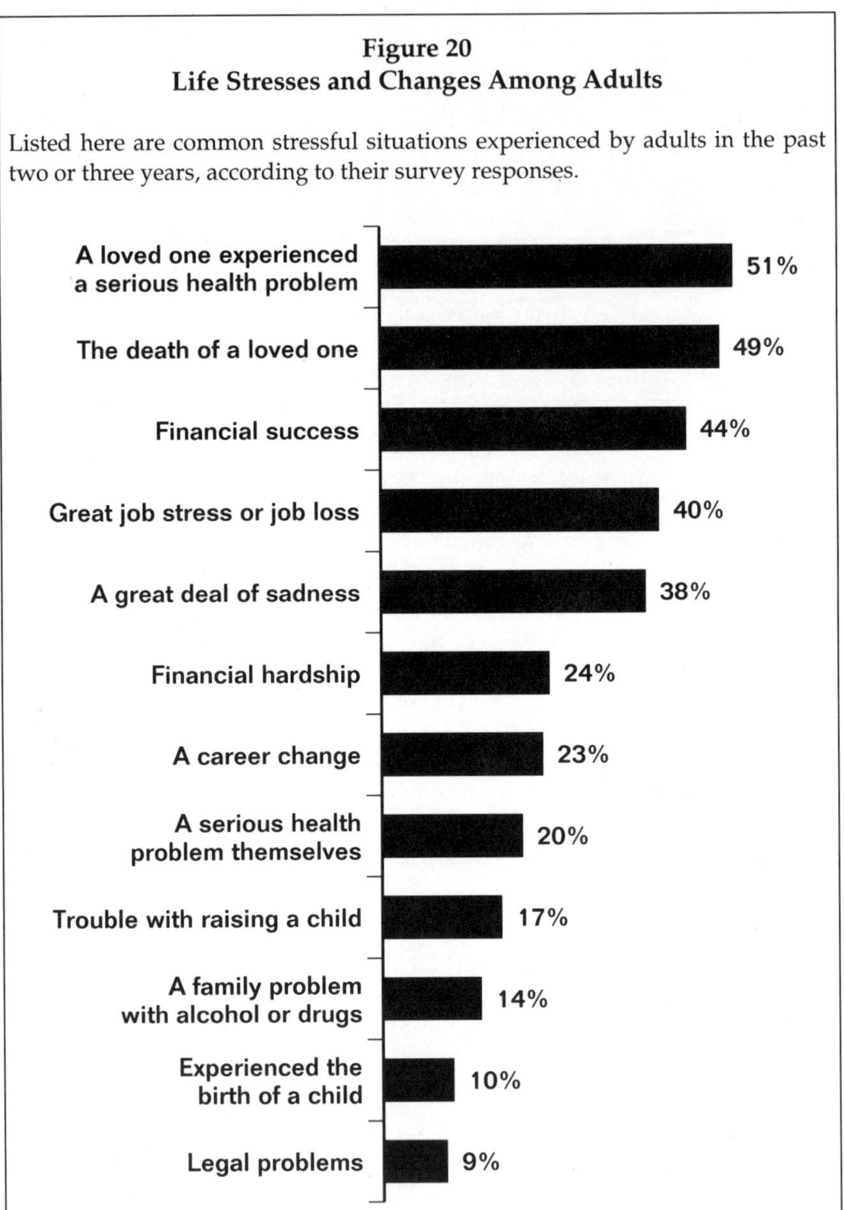

commitment.[25] If this relationship is generally true, it may indicate the need for particular support and guidance during difficult times.

Multicultural Awareness—In some senses, the United States does not have a culture. Rather, it has many cultures, represented by the spectrum of ethnic/racial groups, ages, religions, languages, and perspectives that fill the nation's salad bowl. The multicultural reality is becoming even more evident for white Americans, who have, for years, been able to ignore or squelch diversity. The growing proportion of ethnic minorities in the country's population, particularly in cities, makes such an approach not only theologically inappropriate, but practically impossible.

Though some Christians may wish to retreat from this diversity, our study affirms that mature Christians understand and accept such diversity. By emphasizing different cultures, an educational program broadens people's understanding of themselves and their world. And it helps them see the similarities among different people, while also learning to respect, accept, and celebrate the differences. William R. Adamson describes this awareness as "recognizing and removing our coloured glasses":

> When people come together in a local church, study the Bible or plan for outreach, they all come, as it were, wearing coloured glasses. That is, they all see things differently. . . . It can be quite surprising, even shocking, to learn that people of other regions, countries and cultures, even people of the Bible, see life quite differently than we do.[26]

Though multicultural awareness is an important key to nourishing faith maturity in adults, it's rarely a part of Christian education. Only 24 percent of churches adequately addresses multicultural concerns. Furthermore, only 17 percent of adults say their church emphasizes "helping members learn about people of different races and ethnic groups." Multicultural awareness can take root through many different avenues. Here are a few possibilities.

- Learn to appreciate the artistic contributions of other cultures through music, painting, dance, drama, film, and other forms, by using the artistic expressions in classrooms and worship.
- Study people from other cultures who have influenced our faith. Connect their stories with your stories.
- Arrange "crosscultural exchanges" with congregations of other faiths or ethnic heritages. Mix Sunday school classes, trade teachers, or invite guest leaders to your adult-education offerings.
- Listen to the stories and experiences of individuals from other backgrounds.
- Use resources from other faith traditions or cultural perspectives. For example, a white congregation might study African American theology or liberation theology.

- Visit other faith communities. Adult classes could easily take prearranged "field trips" to another church's Sunday school, to a mosque or synagogue, or to a contrasting worship service. (A liturgical Lutheran congregation might visit an unprogrammed Quaker meeting!) Then talk about similarities, differences, and new insights.

Global Awareness—People of mature faith see world issues through the eyes of faith. They're concerned about the environment, ecology, world hunger, lack of education in third-world countries, political oppression, and other global issues. They see their lives as intertwined with the lives of their brothers and sisters around the world.

Despite numerous denominational efforts to emphasize these issues, just 31 percent of congregations adequately address them in adult education. Furthermore, these issues fall to the bottom of the list of what adults are interested in studying or learning about. As with multicultural awareness, promoting global awareness involves challenges similar to other social issues. Chapter 10 examines specific responses to these issues.

BALANCING EDUCATIONAL CONTENT

In looking at the many dimensions found to be important for effective educational content, many pastors and educators might react by saying, "We can't emphasize everything!" There's some truth to that. No church can emphasize all the key content issues at the same time. Two approaches suggest possible solutions.

First, many issues should be integrated into other themes if curriculum is well constructed. For example, in youth education, all such issues as Bible study, key theological concepts, moral decision-making, and sexuality could be integrated into a study on sexuality. For adults, all four content issues could be integrated into studies on current issues—capital punishment, Christians in the workplace, the environment, family life, or other adult concerns.

Another appropriate solution would be to take a longer view. How might the church bring all these concerns before the congregation in the next three years, for example? By emphasizing the variety of issues through time, while also touching on other issues, Christian education can nourish a balanced, growing faith across the years.

Regardless of the specific approach taken, however, the goal should remain the same: To help learners build bridges between their faith and their life, so that their faith can grow, their relationship to God can become stronger, and their lives—and the world—can be changed.

Worksheet 5

Content Evaluation

Use this worksheet to evaluate your Christian-education content for youths and adults, based on the emphases in this chapter. Select a number that best represents how well your congregation does in each area. Use the following numbers in your evaluation:

1 = rarely true **3 = often true**
2 = sometimes true **4 = very often true**

Educational Content Emphases	U.S. Churches*	Your Church
Youth		
Emphasizes education about human sexuality.	27%	____
Emphasizes education about drugs and alcohol.	20%	____
Emphasizes moral values and moral decision-making.	60%	____
Emphasizes responsibility for poverty and hunger.	30%	____
Effectively teaches the Bible.	66%	____
Effectively teaches core theological concepts.	74%	____
Effectively teaches good friendship skills.	65%	____
Effectively helps develop concern for others.	66%	____
Adult		
Emphasizes biblical knowledge and understanding.	74%	____
Emphasizes multicultural awareness.	24%	____
Emphasizes global awareness and understanding.	31%	____
Emphasizes moral decision-making.	44%	____

**Based on congregations in the five mainline denominations that were part of the* Effective Christian Education *study.*

Chapter 9

How Do We Study?

Jay Leno is one of the country's premiere comedians. At one point, Leno performed about 250 times a year around the country. Now successor to Johnny Carson as host of "The Tonight Show," Leno was chosen by *Time* as the most popular TV comedian of the 1980s.

But his act wasn't always so popular. The first time Carson heard Leno, he told the comedian, "You seem like a very funny young man, but you're not right for the show." What was the problem? Leno's timing was off. He would tell two or three jokes, then rely on his trademark clowning and gestures to keep the laughs coming. Then Leno watched "The Tonight Show" and realized that Carson was telling 15 or 20 jokes in the same amount of time Leno himself would tell three.

"I resented what Johnny said, but I took it to heart and began honing the material, adding more jokes, better jokes," Leno recalls. "I've always been grateful to him for being so straight, for giving me the *real* advice, hard as it seemed at the time."[1]

Jay Leno's material is part of what makes him a funny, popular comedian. But he never would have gotten where he is if he hadn't learned timing. Telling the joke depends on more than simply having the right script. The process makes all the difference.

A similar truth applies to Christian education. While solid, appropriate content is essential (only master comedians can make people laugh at a bad joke!), "good delivery"—an effective educational process—is also vital. Without it, the material never realizes its potential impact.

MERGING CONTENT AND PROCESS

Effective teaching involves conveying appropriate information in ways people can best learn it. Unfortunately, churches too often focus their energy entirely on *what* is being taught, placing much less emphasis on *how* it is being taught and how people learn. As a result, they rely on one-way communication: lectures, sermons, and so forth.

In *Empowering Disciples: Adult Education in the Church,* William R. Adamson seeks to apply many of these effective-education findings to adult education in the church: "The theory of adult education today stresses the autonomy, responsibility and self-initiating qualities of the adult person." He then challenges the church to "develop a style quite in contrast to the directive and dependency-building modes of our academic system and our culture."[2]

In the past, Adamson says, teaching models in the church have focused almost exclusively on content. "In traditional forms of education . . . the teachers decided in advance what knowledge or skill to transmit, arranged this content material into logical units, selected a set of methods, and prepared a plan for presenting these content units in a sequence." But, he argues, a process model is more appropriate for adults (and, I would argue, for most youths as well):

> In this model the teacher functions more as a consultant or facilitator who prepares a set of procedures for involving adult learners in their own learning tasks. . . . This process model neither ignores nor excludes content material, but it does emphasize a different way of operating, a different way of *appropriating* the necessary content.[3]

The *Effective Christian Education* study confirms the imbalance. Overall, churches tend to do better with content than with process. The average percentage of churches that exhibit the content qualities are 49 percent for youth and 43 percent for adults. In comparison, only 41 percent of churches exhibit the qualities of an effective-education process for youth, and 38 percent for adults.

Looked at from the perspective of the teacher, we find a similar lack of emphasis on educational process, reflected in the percentage of those who know educational theory and practice. Only 44 percent of adult-education teachers exhibit this knowledge, while only 34 percent of youth-education teachers do.

"The effective program not only teaches in the classical sense of transmitting insight and knowledge," the study's summary report concludes, "but also allows insight to emerge from the crucible of experience. . . . Both ways of learning are powerful, and the two in combination produce stronger growth in faith than either one alone."[4]

Before examining the study's specific findings, it may be helpful to put them into the context of educational theory, using John Dewey's philosophy as an example. In *Experience and Education,* he suggested four key concepts for effective teaching.[5] These can be translated easily for the Christian-education setting.

Experience—Before we became parents, my wife and I read several books on parenting. That reading helped focus our thinking so we would know some of what to anticipate. But we did not really begin learning what being a parent was all about until we left the hospital with our son. Then the true education began!

"All genuine education comes about through experience," Dewey wrote. In the church, such experiences might include direct involvement in a particular concern, such as poverty or peacemaking (see chapter 10). It may involve reflection on daily life experiences. Or it might involve games, simulations, or other designed experiences.

Democracy—In theological terms, this emphasis corresponds to respecting the individuality of each person and recognizing that God works and speaks through each learner, not just the teacher. In this model, then, effective education is student-centered, not teacher-centered.

In an important book, *The Adult Learner: A Neglected Species*, adult-education pioneer Malcolm Knowles describes how he discovered the power of this principle. In his first year of teaching in college, he did a good job of transmitting information to his students. They seemed to enjoy his lectures, and he enjoyed being in the spotlight.

Then he began working on a master's degree and took a seminar in psychology, in which the facilitator didn't teach, but let the graduate students guide the process. Knowles and the other students plunged into the topic and took responsibility for their own learning. "That was the day," Knowles asserted, "I decided to switch from being a teacher to being a facilitator of learning. . . . I have never been tempted since to revert to the role of teacher."[6]

A similar emphasis on respecting students and letting them take responsibility for their learning applies to youth education as well. As Thom and Joani Schultz state in *Do It! Active Learning in Youth Ministry:* "Active learning depends on students making discoveries rather than teachers imparting facts and ideas. Active learning starts with the students and moves at their pace."[7]

Continuity—Learning doesn't take place in isolation. Each experience connects with what has gone before and shapes what is still to come. Growth, change, and learning take place as one experience and insight builds on another. In this sphere, the leader's role is to be alert to the group's setting, attitudes, and dynamics, and shape the learning experience so that true, worthwhile growth can take place. Writing about adult education but with conclusions applicable to youth education, Adamson explains:

> Usually, adults have interests or concerns in the back of their minds when they sign up for a course or a group project. Sometimes the concern is vague and nebulous, sometimes sharply defined. . . . Planners and resource leaders need to assist adults to sort their experiences, focus their hopes and motivations, and contrast their present knowledge or skill with the knowledge or skill desired. . . . It is not satisfactory to try to run adults through a preconceived set of hoops, or to leap over an arbitrarily appointed set of hurdles.[8]

Youth too!

Interaction—This concept balances the external and internal conditions of learning. In other words, effective teaching looks not only at what is happening around the student (the experience) but also at what is happening inside the student. How does the student respond to the situation?

This interaction demands the development of learning experiences appropriate to the students' intellectual, spiritual, physical, and emotional development. In selecting appropriate teaching styles and experiences, the teacher builds a bridge between the content to be learned and the learner. Thus, Dewey writes, "The teacher loses the position of external boss or dictator but takes on that of leader of group activities."[9]

In many ways, the *Effective Christian Education* study affirms some of Dewey's emphases (which, of course, have parallels in other theories). In this chapter, we'll examine specific process emphases for youth and adult education uncovered by the study, then discuss a variety of teaching styles that parallel some of the study's emphases.

YOUTH EDUCATION PROCESSES

When the U. S. Department of Education released its report on public education titled *A Nation at Risk,* a group of experiential education specialists criticized the report, in part, because "it ignores the large body of research about how and why individuals learn, how they develop cognitively, morally and socially, and how they differ among themselves." The group went on to suggest that learning be refocused so that "the learner is directly in touch with the realities being studied rather than simply reading about, hearing about, or talking about these realities."[10]

A similar critique and challenge could be directed at youth-education programs in churches. The *Effective Christian Education* study affirms what learning theorists have said for years: Teenagers learn best when insights and knowledge emerge from experience. By combining creative learning techniques with solid biblical and theological knowledge, teenagers are more likely to grow in their faith. The study identifies seven process emphases that lead to more effective Christian education with youths.

Emphasize life experiences as occasions for spiritual insight. The study's approach to faith maturity emphasizes nourishing a life-transforming faith. For this to take place among young people, they need to see the connections between faith and human experience. This emphasis helps them see how faith makes a difference now; it's not just an otherworldly commitment.

This emphasis parallels much of the thinking in education circles of the way people—children, youths, and adults—learn best: by reflecting on experience. Yet only 36 percent of churches effectively embody this characteristic in youth education. These experiences can take several forms.

- Some opportunities for reflection may involve direct, purposeful participation. Young people learn about responsibility to the poor by working in a homeless shelter or soup kitchen. Or they learn about loving enemies by having a meal with someone they thought was an enemy.

  As Christian educators, we need to look for opportunities to directly involve young people in issues and situations that have a bearing on our faith. But we also must provide opportunities for personal and theological discussion, wherein young people can sort out their feelings and beliefs in light of the experience.
- Other opportunities for reflection may simply emerge from young people's everyday lives. When interviewers visited the youth classes at a Los Angeles church, the students faced an impending teacher strike the next morning. Recognizing the concern among the students, the teacher began by asking questions that helped the young people focus their discussion on how they should respond to the strike as Christians. The result was a powerful, relevant class on responsibilities, political involvement, and priorities.
- Since direct involvement in many concerns or issues is often difficult—if not impossible—in many Christian-education settings, Christian educators must create experiences that simulate the emotions, issues, and problems associated with the issue. This creates sometimes powerful opportunities for reflection. In *Do It! Active Learning in Youth Ministry,* Thom and Joani Schultz illustrate this process by describing the difference between active and passive learning:

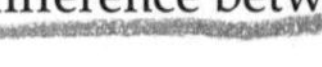

> Visitors to any church's youth ministry can quickly see whether the leaders prefer passive or active learning. In the passive-learning churches, young people sit still (more or less) while the adult leader talks. In the active-learning churches, the visitor may find kids learning about leadership by building towers made of uncooked spaghetti or celebrating forgiveness by tossing confetti in the air.[11]

At their best, simulated learning experiences include four elements found in direct experiential learning. Put together, these elements form the experiential learning cycle below, described by Jane Kendall, executive director of the National Society for Internships and Experiential Education.[12]

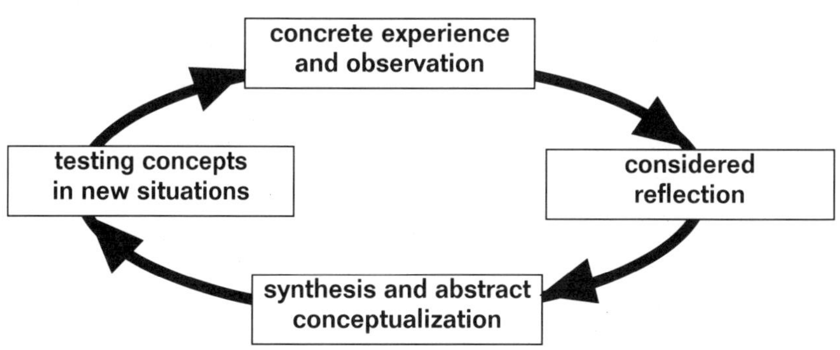

When designing learning experiences, the leader must think through, anticipate, and plan for each stage in the process. Here is a planning process you can use in designing active learning experiences for youths. A similar process can be used in developing experiences for adults.[13]

1. *Identify the theme or goal*. Unless a goal or theme is clearly understood, a learning experience will be difficult to create and lead. This purpose may emerge from several places—scripture, life experiences, or theological themes, depending upon your purpose and context.

2. *Identify feelings or needs*. What feelings or needs are involved in the theme you chose? What elements will grab learners' interest, feelings, or curiosity? How might this theme be simulated? Usually, you can identify several different emotions or attitudes or needs. The task, then, is to isolate the one that can be most effectively communicated.

3. *Create and lead the experience*. This is where creativity really comes into play. It involves almost stream-of-consciousness thinking to identify concrete experiences that evoke the feelings, attitudes, or needs you

identified. It requires flexibility and creativity. Sometimes it helps to think about different senses, media, games, and props that might elicit response. Old activities can often be reused with new twists. Instead of just having people draw pictures, for example, have them draw with their weaker hand—or by holding the crayon in their teeth.

In the process of designing the experience, be careful not to manipulate. Activities need to be open-ended enough to allow for a variety of responses and interpretations. Furthermore, be sure to include all learners in the experience. Interaction increases the effectiveness as learners work together.

4. *Guide reflection.* Reflection is integral to the activity and the learning. Reflection is best guided by open-ended questions that ask participants to express their feelings, insights, and connections. Throughout the group process, trust the Holy Spirit to reach appropriate conclusions.

5. *Focus on application.* Before concluding the activity, encourage participants to make connections to their own lives and experiences. As people apply the insights to new experiences, the experiential cycle is complete.

6. *Evaluate.* As with any learning experience, it is important to assess the effectiveness of an experience afterwards. This involves both an evaluation of the process and a reassessment of new issues that may have emerged and need to be addressed.

Apply faith to everyday decisions. What do I do when I see a fight at school? How do I respond to someone who wants to copy my paper? How do I respond to pressure to buy the latest fashions? How do I deal with a sexually explicit movie or song?

These are real questions in a teenager's world. If the church doesn't help kids think about appropriate responses in a faith context, young people will often make their decisions based on something they saw on television or heard in the locker room.

Effective youth education gives young people a safe, trusting environment, where they can ask those questions and talk about how they would make decisions. Despite its importance, only 49 percent of churches effectively embody this characteristic.

One church that emphasizes this kind of dialogue is Bethel African Methodist Episcopal Church in Baltimore, Maryland. Faced with all the problems associated with urban life, the young people in this church gather monthly on Friday evening for "Teen Rap." Young people choose what they want to talk about. Parents and adults are welcome to attend, but they are not allowed to say anything. Even the youth leader talks only to highlight or clarify scripture.

"There are sessions in which the kids really lay their stuff out," the youth leader says. She remembers one session in which a teenage girl told about the pressure she felt from her boyfriend to have sex. The group helped her by supporting her and encouraging her to make a responsible, faithful choice.[14]

Create a sense of community in which people help one another develop their faith and values. United Methodist pastor Dean Feldmeyer describes an incident that illustrates the importance of community. His church began a "Breakfast Club" for youth that was intended to focus on multitudes of kids eating, laughing, and listening to a speaker. Only ten kids showed up.

So he switched gears and replaced the long cafeteria tables with round tables. Instead of relying on singing and a speaker, he distributed discussion-starter sheets to each table. Questions focused on sharing life experiences. After 45 minutes, the sessions close with a brief devotion. Before long, the church was serving breakfast to ten tables of five kids each. "The message is out," Feldmeyer announces. "Free acceptance and support available here."[15]

Too often, churches plan myriads of programs and activities, hoping to keep young people's interests by imitating M-TV. But we cannot really compete with the flashy, fast-changing, provocative images of a teenager's world.

We can, however, meet another, more basic, need: The need for love, acceptance, trust, and support. By integrating youths into the faith community, we keep them from looking elsewhere for support when they are struggling with and asking tough questions. However, only 31 percent of churches in the study effectively emphasize building a community of faith.

Building community with youth can take many different forms. One approach is found in Denny Rydberg's *Building Community in Youth Groups*. He describes a five-step process for creating community:

1. *Bond Building*—This step involves breaking down barriers between students and establishing a trust relationship. This occurs, Rydberg suggests, through joint problem-solving and cooperation. This problem-solving can take place in the classroom through a variety of structured noncompetitive games and simulated experiences.

2. *Opening Up*—In the second stage, people begin sharing nonthreatening areas of their own lives. If others listen and are perceived to care, a major step is taken in building community. By giving opportunities for people to share prayer requests and personal stories (either with the whole group or one-to-one), we promote this opening up.

3. *Affirming*—Rydberg advises: "After revealing their inner selves during the opening-up step, students need positive feedback to reassure them that

others think they are still okay before they will consider sharing further." Though often awkward to do, even simple affirmation is cherished.

4. *Stretching*—At this stage, people begin to share one anothers' burdens. This may occur naturally as young people experience and seek support during crises in their own lives. Or it may occur by placing young people in unfamiliar surroundings, where people can no longer rely on established patterns. Service projects, group trips, and camping experiences often serve this purpose.

5. *Deeper Sharing and Goal-setting*—In this final stage, the group truly becomes a community, a setting where young people can express their deep feelings, struggles, and longings without risk of condemnation or humiliation. Though rare in many Christian-education settings, this experience can be invaluable in faith formation.[16]

Emphasize individual spiritual growth. Young people grow in faith at their own rate. Some young teenagers may be relatively mature in their faith, while older youths may have a much more superficial faith. If we fail to recognize the differences and respond appropriately to each, we risk losing young people who feel either unchallenged or inadequate, depending upon which end of the spectrum we emphasize.

The study affirms the need to emphasize the natural unfolding of faith and to recognize the uniqueness of each person's faith journey. And about half of all churches (47%) do well in this area. On the positive side, 77 percent of teenagers say it is "true" or "very true" that they can be themselves at church.

This emphasis requires providing opportunities in which youths with different levels of faith commitment can grow. While this emphasis might involve providing a variety of learning opportunities—from introductory faith basics to serious discipleship—it also must occur within each educational setting. How might this happen? Consider these possibilities:

- Get to know each person individually. Unless pastors, teachers, and leaders know where young people are on their spiritual pilgrimages, it's difficult, if not impossible, to affirm each young person's uniqueness.
- Affirm the variety of responses in the classroom. Instead of listening only to those young people who are more mature, encourage all students to learn from one another. Often, simple expressions of faith remind those with more maturity of central issues, while more mature responses can challenge others to grow.
- Use learning styles that allow for diversity of responses. Open-ended questions and activities allow all to participate and express themselves. Lectures, memorization, and reiteration limit participation.

Encourage independent thinking and questioning. Young people are naturally critical. They have begun asking tough questions to discover a faith they can live by. Instead of stifling these questions as signs of "unfaith," we need to affirm—even encourage—the questioning. Of all the process areas, this one is strongest in mainline churches. Sixty-two percent effectively promote questioning.

Yet young people do not always feel that their questions are welcomed. Only 45 percent say their church encourages questions. And only 42 percent say their church challenges their thinking.

Churches can provide a supportive, warm "laboratory," where youths can test and experiment with their faith without risk of rebuke. Otherwise, young people may take their questions outside the church. And they may never return.

Promote intergenerational contact. In *Effective Youth Ministry: A Congregational Approach,* Roland D. Martinson states: "Young people spend most of their time with their peers. School, sports, and leisure activities separate them from children and adults. Congregational life offers an opportunity to integrate young people with persons of all ages." Yet, Martinson adds, "Integration of youth in the congregation does not always happen."[17]

Indeed, only 20 percent of congregations adequately promote intergenerational contact. And just 39 percent of youths say their churches do a good or excellent job of helping them get to know adults in the church.

The *Effective Christian Education* study found, however, that intergenerational contact helps young people grow in their faith. The study suggests several reasons to encourage such contact.

First, contact with older adults is more likely to give young people mentors with mature faith. This maturity can have a positive influence on teenagers' growth in faith.

Second, it builds for young people a sense of community in the congregation. As young people get to know people of all ages, they feel more comfortable in the church and more like part of the family of God.

Third, intergenerational contact can build mutual respect among the generations. As older adults get to know the youths, they will be less suspicious about innovations in the youth program. And as a result, the congregation as a whole is more likely to support youth education.

Finally, intergenerational education is another way to build shared experiences for youth and parents, which can open doors for formal and informal faith conversations at home. Discovering ways to make intergenerational interaction beneficial for all generations can have a significant impact on young people's faith maturity, as well as on the life of the church. Such interaction can take place in many ways. Effective congregations visited by researchers highlight some of the possibilities:

- In one church, young people who become new church members are assigned a church elder as a mentor. This one-to-one interaction is a powerful, faith-shaping experience for the young people.
- Another church has a quarterly intergenerational Sunday school class that emphasizes community building. One year, each class was given an "award" that symbolized its life together. An adult class received the "Beat-up Bible" award for its diligent, inquiring Bible study.
- Many traditionally age-segmented events in one church have been restructured to include all ages. Vacation Bible School, and even the "youth" group include opportunities for all ages. And each fifth Sunday is used for family outings that build community and fellowship. As one fourth-grader put it, "Well, if we didn't have Sunday school and youth group, what would the adults have to do?"

In order for intergenerational learning to be effective, it must allow for differences in development and abilities. Experiential learning is often most appropriate, since it begins with a shared experience in which all can participate. Presentations such as dramas or films can also be effective in creating a common experience upon which to build.

Promote participation in service projects. Some of the best faith learning takes place when young people give themselves away. Indeed, service blurs the line between content and process, as their involvement shapes their thinking. Popular youth speaker Anthony Campolo writes, in his usually provocative way:

> A church which provides its young people with opportunities and challenges for social change gives them the opportunity to explore some of the primary reasons for their salvation. Through these activities they will come to see that Jesus is not only interested in saving them from sin and getting them into heaven, but also wants to make them into instruments through which He can do His work in the world.[18]

Despite the value of service in nurturing faith, half of all teenagers say they rarely or never participate in service projects for other people. Through their whole lives, only 29 percent of young people say they have spent more than ten hours doing projects to help people in their town or city.

Similarly, most congregations do not place a strong emphasis on providing youths with opportunities to serve others. Only 40 percent of Christian education coordinators say this is a strong emphasis. Similarly, just 41 percent of teenagers say their church does a good or excellent job of helping them become involved in helping people in their town or city.

Service projects, either locally or out of state, become important vehicles for nourishing faith. They also plant the seed in young people to begin noticing the systemic social issues that underlie the problems of poverty and other social ills. Furthermore, the process of taking young people out of familiar settings also causes them to reassess values, priorities, and perspectives. Chapter 10 suggests ways to address service and justice themes in Christian education.

ADULT EDUCATION PROCESSES

For at least the past twenty years, education theorists have focused considerable energy on adult education. In fact, according to Malcolm Knowles, the bulk of learning theorists and interpreters since 1970 have "been concerned almost exclusively with adult learners."[19]

The hallmark of current thinking about adult education is that it shifts responsibility for learning from the teacher to the adults in the group. By taking responsibility for their own learning, adults become actively involved in their own growth. This shift in thinking has profound implications for all areas of adult education. Instead of teachers being all-knowing databases of information about the faith upon which they expound, they become facilitators who find responsible ways to draw learning and growth out of the adults themselves.

It's interesting and discouraging to note how few publishers of adult Christian-education resources recognize the implications of this emphasis for curriculum development. For example, most Sunday school curriculum gives the teacher detailed background information on the scripture and theme, but gives virtually none to the class participants.

This standard practice creates a hierarchy that contradicts adult learning theory—as well as a theology of priesthood of all believers. Teachers begin with more knowledge than others in the class, which often results in the teacher spending the class explaining what he or she knows. (One teacher effectively dealt with this problem by distributing the background information in the teacher's book to all the class participants.)

Some people may imagine that shifting from a teacher-centered to a student-centered model of adult education makes the teacher an unnecessary element in the classroom. Yet the teacher still has a vital role in the learning process. Clinical psychologist and educator Carl Rogers suggests ten guidelines for teachers, paraphrased below, which have important implications for adult Christian education.[20]

1. The facilitator sets a mood or climate of trust and openness for the group or class experience.

2. The facilitator elicits and clarifies the purposes (why they came) of the individuals and the purposes of the group as a whole (why it exists).

3. The facilitator relies on the inner motivation and needs of the students to guide the group.

4. The facilitator organizes and makes available a wide range of resources for learning.

5. The facilitator sees his or her role as a flexible resource to be used by the group. The facilitator is valuable to the group for whatever experience or information he or she can bring to the group.

6. The facilitator accepts both intellectual content and emotional attitudes that arise in the group process. Neither is discounted.

7. As the class or group becomes established, the facilitator can participate more actively as one of the group, expressing views as an individual who is part of the group.

8. The facilitator expresses his or her own feelings and thoughts in ways that model honesty and sensitivity.

9. The facilitator remains alert to expressions that indicate deep or strong feelings, then sensitively discerns whether or not to elicit those feelings for constructive sharing and understanding.

10. The facilitator recognizes his or her own limitations, both in knowledge and comfort, in sharing himself or herself.

The *Effective Christian Education* study underscores the need for focusing new energy on educational process for adults. It identifies five elements of an effective educational process which encourage growth in faith, few of which are strong in most congregations. Naturally, some of these emphases parallel youth process.

Create a sense of community in which people help one another develop faith and values. One of my most profound faith experiences took place late one Friday night in a Chicago apartment. I was leading a small-group study of Stanley Hauerwas' book *The Peaceable Kingdom,* which focuses heavily on creating a community of faith. Early in the discussion that evening, someone interrupted, saying, "We keep talking about the importance of faith stories, but we never really talk about them. Why not?"

And for the next three hours, each of us told our stories—the ups, the downs, the questions, the concerns, the hopes, the dreams. For perhaps the first time, I knew something of what it meant to have brothers and sisters in Christ. But it happened only because we interrupted my carefully prepared discussion in order to share ourselves with one another and, in the process, developed lasting Christian community.

Before effective education can take place, participants must have a sense of community—a sense that they are, indeed, sisters and brothers in Christ. According to Thomas H. Groome, "To the extent that a Christian community can be created within an educational context, that context is likely to be effective in sponsoring its members toward lived Christian faith."[21]

As important as community is for education, few churches emphasize it. Indeed, only 16 percent of educational programs adequately include this element—the lowest process emphasis in adult education.

Community forms as participants share part of their own lives with others and speak about their faith. Teachers also encourage community by creating an atmosphere of trust, support, and openness. This atmosphere forms as teachers themselves risk openness, then respond sensitively to other people's openness. The community-building process described in the youth-education section can be adapted for adults.

Use life experiences as occasions for spiritual insight. Each adult brings numerous life experiences and struggles to the classroom. These are invaluable vehicles for helping people gain spiritual and theological insight. Indeed, adults feel cut off and unappreciated if their experiences and insights are not taken seriously.

Adamson explains that children in school often learn knowledge and skills they will (perhaps) use later. In contrast, "Adults involved in making a living, carrying responsibility, and coping with life issues prefer *immediate application* of their learning. . . . They are eager to learn things which will help them be more capable and will relate constructively to their present situations."[22]

According to our study, 61 percent of congregations effectively allow spiritual insight to emerge from life experiences in their adult-education programs. At the same time, research conducted for the Religious Education Association of the United States and Canada found that many people do not find "support for their faith or help during life crises from their religious organizations." A report titled *Faith Development and Your Ministry* concludes: "When dealing with personal challenges, far more people turn to private activities such as prayer, music, and inspirational reading, than to their religious community."[23]

Helping adults use life experiences to gain spiritual insight involves developing a learning process that actually uses the learners' experiences. In a sense, the people become the curriculum. Knowles suggests three teaching principles that facilitate this process:

1. The facilitator helps students use their experiences for occasions for learning through discussions, role-plays, case studies, and other teaching methods.

2. The facilitator presents his or her own resources at a level appropriate to the students, so that they can connect the resources with their own experiences.

3. The facilitator guides and encourages students to apply new learning to their experiences, so that the learning becomes more meaningful and integrated.[24]

Apply faith to political and social issues. When war breaks out in the Middle East or riots erupt in Los Angeles, social issues dominate conversations in churches. Most of the time, however, social and political issues are less important than social hours and in-church gossip. Only 17 percent of mainline churches emphasize the social and political dimensions of life in their Christian-education programs.

Americans have bought the false notion that religion and politics don't mix. Their faith has little to do with the ballot box or the way they respond to social concerns. In fact, 58 percent of adults say they do not want churches to be involved in political issues. But 50 percent say they often or always try to apply their faith to political and social issues.

If, indeed, the gospel calls us to address social inequities and injustice, we must find ways to overcome this general avoidance of these issues in Christian education. Adamson is convinced that "in order to assist adults to nurture their faith, we need to focus on the liberating work of Jesus Christ for our *social systems* as well as [for] ourselves. Our social systems condition us with implicit assumptions and values. We need to remove our coloured glasses so that we may see our systems and our context with fresh eyes."[25]

Such a challenge is sometimes difficult to respond to. Though important, challenging cultural assumptions and values is threatening and difficult. Other process elements (building community, applying faith to life) can make the process somewhat easier. Chapter 10 focuses on ways to deal with controversial issues.

Respect the importance and uniqueness of each person's faith journey. Different people are at different places on their faith journeys.

Some may just have pulled out their maps, looking for direction. Some may have taken long detours and lost their way. Others may have traveled many miles through the years. And still others may have taken a break at a rest stop.

But each person is on the journey. And each person can learn from the others. As they talk together openly and with respect, affirming each other regularly, people will learn and grow together. Adult Christian-education participants need encouragement and support in order to travel on the faith journey at their own speed and in their own way. Yet only 25 percent of churches embody this trait in their adult-education activities.

Accepting and affirming people who are at different stages, with different perspectives, is not an easy task. "It is not enough simply to bring the people of God together and expect unity to happen as if by magic," argues Stephen Kliewer. "We must develop some strategies which will help people draw together in love."[26] As with building community, it requires helping people see the value of others, creating an atmosphere of trust and openness, and respectfully listening to each person's story.

Encourage independent thinking and questioning. Adult Christian education rarely deals with foregone conclusions. The ethical, theological, and doctrinal issues usually are too complex for simple answers. And they usually are not questions with which adults struggle, so they can have little apparent relevance.

In an effective program, questions are often posed with no answer in mind. And people need the freedom to ask their own questions and suggest their own responses, without fear of being censured or ridiculed. Many congregations—71 percent—already foster such an atmosphere.

The discovery-learning or problem-solving teaching approaches highlight this emphasis in the educational process. In this model, the teacher's primary role is to engage students in questions that are designed, in the words of proponents N. Postman and C. Weingartner, "to open engaged minds to unsuspected possibilities."[27]

Related to inductive teaching, discovery learning sees content as material to be explored, rather than merely as knowledge to be remembered. Appropriate for all ages when the media are designed correctly, this style can be particularly effective with adults because it respects and builds upon their own experience and knowledge.

Worksheet 6
Educational Process Evaluation

Use this worksheet to evaluate your congregation's educational processes for youths and adults. Read each statement, then select a number that best represents your congregation. Use the following numbers in your evaluation:

1 = very weak **3 = pretty good**
2 = okay, but not great **4 = excellent**

Educational Process	U.S. Churches*	Your Church
Youths		
Emphasizes intergenerational content.	20%	_____
Emphasizes life experiences as occasions for spiritual insight.	36%	_____
Creates a sense of community in which people help one another develop their faith and values.	31%	_____
Emphasizes the natural unfolding of faith and recognizes that each person's faith journey is unique.	47%	_____
Encourages independent thinking and questioning.	62%	_____
Effectively helps youths apply faith to daily decisions.	49%	_____
Emphasizes involving youths in service projects.	29%	_____
Adults		
Emphasizes applying faith to political and social issues.	17%	_____
Emphasizes life experiences as occasion for spiritual insight.	61%	_____
Creates a sense of community in which people help one another develop faith and values.	16%	_____
Emphasizes the natural unfolding of faith and recognizes each person's faith journey as unique.	25%	_____
Strongly encourages independent thinking and questioning.	71%	_____

**Based on congregations in the five mainline denominations that were part of the* Effective Christian Education *study.*

SHIFTING TO EFFECTIVE PROCESSES

I once participated in a church conflict-management workshop, in which the facilitator tried using experiential role-plays with adults. He divided the group into teams, each taking a particular perspective on whether to buy a new pipe organ.

Few of the adults even knew what to do, and the simulated debate never really took on life, as it was designed to do. In trying to encourage the process, the facilitator asked one member about her perspective. "I don't know what's going on," she said, obviously frustrated. "I didn't even know anyone *wanted* a new pipe organ at this church!"

Due to their experience with a more teacher-oriented approach, many people in the church—particularly adults—may resist the active-participation approach to Christian education. No longer can they sit passively and listen. It makes them feel more vulnerable, and they may not be sure they are actually learning anything.

Thus leaders need to assure participants that learning does take place, but that the emphasis is on receiving information rather than just transmitting it. Having them look back on previous experiences may help them discover—from their own experience—that learning truly does occur. They are likely to remember much more than they did in a more passive learning situation.

The issue of vulnerability is a real concern, particularly in a group just beginning to form. Most people may be comfortable with sharing ideas, but many are uncomfortable with sharing their feelings and struggles. Here is where the importance of community and trust come in. And by taking risks themselves, leaders model the approach and make it less threatening.

If at first people don't respond well to a more process-oriented educational approach, it may be tempting to fall back on the older comfortable methods. However, after a few experiences, most people begin to understand and to feel comfortable with an active, involving process. And the long-range results are certainly worth the handful of awkward sessions.

"Mary/Martha" and "Woman to Woman"

Worksheet 7
Youth Curriculum Checklist

The *Effective Christian Education* study suggests numerous implications for curriculum development and selection. Use this checklist in evaluating and selecting curriculum for youth. You may have other evaluation points to add that were not directly addressed in the national study.

Curriculum Title: ______________________________

Publisher: ______________________________

❑ Yes ❑ No Gives teachers guidance and insight into the educational theory and methods for youths.

❑ Yes ❑ No Effectively teaches the Bible and core theological concepts.

❑ Yes ❑ No Emphasizes youth life issues such as sexuality, and alcohol and other drugs.

❑ Yes ❑ No Emphasizes moral values and decision-making.

❑ Yes ❑ No Emphasizes responsibility for poverty and hunger, and suggests ways to involve youths in service.

❑ Yes ❑ No Is compatible with the denomination's theology and tradition.

❑ Yes ❑ No Teaches friendship skills and developing concern for others.

❑ Yes ❑ No Uses educational processes that create a sense of community among the youths.

❑ Yes ❑ No Uses life experiences as occasions for spiritual insight, either through simulated learning or direct involvement.

❑ Yes ❑ No Recognizes and affirms the uniqueness of each person's spiritual journey.

❑ Yes ❑ No Encourages independent thinking and questioning.

❑ Yes ❑ No Offers suggestions for intergenerational contact.

❑ Yes ❑ No Provides materials to promote faith conversations in families.

❑ Yes ❑ No Provides for coordinated study so that all ages study the same issues or Bible passages simultaneously.

Overall Assessment and Comments: ______________________________

____

____

Worksheet 8
Adult Curriculum Checklist

The *Effective Christian Education* study suggests numerous implications for curriculum development and selection. Use this checklist in evaluating and selecting curricula for adults. You may have other evaluation points to add that were not directly addressed in the national study.

Curriculum Title: ____________________

Publisher: ____________________

❑ Yes ❑ No Gives teachers guidance and insight into the educational theory and methods for adults.

❑ Yes ❑ No Emphasizes biblical knowledge and understanding.

❑ Yes ❑ No Emphasizes multicultural awareness.

❑ Yes ❑ No Emphasizes moral decision-making.

❑ Yes ❑ No Emphasizes global awareness and understanding.

❑ Yes ❑ No Emphasizes applying faith to political and social issues.

❑ Yes ❑ No Is compatible with the denomination's theology and tradition.

❑ Yes ❑ No Uses educational processes that create a sense of community among the adults.

❑ Yes ❑ No Uses life experiences as occasions for spiritual insight, either through simulated learning or direct involvement.

❑ Yes ❑ No Recognizes and affirms the uniqueness of each person's spiritual journey.

❑ Yes ❑ No Encourages independent thinking and questioning.

❑ Yes ❑ No Provides materials to promote faith conversations in families.

❑ Yes ❑ No Provides for coordinated study so that all ages study the same issues or Bible passages simultaneously.

Overall Assessment and Comments: ____________________

____

____

____

Chapter 10

Faith in Action: Educating for Service and Justice

Throughout this book have been references to the troubling truth that most mainline church members don't become involved in, or express concern for, social and political issues. Few spend significant hours helping the poor, hungry, or sick. Few participate in marches, meetings, or gatherings to promote social change. Few people think the church should be involved in political issues. And few churches are emphasizing these issues—particularly those that move beyond service to social action (see Figure 21).

Perhaps the most common response to these realities is acquiescence, arguing that you can't force people to do things they don't believe in. If people aren't interested, why push them? Let's nourish the faith in the protective context of the congregation, and only later begin outreach and service. Maybe they'll get involved after we meet their needs.

Figure 21
Social Concerns: Low on Churches' Agendas

How much do churches emphasize social issues? Some people would say too little, while others would say not enough. Here are the percentages of adults in the *Effective Christian Education* study who say their church places a "strong" or "very strong" emphasis on each issue:

- Reaching out to the poor and hungry: 48%
- Involving members in helping people in their town or city: 40%
- Helping members learn about people of different races and ethnic backgrounds: 17%
- Discussing national and international issues: 12%
- Getting members to work for social justice and peace: 12%

This approach ignores the value of service and outreach in nurturing faith maturity and loyalty. It also ignores the educational reality that people learn best through direct, personal involvement. Furthermore, it undercuts a balanced theology. The faith-maturity scale that underlies the *Effective Christian Education* study emphasizes the importance of a multidimensional faith, which balances faith's horizontal and vertical dimensions. To ignore the horizontal dimension is to ignore scripture's call to combat injustice and work for God's *shalom.*

If the horizontal dimension is so important to a balanced faith, why is it emphasized in so few churches? In *Revisioning the DRE,* Donald G. Emler attributes the problem, in part, to the fact that until recently, educators tended to ignore social concerns, focusing instead on institutional concerns and outlooks. "Still today," he adds, "even with the church finally responding to societal issues, religious educators do not seem to adequately know how to equip and enable learners to participate in the ministries of peace and justice. The most religious educators seem to know how to do is tell learners that they should be concerned."[1]

How can churches work toward more balanced expressions of faith? How can Christian-education leaders overcome roadblocks that keep members from becoming involved in social issues? These three "I's" seem imperative: Information, Involvement, and Integrity with the mission of the local church.[2]

CONVEYING INFORMATION

In the mid-1980s, the world was riveted by news coverage of the famine in the horn of Africa. Americans responded with millions of dollars in donations and great outpourings of concern and interest. Though relatively short-lived, the response illustrates the power of information about issues in motivating people to action. Unless people know about an issue or need, they can't respond to it.

Of course, part of the problem with many social issues is that they can polarize congregations, which often leads to in-fighting, not outreaching. In *Peacemaking Without Division: Moving Beyond Congregational Apathy and Anger,* Patricia Washburn and Robert Gribbon suggest a progression of four elements in the information process, which they find help congregations deal with peacemaking and other controversial social issues.[3]

Figure 22
Social Attitudes of Adults and Youths

Here are the percentages of youths and adults who say they "tend to agree" or "definitely agree" with each statement.

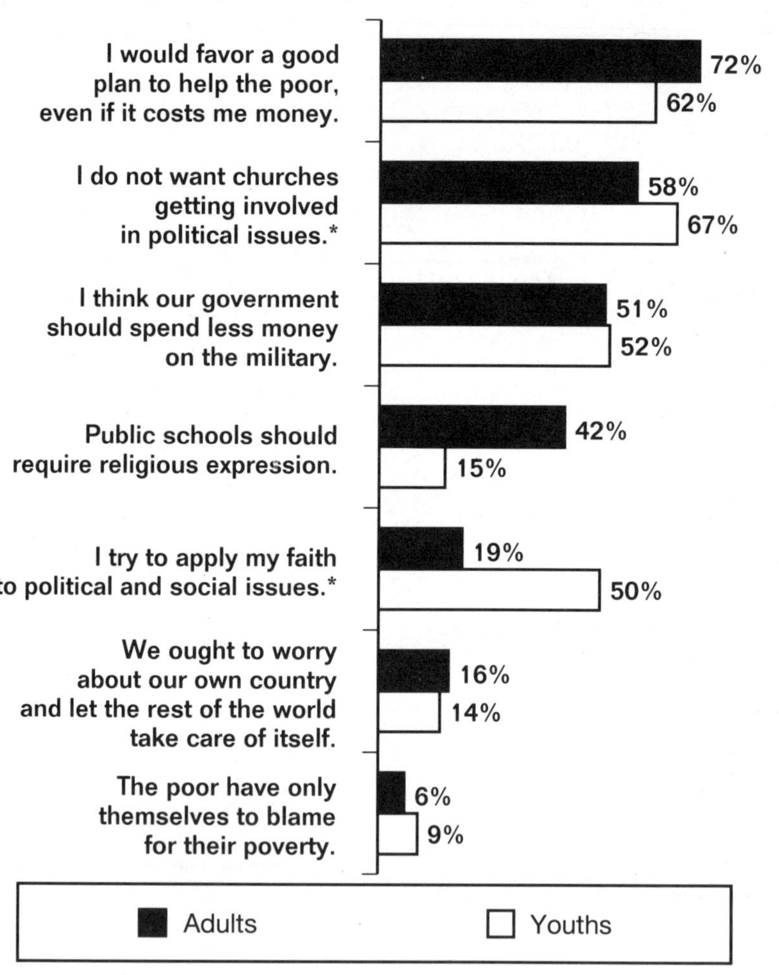

I would favor a good plan to help the poor, even if it costs me money.
72%
62%
I do not want churches getting involved in political issues.*
58%
67%
I think our government should spend less money on the military.
51%
52%
Public schools should require religious expression.
42%
15%
I try to apply my faith to political and social issues.*
19%
50%
We ought to worry about our own country and let the rest of the world take care of itself.
16%
14%
The poor have only themselves to blame for their poverty.
6%
9%
Adults
Youths

Based on those who answered sometimes, often, almost always, and always true.

Feelings—The first step involves having people identify their feelings about the issue. What are their fears?; their worries?; their insecurities?; their pleasures? "The feelings are basic," Washburn and Gribbon write, "and probably shape the tone and content of what we later express in thought."

This beginning point fits well with the educational model of experiential learning, in which experiences are designed to elicit feelings (see chapter 9). I once participated in a hunger workshop in which half the participants were served a bountiful cafeteria of food, while the other table received a bit of rice. Feelings emerged as both groups sat silently and awkwardly, wondering what to do. Some people at the bountiful table suggested that their food be shared—which elicited much debate. Some people at the empty table talked of going over to steal food. Though people participated in light-hearted ways, the activity opened up a plethora of serious feelings about issues of hunger and development.

Feelings create connections between faraway issues and individuals. If people identify with the feelings of the oppressed, they are more likely to be compassionate and responsive. This feeling level is also the level at which direct personal involvement can be vital in evoking deepseated feelings. Debriefings after service projects, mission trips, and other activities can help people express their feelings and begin to put pieces together.

Story—At this stage, people begin articulating their own story and making connections with the issue at hand. Washburn and Gribbon ask people to describe living in a nuclear age. In the process, people "own" some of their feelings and begin to develop an understanding of those with different views. At this stage, Washburn and Gribbon also suggest building bridges to the biblical story as it relates to people's fears and hopes.

Community—The community stage builds on the experiences of storysharing. At this stage, the group examines statements about the issue by people of authority or those who are respected in that particular community. These might be denominational statements (which people may or may not agree with), books by respected authors, or people within the congregation. The goal is not to force a perspective, but to begin forming a community response to the issue.

Ideas—Saving the sharing of ideas until the end is not the way most churches operate; most start with a statement they plan to either adopt or reject. But Washburn and Gribbon argue that the common approach of such position statements and study groups leads people to respond out of guilt or fear, not out of hope. "One great contribution of the church to the world order," they suggest, "can be to help people move from fear to hope as a basis for action."[4]

This sort of process was followed by one congregation that sensed a growing concern about how Christians should respond to homosexuality. Instead of beginning with an idea (such as, We want a statement on whether or not to accept homosexuals into the fellowship), the congregation began by examining issues and feelings, with no specific outcome in mind. Through time, participants examined scripture, other literature, other perspectives, and their own experiences. Though the issue could have been divisive, the congregation concluded its study by drafting and accepting a congregational statement regarding sexual orientation.

Of course, such a process takes a lot of time, energy, and patience. And since churches usually handle conflict by avoiding it, Washburn and Gribbon suggest focusing on conflict-management skills before focusing on people's ideas and opinions. They particularly emphasize shifting from a win/lose mentality to a win/win mentality. After leading workshops on peacemaking for a number of years, they say this approach is well-received and accepted. They conclude:

> Pastoral care and prophetic ministry need not be at odds. Issues affect people, and people bring the issues. If we take individuals seriously, we will create contexts into which people can bring all their hopes, fears, stories, commitments, and ideas. When we allow all of reality to be dealt with in a religious context, we find that both issues and people are transformed.[5]

PROMOTING APPROPRIATE INVOLVEMENT

Information alone is never enough to make people committed to issues. At some point—often in the process of receiving the information—people need to become personally involved in the issues. Then the issues become real and vital and, sometimes, life-changing.

In addition to building awareness for the issues, service involvement has positive byproducts. Experts in service-learning (which combines service with related educational subjects, from elementary school through college) have identified numerous ways in which appropriate service involvement appears to have a positive impact on both young people and their communities. These benefits would likely "rub off" on adults and the church as well.[6]

Building Learning Skills—Being involved in service enhances one's own skills. This outcome seems strongest when service involves tutoring of peers or young children. But there's also some evidence that service involvement can improve problem-solving abilities, critical thinking, and open-mindedness.

Enhancing Self-esteem and Personal Responsibility—Community service appears to have a positive influence on teenagers' social and psychological development. It also gives them a sense of being part of—and contributing to—something bigger than themselves. In focusing on the importance of service, a major report on young people by the William T. Grant Foundation concluded: "There is virtually no limit to what young people—with appropriate education, training, and encouragement . . . can do, no social need they cannot help meet."[7]

Promoting Positive Values—Experiences of giving of themselves can change the way people look at their own lives. Personal journals of young people who serve others sometimes show altered career plans, personal changes, and new perspectives on the world. Furthermore, young people often learn new skills in relating to others and develop empathy for those in need.

Building Bridges Across Barriers—Whether it involves working with those in poverty, the elderly, people of a different ethnic background, or people with different learning abilities, service can be an important element in building understanding and empathy.

Researchers Dan Conrad and Diane Hedin quote the following journal excerpts from a young woman after she had worked in a nursing home for one day: "Honestly, I doubt if I can respect these people who wear diapers, drool gallons of saliva a day, speak totally incoherently and [are] totally dependent on youth."

By the end of the first week, however, her feelings had begun to change: "I think those insecurities you feel when you start working with elderly people disappear when you begin to really *love* them."[8]

Knowing these benefits—as well as the biblical mandate to help others, how can we best encourage people in the churches to become involved? Without seeking to be exhaustive, some ideas that follow will point to some useful directions.

Think through strategies and issues. A poorly planned service or action experience can do more harm than good, both for those being served and those serving. One first experience could dampen any interest in further involvement. A network of national service-learning organizations has developed a series of guidelines which the church would do well to study and use as appropriate.[9] They suggest that an effective and sustained service-learning program does the following:

1. Engages people in responsible and sustained actions for the common good.
2. Provides structured opportunities for people to reflect critically on their service experience.
3. Articulates clear service and learning goals for everyone involved.
4. Allows for those in need to define those needs.
5. Clarifies the responsibilities of each person and organization involved.
6. Matches service providers and service needs through a process that recognizes changing circumstances.
7. Expects genuine, active, and sustained organizational commitment.
8. Includes training, supervision, monitoring, support, recognition, and evaluation to meet service and learning goals.
9. Ensures that the time commitment for service and learning is flexible, appropriate, and in the best interest of all involved.
10. Is committed to program participation by and with diverse populations.

Provide involvement opportunities. It should be obvious, but we sometimes forget that people will not be involved if we don't provide opportunities. Are those opportunities readily available for those who do become interested? Or must people already be strongly committed to find them?

In *How to Mobilize Church Volunteers,* Marlene Wilson describes her experience as director of a volunteer agency that sought to match calls for help with organizations, churches, and individuals who could help. She made intentional efforts to include all 75 churches in her city, Boulder, Colorado, but encountered two responses:

> One was ignorance of the need (most congregations simply had no idea there were unmet needs like that in our city); the other was "ignorance" (that's knowing about the needs, but doing nothing that really helps them). I found that often this kind of response was not because the people didn't care enough; it was because they simply did not know any other way to respond. Their churches had not equipped them to be the scattered church in the hurting world.[10]

Plan developmentally appropriate experiences. Service opportunities must be planned with the developmental needs of participants in mind. Adults can do different things from high schoolers, who can do different things from junior highers. For example, most experts agree that the best projects for younger teenagers involve interpersonal contact. Senior citizens have a wealth of expertise and experience to share, but may not have the stamina of younger adults (although some might!).

Furthermore, service opportunities should fit the skill levels of people, so that they do not become frustrated or feel that their skills are undervalued. Whatever the role, the tasks must be real, not "busy work" or work that staff people do not want to do. People are quick to sense phoniness and to resent being exploited.

Process the experiences. Research in the effectiveness of service-learning shows that the most important influence on positive change is a regular, formal opportunity to discuss what is being learned. People need to talk about what they see and perceive. They need to express their feelings about themselves, the people involved, and the issues being addressed. Such discussion helps people articulate and assimilate their experiences in meaningful ways.

Many churches take groups on weeklong work camps to rehabilitate or build homes in low-income communities. These can be extremely positive experiences of growth and personal evaluation. But they can also lead to cynicism about the poor ("Why do we help them when they have big cars?") or a misunderstanding of the cycle of poverty. The key difference lies in taking the time and effort to talk about their perceptions, feelings, insights, concerns, and responses.

Provide ongoing opportunities. Ongoing service involvement tends to have a greater impact than one-shot experiences. It takes more than a day or week to assimilate experiences, get over initial barriers, and build meaningful relationships. Thus long-term projects within the church's own community will likely have a much more lasting impact than the work camps in faraway places.

MAINTAINING INTEGRITY WITH A CHURCH'S IDENTITY

One of the problems with getting people involved in social ministry is that we too often assume that a church has to be a particular kind of church to become active in social ministry. These churches are the ones whose pastors are quoted on the evening news whenever a hot issue is in town. They're churches whose identity centers around social ministry. As a result, we may push churches to become active in ways that don't fit their own sense of mission and culture. It rarely works. For social ministry to be effective in a congregation, it must grow out of, and be integral to, the church's own sense of calling.

The good news is that social ministry can be effectively integrated into different congregational styles. Many different kinds of churches can and do address and respond to social issues. Indeed, a mixture of congregational styles actually enhances the vitality and diversity of the church at large.

Carl S. Dudley, of the Center for Church and Community Ministries, has undertaken what is perhaps the most comprehensive research in this area. Through a multifaceted, longitudinal study of about 100 Midwest churches, Dudley and his colleagues suggest that "typical congregations can develop and institutionalize effective social ministries, with a wide variety of leadership styles." Thus, Dudley argues, rather than undercutting the congregation's identity to make this ministry happen, taking those dynamics seriously is the key to the ministry's success. Dudley identifies six congregation types and discusses how they organized their social ministries. Of course, most actual churches include elements of several types.[11]

Crusader Churches—These fit the pattern of highly visible congregations in social ministry. "They turn every issue into a campaign, every crisis into a larger cause," Dudley writes. They march on the front lines of social causes, raising issues where others might let them slide. However, they aren't necessarily the most liberal congregations. In fact, in a chapter on the subject, Dudley and Sally A. Johnson suggest that they tend to be theologically moderate or evangelical, but hold liberal views on social issues.

As a rule, these churches are pioneers that clear the way for others—and for denominations to become involved in controversial issues. Their members tend to be more active in issues than are people in other churches, and they are very energetic and innovative. Dudley and Johnson conclude: "Admirers are tempted to make them the normative model for congregational social ministry. Yet the majority of American Christian congregations build on other identities to generate effective social ministries."[12]

Survivor Churches—These churches don't seem like good candidates for social ministry. They are "reactive, and always on the verge of being overwhelmed by emergencies." You might think they have too many problems of their own to worry about problems in society.

But survivor churches can effectively respond to crises. "They may be reacting with their backs to the wall, but it works," say Dudley and Johnson. "These are activist congregations, second only to crusaders in their corporate commitment to respond to social problems."[13]

These churches, Dudley and Johnson suggest, find their identity in their survival and persistence. These characteristics become positive motivating forces for helping others in crisis. Indeed, because of their own struggles, the survivors can cope where other congregational styles might collapse.

Pillar Churches—These churches support and undergird the community as did the "old First churches," with resources and status. When they become involved in social and public issues, they do it out of a sense of civic duty. They tend to study issues longer and seem slow to act to some issues. When mobilized, though, "these churches can have a powerful impact."[14] They offer stability to movements. Because they tend to be larger, they can provide resources and facilities for community groups. Their methodical, in-depth study often leads them to develop more comprehensive strategies than other congregations, meeting multifaceted needs when they address the problem.

Though the pillar churches in Dudley's study tend to be liberal on theological issues, they are more conservative on social issues. But the pillars can legitimate change where others might ignore it. And when they do become involved, they often quickly move to advocacy due to their prominence in the community.

Pilgrim Churches—These, which often have an ethnic makeup, are rooted in people and a heritage, not a place. Family ties are vital, and ministries generally happen through familial or cultural networks. These churches have a deep sense of responsibility to society's outcasts.

Pilgrim churches might not think of themselves as activists. Yet they are among the most active in caring for "our people" and, in time, those beyond themselves. Because they themselves had arduous journeys to find their viable place in society, they often focus their ministry priorities on long-term improvements in the lives of others. They tend to sponsor, for example, educational efforts such as job training, English classes, parenting skills, and other life skills. And, due to their history, they tend to be conscious of systemic and global issues, which quickly push them into advocacy roles.

Servant Churches—These churches focus their social ministries on quiet care for individuals—individuals who might otherwise be lost in larger social agendas. Theirs is a pastoral, personal ministry, revolving around visiting the sick, taking food to the bereaved, providing basic necessities to neighbors in need. They aren't motivated by causes, but they faithfully help people.

As might be expected, they tend to be socially conservative and theologically moderate. They take public stands or advocacy roles only when they feel forced to do so by circumstances. For them, caring for people is a natural part of their faith. As a result, they effectively help individuals in need to "get back on their feet" by doing home repairs, helping with insurance paperwork, or finding a job.

DOING THE WORD

These diverse images of congregations and their potential involvement in social issues open the doors for all types of congregations to become involved in social ministries. And as different congregations minister out of their own identities, the patchwork of ministries among churches becomes rich with possibility. As Dudley and Johnson suggest: "Each self-image has special, irreplaceable gifts that these congregations can alone offer to others through social ministry, gifts that make them stronger and richer in the act of giving."[15]

This kind of service and action may not seem like a traditional task of Christian education. But consider what takes place in the context of outward ministry. Through personal contact and involvement, people learn about issues and needs. They struggle with how their faith speaks to the concern. They discover ways to translate the gospel into meaningful action in the world. At each stage along the way, they are shaping, renewing, nurturing their faith in the crucible of experience in "doing the word."

Chapter 11

Nurturing Faith in Families

Suppose your church included 100 families. And suppose those families reflected the population of the United States. Here's what your church would look like:

- It would have about 321 parishioners, reflecting an average family size of slightly more than three people.[1]
- Fewer than ten of the families would be "traditional"—intact marriage, father working outside the home, mother not, at least two children.[2]
- Fifty-nine of the families would be married couples. Of these, 29 would have children under age 18. Well over half of these families would have two working parents.
- Eight families would be single-parent families—seven of them headed by a mother.
- Twenty-three adults would live alone.
- Two unmarried couples would live together.
- The remaining eight households would have some other living arrangement.[3]

These kinds of statistics aren't surprising anymore. We've been reading about them and hearing about them and even living with them for years. But we sometimes fail to evaluate the church's role in responding to these and other family dynamics.

Such a response is critical, not only because the family needs support and guidance, but because the family is vital to the church's efforts to promote faith. For better or worse, our families have more influence on our character, values, motivations, and beliefs than any other institution in society, including churches and schools.

Sometimes the reality of the family's influence on children and youth is difficult to accept. Middlebury College President Olin Robison describes a common encounter on parents' weekend at the college. He writes:

> Almost every year when I'm fielding questions, some parent will stand up and say: "My son or daughter is having a very good experience here, and I really appreciate it. However, I've looked in your college catalogue, and I want to know why you don't do more on the free-enterprise system. I don't think you're doing enough." There's a rustle in the room.
>
> Not wanting to disturb the pleasant atmosphere of the weekend with a philosophical debate, I simply respond: "Why don't you leave them alone? They're going to grow up and be just like you."[4]

In many ways, Robison is right. A family's positive influence can overcome many obstacles. A determined and loving single-parent mother in Brooklyn can keep her children from caving in to pressure to use drugs. A caring, gentle father can nourish pride and self-esteem in a child with a learning disability.

Indeed, a Search Institute study of 47,000 teenagers, *The Troubled Journey,* found that youths who have a positive family life, where they feel love and support, are less likely to engage in at-risk behaviors. In fact, this factor had the strongest negative correlation to at-risk behavior of any of the 11 positive factors.[5]

At the same time—as family systems experts have taught us—a negative influence at home during childhood and adolescence can be difficult (albeit not impossible) to overcome. A sexually abused daughter may never be able to form intimate, trusting relationships. A neglected son may never develop the self-esteem to stand up for himself, because he is afraid of losing someone's love.

According to John Bradshaw, "Our lives are shaped from the beginning by our parents. After birth our self-image comes from our primary caregiver's eyes. How I see and feel about myself is exactly what I see in my caregiver's eyes. How my mothering person feels about me in these earliest years is how I will feel about myself."[6]

The *Effective Christian Education* study confirms that families have a similar influential role in faith growth and maturity. Family religious experience has more influence on young people's faith than does Christian education, which also has a strong relationship to faith maturity. Lifetime church involvement, friends' religiousness, a caring church, nonchurch religious activities, and serving others also have a positive, albeit less influential, impact on youths.

Figure 23
Positive Faith Influences on Adults

Adults were asked to identify which factors in their lives they thought had the greatest positive influence on their faith. Out of 30 possibilities, here are the top ten choices for all adults, men and women. (Each person could choose 5.)

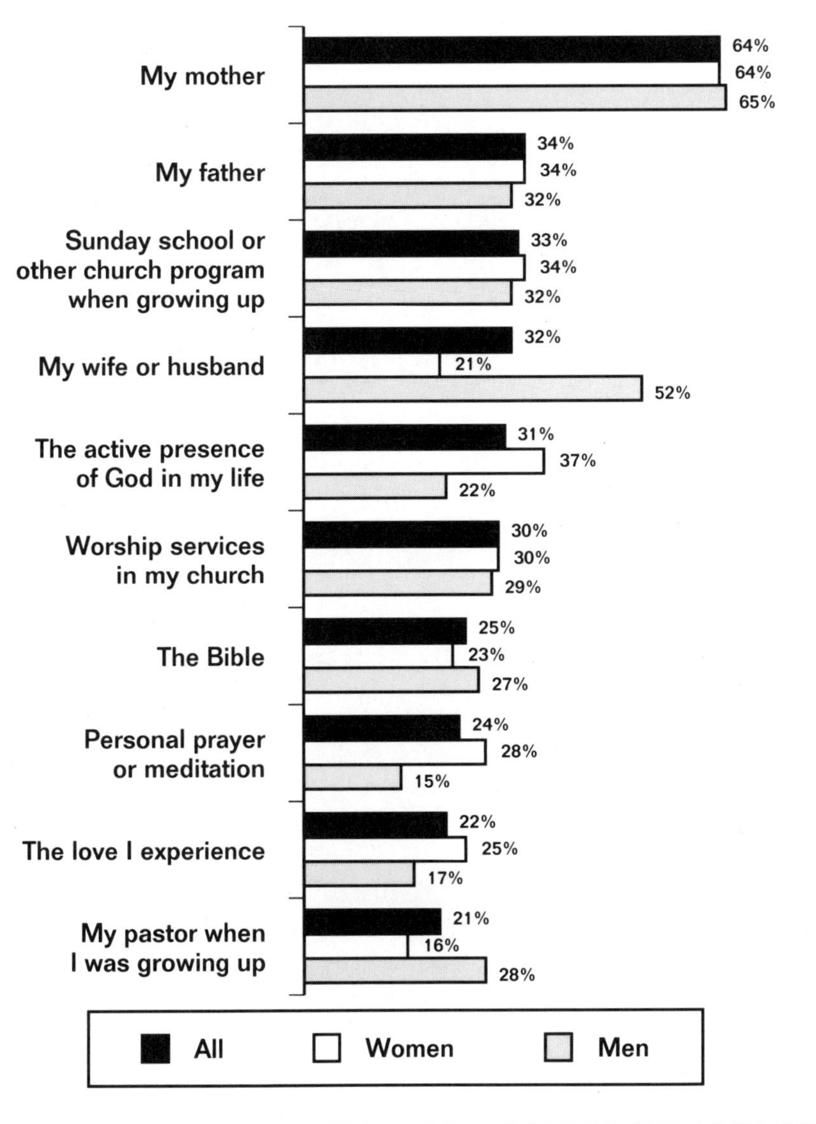

Furthermore, the study found the three following elements have the greatest impact on young people's faith maturity:

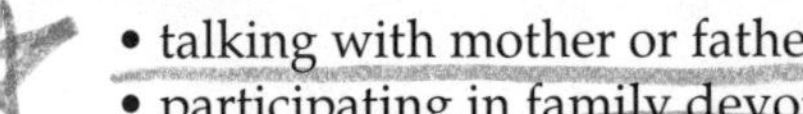

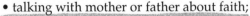

- talking with mother or father about faith;
- participating in family devotions, prayer, or Bible reading;
- being involved in family service projects.

The more young people experience these family activities, the more likely they are to develop a mature faith. Unfortunately, relatively few families do each of these things. Thus the church can play an influential role in helping families nourish faith.

Family life is also influential on adult faith, though lifetime church involvement and lifetime Christian education involvement have the strongest relationships to faith maturity. Biographical factors holding modest relationships are: spouse and friends' religiousness, a caring church, involvement in nonchurch religious activity, serving others, and family religiousness as a young person.

MISSING INGREDIENTS

Parents want their children to have a lifelong faith. An earlier Search Institute study, *Young Adolescents and Their Parents,* found that 68 percent of parents are "very" or "quite" interested in learning "how to help my child grow in religious faith." Even more parents (87 percent of mothers and 76 percent of fathers) say they would like to talk more about God and other religious topics.[7]

In interpreting the data of that study, Merton P. Strommen and A. Irene Strommen note that both parents and their children say religion is very important in their lives. Yet despite this importance, religion "is almost a taboo subject in the home." They continue: "Apparently the Old Testament command to parents, 'You shall teach these words of mine to your children, talking of them when sitting in your house, and when you are walking by the way, and when you lie down, and when you rise,' is largely ignored."[8]

The *Effective Christian Education* study affirms and augments the earlier study's findings. Key factors that nurture faith maturity are missing from most families in mainline churches:

- Two-thirds of families rarely or never have family devotions.
- More than half the teenagers don't talk to their fathers about faith or God. A third don't talk to their mothers.
- Two-thirds of families don't do family projects to help others.

Figure 24
Positive Faith Influences on Youths

Teenagers were asked to choose the top five positive influences on their faith. Out of a possible list of 28, here are their top 12 choices, ranked in order of perceived influence.

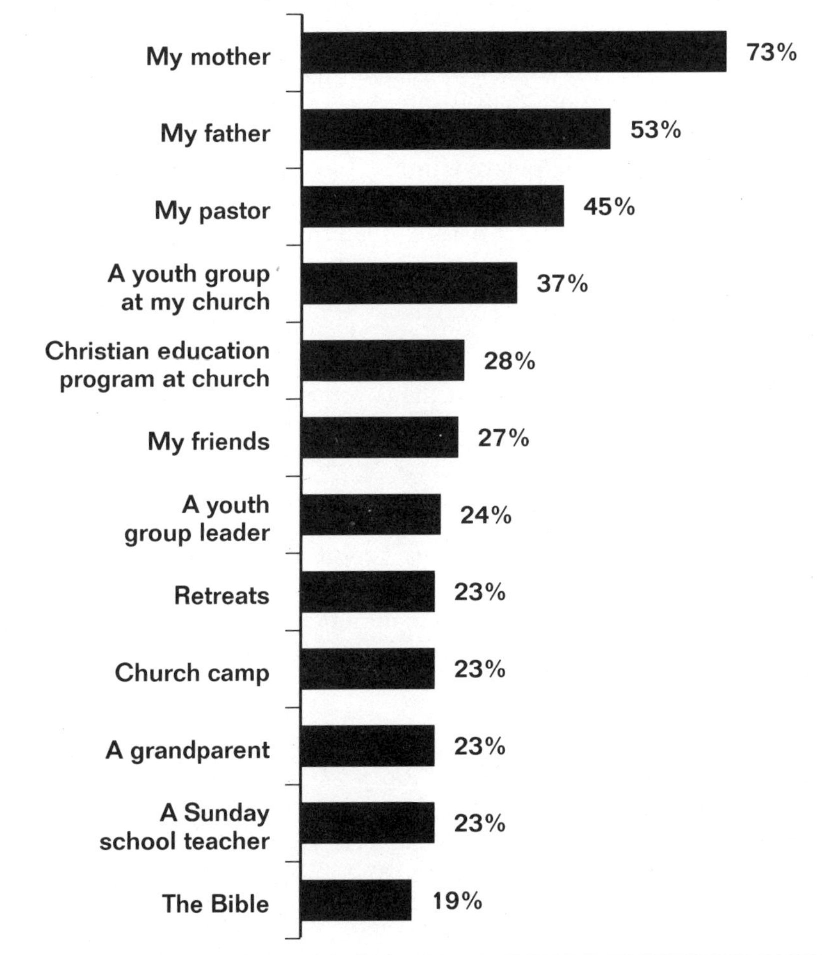

A disturbing trend emerges when we compare the family religiousness of today's youth with the memories of adults from that age. Family religious activity appears to be declining from one generation to the next, though it's difficult to assess the role of memory and reminiscence in the responses. If these figures reflect realities, there's a serious danger that tomorrow's adults could have in place even fewer of the biographical factors to nourish faith maturity through their lifetime.

Another notable finding concerns differences regarding mothers and fathers. While 62 percent of teenagers say they talk to their mothers about religious faith, only about 40 percent say they talk to their fathers. Furthermore, 93 percent see their moms doing religious things, while 80 percent report such observations about their dads.

Young people perceive these differences regarding their mothers and fathers. When asked how religious their parents were, 42 percent said their mothers were "very religious." Only 33 percent chose this response for their fathers. In addition, 73 percent said their mother was one of the top five positive influences on their faith (the number-one influence in a list of 28 possibilities). Fifty-three percent listed their father among the top five influences—the second-highest response.

Though the study can't definitively explain why these differences between mothers and fathers occur, two factors may be at work. First, as we noted in chapter 2, women generally have a higher faith maturity than men. Furthermore, men in their forties (when they'd be likely to have teenagers in the house) experience a marked dip in faith maturity. Perhaps dads are struggling so much with their own issues that they feel inadequate to nourish faith in their children.

Second, fathers tend to spend less time than mothers with their children. A study reported in *Phi Delta Kappan,* a magazine for educators, found that teenagers spend, on average, only five minutes a day alone with their fathers. This compares to 40 minutes with their mothers and an hour with both parents.[9] Thus children simply aren't around their dads enough to be influenced as strongly.

ASSESSING THE DECLINE

What factors have played into the generally low levels of religious activity in church families? No definitive response can be found for that question, but several scenarios outlined by the Strommens are possible.

We may be seeing the effects of several decades of declining religious involvement. The Strommens note that Gallup polls show a declining interest among adults in religious training for their children since the mid-1960s. "Parents who have received scant biblical training, and little opportunity to verbalize what they do believe, feel inadequate to teach at home," they write. "They reason that if their child should begin to question them and they do not know the answer, it would be humiliating and confusing."[10]

Structured opportunities can take many different forms, depending on family styles. Carol Rose Ikeler suggests several:

- Prayers of thanksgiving before meals may be recited, spoken, sung, or said silently.
- Bedtime prayers give quiet reassurance to children.
- Regular family devotions may consist of scripture reading or use of a published devotional guide.
- Observe holidays (Christmas, Easter, Lent, etc.) with family traditions that include worship.
- Family traditions can also celebrate special events such as birthdays, entering school, vacation, graduation, and so forth.[15]

Churches can promote family devotions by providing resources and teaching parents skills for leading these and other structured family devotional activities. And with creativity, some of the same educational techniques essential for effective Christian education can be translated for home devotions.

FAMILY SERVICE PROJECTS

The now-famous story of Trevor Ferrell illustrates the potential power of family involvement in service on faith maturity. The 11-year-old and his family lived in a middle-class Philadelphia suburb. One night on the evening news, he saw a story about the homeless in the city. Concerned that people could be freezing on the city streets right then, he finally convinced his parents to take him downtown, where he gave a blanket and a pillow to a homeless man.

That single incident transformed the family. Trevor went back day after day, delivering all the extra blankets in their house. He began receiving supplies from church friends, then the neighborhood. By the time Trevor was 16, his efforts had become an extensive ministry with three food vans, a thrift shop, and a halfway house for the homeless.[16]

Unfortunately, families like the Ferrells are rare. James McGinnis and Kathleen McGinnis write: "Faced with so many problems of their own, many families are not inspired to work with and for others . . . . Often isolated from the victims of injustice, from people working for change, and from a supportive community, many families have just not been touched or moved to act."[17]

Such a lack of involvement or concern is troubling for a number of reasons. First, it shows that the gospel's call to service and ministry has largely been unheeded by many families. Second, it means that young people and parents miss influential opportunities to grow together and to grow in faith. Finally, families miss shared experiences out of which they can discuss their values and priorities.

How can churches encourage families to serve together? The following suggestions may be useful as discussion starters.

Raise awareness in intergenerational contexts. Though it can be useful to talk about hunger with the youth group, a young person's eagerness to be involved could be stifled by parents who are not aware of the needs. Offer service opportunities as family events. There's no reason youth groups should be the only ones to paint houses for the elderly or repair roofs for low-income neighbors. Moms and dads and sons and daughters can do those things together.

Find connections with everyday life. If you can avoid adding time commitments to families, you're more likely to have early successes. Look for ways families can serve and promote justice in their daily lives. This could involve joining boycotts to support migrant workers, making lifestyle choices to reflect inequities in the world, and so forth.

Provide opportunities that relate to family life. For example, ask a family with teenagers to be a sponsor for a refugee family with teenagers. Personalizing service in these ways can nourish a long-term sensitivity to service and justice issues.

Create a community of support by bringing together families in service. Each family can encourage the other and make the other feel it's not alone in its ministry. All the suggestions for service and action in chapter 10 can be appropriate avenues for families to serve together through the congregation.

In their landmark book, *Parenting for Peace and Justice,* Kathleen and James McGinnis suggest that direct service (works of mercy) and social change (works of justice) are the "two feet" needed to walk the path of service. They suggest six principles for such involvement, which are helpful guides for churches that seek to encourage family involvement in service and social justice.[18]

1. Regularly invite children to join in social action. It takes time to explain issues and to discuss questions. Children need the freedom to say "no," and the decision should be a family decision.

2. Expose children to advocates, victims, and situations. This provides motivation and overcomes the major obstacles to involvement—ignorance and fear. Exposure can come through guests in the home, parents themselves, reading, television, movies, the neighborhood, and travel.

3. Actions should be within children's capacities. Relate actions to home and family living, and build on prior experiences. Look for opportunities in which children can play a specific role, and respect their limits.

4. Integrate fun whenever possible. Combine the action with a fun event. Join with others—especially other families. Learn about issues in an enjoyable context, such as a good movie. And involve children in doing and making.

5. Do "with" instead of do "for." Respect and promote the dignity of others. Learn from those you hope to serve. Arrange exchanges and promote self-help efforts.

6. Include both works of justice and works of mercy. In addition to caring for victims, work to change systems that victimize them.

PROMOTING FAMILY EDUCATION

Together, these emphases (faith conversations, devotions, and service) point toward the need for systematic efforts to include the family as an emphasis in Christian education. Yet relatively few churches intentionally address the educational needs of parents.

For example, Christian education coordinators were asked to assess whether their church emphasizes family/parent education. In evaluating grades one through six, only 7 percent of the coordinators said their church has a strong emphasis on "providing classes to help parents learn how to promote faith in their children." And only 8 percent said their church emphasizes "providing classes for parents on effective parenting or communication" for this age group.

Similar results appear among parents of teenagers. Only 6 percent of Christian education coordinators suggested an emphasis on "providing classes to help parents learn how to promote the faith of their children." And only 9 percent said their church emphasizes "providing classes for parents on effective parenting or communication" for this age group.

Several models for family ministry and parent education are used and promoted as effective for nourishing and supporting families. Some churches add programs that specifically address family issues. These might include family nights, parent classes and workshops, and family retreats.

Other congregations integrate family issues into existing programs. For example, many provide a parent-education class as an option in Sunday school. Or they emphasize family issues in the worship, education, and fellowship life of the congregation.

Whatever specific model is implemented, Richard P. Olson and Joe H. Leonard, Jr., suggest that an effective family-education program needs to address intentionally two broad areas:[19]

Content—Families need churches to help them understand themselves and others, particularly in light of the changing shape of families today.

Olson and Leonard suggest four primary content areas: growth in faith; sexuality; family relationships; and stages of life, including common transitions and crises.

Skills—This emphasis focuses on skills for family life. These basic skills include communication; planning; and organization.

Of course, each congregation must develop its own ministry to families, based on specific dynamics in the congregation. As Leonard stated in an

Worksheet 9
Family Ministry Evaluation

Use this worksheet to evaluate your congregation's ministry to families. For each of the possible emphases listed, check whether you believe your congregation needs to emphasize more, emphasize less, keep the same, or study more. Compare your answers with the answers of other education planners in the congregation.

	Emphasize More	Emphasize Less	Keep the Same	Study More
Teaching parents to promote faith in children.	☐	☐	☐	☐
Providing classes for parents on family communication.	☐	☐	☐	☐
Encouraging families to talk about their faith at home.	☐	☐	☐	☐
Teaching families to have meaningful family devotions.	☐	☐	☐	☐
Helping families become involved in service.	☐	☐	☐	☐
Dealing with the needs of non-traditional families.	☐	☐	☐	☐
Giving families opportunities to worship together.	☐	☐	☐	☐
Nourishing the faith of parents.	☐	☐	☐	☐
Other:	☐	☐	☐	☐

earlier book: "If family ministry is based on the actual needs of real families, and seeks to help real families fulfill their callings, then each church's approach to family ministry will be unique. . . . The emphasis in each congregation will reflect the particular families that belong to it."[20]

How well does your church nourish families? Use the following questions, along with Worksheet 9, to evaluate your congregation's ministry with families:

- What are the biggest problems you've seen in the families in your congregation? How does your church help families with these issues?
- What elements of your congregational life tend to pull families apart instead of bringing them together? Is the approach appropriate in these cases? If not, how could programs be changed?
- Which of the elements of promoting family religiousness is strongest in your congregation? What can you do to celebrate that strength and ensure that it remains strong?
- What factors in promoting family religiousness do you see missing in your congregation? How have you seen these factors helping families grow in their faith?
- What ministries does your church have that directly address the needs of families? What ministries indirectly touch families' needs?
- What untapped resources does your congregation have that could be used in ministry with families?

PUTTING PIECES TOGETHER

The possibilities of family education highlight how much the different aspects of promoting faith are interrelated, and how the family is central to the cycle. By promoting adult involvement in Christian education, we involve more parents. As parents' own faith matures, that growth translates into their families. The children grow in their faith, which, in turn, increases the effectiveness of youth programs. When the teenagers become adults, they'll have a stronger faith foundation on which to build, so they are more likely to be involved in Christian education when they are parents. And the cycle continues.

Of course, some youths and adults don't come from families with a strong faith base. That doesn't mean they cannot grow in their faith. Instead, it becomes a greater challenge to the church to create an environment where faith can mature.

Many churches haven't looked seriously at how to encourage parents to become effective Christian educators. But this study renews the challenge to discover innovative ways to encourage families to grow in faith.

Chapter 12

Where Have All the People Gone?

Tim had never been really big on church. His wife and children participated faithfully in Sunday school and worship. Tim occasionally came to worship but never to Sunday school. He wasn't opposed to church; he just didn't see any reason to participate.

Then Tim and his wife were invited to a party at someone's house with a bunch of young adults from church. While there, several people asked Tim about his job and what he liked to do in his spare time.

"It was really neat," Tim recalled later. "I had always felt out of place at church—I really didn't know anybody. Now I know some people."

The next fall, Tim joined a Sunday school class for young adults. The interactive, discussion-oriented sessions attracted him and made him a regular participant. First he came simply because of the topic of the four-week series. But soon you could count on Tim, regardless of the topic. One late winter Sunday, class members each told something they were thankful for. "This class," Tim said.

Tim's story is just one illustration of how interest in Christian education can be rekindled in inactive church members. The *Effective Christian Education* study suggests a variety of possibilities for renewing interest and involvement in Christian education.

BECOME INTENTIONAL

Despite constant hand-wringing in many congregations about people not participating in Sunday school, the worry appears not to translate into action. When Christian education coordinators were asked if their churches made efforts to encourage participation of inactive members, relatively few indicated much emphasis. Only 34 percent said it is "very true" that their Christian education program encourages participation of inactive children and youth. For adult education, just 25 percent do.

For Christian education to move to center stage in congregational life, Christian educators must become intentional about attracting new participants and rekindling interest in programs.

REEXAMINE PROGRAMS

Are the existing programs effective at reaching people and providing ministry? While the national study discovered that the *number* of programs is not vital for nurturing faith maturity, the *quality* of programs does make a difference. And just because programs have been effective in the past does not mean they are necessarily effective today. As suggested in chapter 6, we need to develop specific programs, based on our mission, goals, and objectives, rather than maintaining programs that are ineffective in fulfilling the church's mission.

To illustrate, consider confirmation, which takes place in many mainline denominations during early adolescence. The goals of confirmation are important, but do current models most effectively enhance those goals?

Possible problems emerge when we note that those denominations with confirmation programs tend to have higher dropout rates among high schoolers than denominations without a similar emphasis in middle school or junior high. After "graduating" from confirmation, many teenagers apparently see no reason to keep going to church.

Congregations must discover ways to help young people see faith as a journey that continues throughout life, not an initiation rite (or marathon) to complete. Roland D. Martinson, in *Effective Youth Ministry: A Congregational Approach,* believes that "confirmation ministry constructed as one, two, or three years of weekly classes over the school year will always be an uphill battle. Confirmation becomes a marathon; the goal is to get through."[1]

Martinson suggests replacing this traditional model with a series of short, varied learning experiences (retreats, camps, classes, research projects, inner-city experiences, internships, etc.) over a long period of time. He would like to involve parents, pastors, and the congregation in a process that truly integrates young people into the community of faith. "Understood in the context of lifelong learning," he continues, "confirmation can afford to be less ambitious. It does not have to impart the whole counsel of God. It is not the final indoctrination in adult faith."[2]

Similar thoughtful consideration needs to be given to all phases of Christian education. Why do adults stay away from Christian education? Are any of these reasons related to program structures? Would there be other, more effective media for nourishing faith than are currently being used?

These are sensitive, difficult questions in congregations that have a we've-always-done-it-this-way-and-why-should-we-change attitudes. But they must be asked, struggled with, and responded to in creative ways.

BUILD ON INTERESTS AND NEEDS

Clarisse was a fairly typical mainline Christian teenager. After her confirmation, she kept going to church. But the congregation offered little for the high-school youth group. In college, her young-adult searching began in earnest. But since no churches in the small town appealed to her, she took her curiosity to college classes. Her class on atheism brought out more questions about faith and the world.

After moving to a major city, the recent college graduate began to look for a church that would let her ask those questions without giving easy answers. The church she chose met her need with a unique "Sermon Talk-back" Sunday school class. The worship service took place before the church school. So young adults would gather in a room, drink coffee, and discuss the sermon with the pastor.

"I had always thought of sermons as like 'sacred cows,'" Clarisse recalls. "That class opened my eyes to a faith that would let me ask my questions. It helped me overcome some of my hang-ups about the church."

People tend to participate in things that meet their needs or build on their interests. Without compromising their integrity, Christian-education programs can address those needs in ways that are faithful to the gospel. In so doing, they can begin drawing people into (or back into) Christian education.

One fascinating finding of the *Effective Christian Education* study is that both active and inactive youths and adults share many of the same interests (see Figures 25 and 26). However, the order of interests is slightly different between actives and inactives. This would suggest the need for the goals to be clear for different offerings. Are they intended primarily to nourish and challenge the faithful? Or are they designed to encourage more active involvement among the nominal?

Another significant finding is that the level of interest is significantly different. In other words, though inactives may share interests with actives, they are not as interested in learning about the subjects. This finding may help explain why active church members often become frustrated by inactives "who don't come even when we plan stuff they're interested in." Furthermore, it suggests that simply addressing interests probably won't be adequate for reaching the inactives. We also must address their needs for community, friendship, and growth in faith when they arrive. Thus it becomes vital to create a congregational climate of warmth, thinking, and care.

These comparisons of interests challenge the notion that the inactive can be reached only through essentially nonreligious activities, such as sports, support groups, and so forth. Though inactive adults' top concerns did focus on parenting and personal development, many of the concerns are overtly religious—applying faith to life, Christian decision-making, building a relationship with Jesus. Thus, addressing interests and needs doesn't necessarily compete with a central focus on nurturing faith.

Figure 25
Active vs. Inactive Adult Interests

The following chart compares the top interests of active and inactive adult church members. The number in parentheses represents the mean response based on a scale of: 1 ("not interested") to 5 ("very interested").

Active Adults' Top Interests	Inactive Adults' Top Interests
1. Learning more about the Bible (4.21)	1. Learning to be a good parent or spouse (3.80)
2. Developing more personal relationship with Jesus (4.17)	2. Improving skills at showing love and concern for others (3.60)
3. Learning how to apply my faith to daily living (4.16)	3. Developing more personal relationship with Jesus (3.56)
4. Learning how a Christian makes moral decisions (4.03)	4. Learning more about the Bible (3.52)
5. Improving skills at showing love and concern for others (4.03)	5. Learning how to apply my faith to daily living (3.36)
6. Making more friends at church (3.99)	6. Learning how a Christian makes moral decisions (3.33)
7. Getting more help with my spiritual journey (3.90)	7. Making more friends at church (3.32)
8. Learning about how to a good parent or spouse (3.86)	8. Getting more help with my spiritual journey (3.19)
9. Having greater sense of community or family at church (3.83)	9. Having greater sense of community or family at church (3.18)
10. Opportunity to help members experiencing hardship (3.80)	10. Opportunity to help members experiencing hardship (3.11)

One final note: In seeking to reach those who are not active in Christian education, it may not be appropriate to assume that they have life experiences similar to those of active adults. As Figure 35 shows, inactive adults are much more likely than active adults to have had several stressful experiences in the past two to three years, including financial trouble, sadness, job stress or loss, or the birth of a child (generally a positive but stressful experience).

It's difficult to interpret these differences in any conclusive way, but they warrant discussion. Do the stresses (such as having a child) pull people away from involvement in Christian education? Do people who experience these stresses not experience support in church during the

Figure 26
Active vs. Inactive Youth Interests

The following chart compares the top interests of active and inactive youth. The number in parentheses represents the mean response based on a scale of: 1 ("not interested") to 5 ("very interested").

Active Teenagers' Top Interests	Inactive Teenagers' Top Interests
1. Learning how to make friends and be a good friend (4.32)	1. Learning more about who God is (3.78)
2. Learning to know and love Jesus Christ (4.28)	2. Learning how to make friends and be a good friend (3.63)
3. Learning more about who God is (4.24)	3. Learning to know and love Jesus Christ (3.60)
4. Help in experiencing God's love and forgiveness (4.12)	4. Learning to love life more (3.58)
5. Learning to love life more (4.08)	5. Gaining a sense of purpose in life (3.49)
6. Developing more compassion and concern for others (4.02)	6. Learning more about the Bible and its meaning for my life (3.46)
7. Learning to make decisions about right and wrong (4.00)	7. Learning how to make decisions about right and wrong (3.40)
8. Learning to like myself more (3.96)	8. Developing more compassion and concern for others (3.33)
9. Learning how I can make a difference in the world (3.90)	9. Help in experiencing God's love and forgiveness (3.31)
10. Discovering what is special about me (3.90)	10. Learning how to make choices and decisions (3.30)

tough times, so they turn elsewhere? Does church involvement lower people's sense of stress and trouble, so that they are less likely to report problems?

Whatever the cause of the differences, the stresses that inactive adults feel suggest some programmatic emphases that may address real needs at crucial times in their lives. For example, might educational programs for those who have lost jobs or who have experienced high job stress meet important needs that currently are not being addressed? These types of questions need to be asked in light of a congregation's priorities.

PUBLICIZE CHRISTIAN EDUCATION

At its best, publicity is simply getting the word out about good programs, so that more people can take advantage of them. Christian-education programs that have something to offer should use a variety of ways to spread the word. Here are some ideas.

Encourage person-to-person contacts. Participants can be the best recruiters for a class or study group. Get them to talk with inactive members about what they are learning and doing. Then inactive members have a point of contact with the class when they actually attend.

Publicize new and ongoing classes within the congregation (which 68 percent of churches do). This could include posters, newsletter announcements, and announcements during worship services or other congregational meetings. These don't need to be dry and boring. Include skits, or even short activities that help people "experience" the class.

Publicize Christian education in the community. Despite the potential attraction of many Christian-education programs to the community at large, only 23 percent of Christian education coordinators say it is "very true" that their programs are well-publicized in the community. This publicity need not consist of large newspaper ads or TV spots. It might just involve news releases to the local newspaper about upcoming events and photocopied fliers posted in appropriate places. (According to C. Kirk Hadaway, churches that spend more on publicity don't necessarily grow more than other churches.)[3]

Develop quality brochures that describe Christian education offerings and distribute them through the congregation. If people don't know about the programs, they are unlikely to attend! Yet just 36 percent of churches have such brochures in order to publicize the churches' education programs.

Highlight Christian-education successes. Let people know what is happening. When my church began using a new youth curriculum, teachers gathered comments from the students about why they liked the new approach, then printed some of the responses in the newsletter. This information can entice others to try out the programs.

REACH ADULTS THROUGH CHILDREN

Alan Jones, Dean of Grace Cathedral in San Francisco, tells about a mother who knew it was time to become involved in church again when her four-year-old pointed to a crucifix and said, "What's that man doing, Mom?"[4]

Though church dropouts and inactive members may have little interest in their own Christian education, they tend to be highly concerned that their children receive it. "I wanted my kids to have the knowledge of religion I didn't have," explains Kris Womer, 29, a mother who returned to the Village Presbyterian Church in Prairie Village, Kansas. "In this crazy world, any kind of positive influence you can give your children is worth the time."[5]

This mother is not alone. According to *The Unchurched American*, 73 percent of unchurched Americans say they want their children to receive religious instruction. And they are particularly interested in summer programs. Summer programs for children and youths rank highest among the activities adults say would be most interesting for their families.[6]

Churches can capitalize on this interest by providing strong Christian education (including Vacation Bible School) that includes occasions when parents will interact with church members. In the process, their interests and church friendships could be rekindled.

RECOGNIZE DIFFERENT COMMITMENT LEVELS

Some church members will want to do everything and are too highly involved in numerous Christian education programs. Others may be only nominally committed, participating only in occasional activities. Though we might sometimes wish everyone would be deeply committed, it rarely happens.

A better approach is to accept the differences, work with each commitment level, and nurture faith and commitment at each stage. For example, special classes with low commitment can give people a taste of Christian education, without making them feel that they would be committing their life. Four-week classes on special subjects can attract people, who then begin to form friendships and interests that draw them in.

On the other end, we must avoid the danger of working only with minimally committed people, and ignoring the needs for growth and challenge of the more committed. They may eventually give up and look elsewhere for nourishment, because they no longer feel motivated to participate.

Our challenge as Christian educators is to find ways to meet both needs. Though this may involve creating a variety of programs, it need not. Often a single class can meet needs for fellowship, spiritual growth, and intellectual stimulation. The key is to recognize and affirm differences, hoping to nourish in people a faith that will grow into a deeper and deeper commitment.

EXPECT INVOLVEMENT

Churches need to begin to see themselves as learning communities. As you work with teachers and leaders to improve your educational process and content, you also will create an atmosphere in the congregation that encourages people to learn. Gradually, the congregation will gain a reputation as a teaching church. And learning and growing in faith are simply natural elements of the congregation's climate and culture.

Bring education into the spotlight by highlighting classes during worship, announcing plans in newsletters, including education issues in sermons, inviting visitors to events and activities. Creating enthusiasm among people who already participate can pique the curiosity of the uninvolved. Their word-of-mouth publicity will be your most effective publicity.

WHAT COULD HAPPEN

Suppose the suggestions in this chapter and other strategies work. Suppose your Christian-education program—and the learning atmosphere that surrounds it—began to attract a great percentage of youths and adults. What might happen?

According to the *Effective Christian Education* study, your program would grow stronger. People would grow in their faith. The enthusiasm

would spill over into the congregation, which would support Christian education more firmly. The study found a direct correlation between churches with high percentages of older youth participation and high adult participation. And it found that strong congregations saw Christian education at the center of congregational life.

But suppose it's the other way around. Suppose people were coming to the Christian-education offerings because the programs were strong. Suppose the high levels of participation have nothing to do with effectiveness.

Does it really make much difference which one comes first: the participation or the effectiveness?; the chicken or the egg? In the end, the overall result is that a greater proportion of church members are growing in their faith and in their loyalty to the church, through effective Christian education programs.

Afterword

Creating a New Future

The church was in crisis. The surrounding culture was going through major transition and upheaval. Much of the world was not Christian, and other religions appeared to be eroding its influence even more. It looked as if the church might become inconsequential in the world, or even disappear.

From some perspectives, that paragraph could describe the church today. But it actually is a picture of the sixth-century church, which faced internal divisions and the rise of Islam in the East. As John H. Leith notes, "The Christian church, from the standpoint of an observer, has always been at risk in the world."[1]

The *Effective Christian Education* study comes at time when many congregations and denominations face discouraging membership statistics and declines in giving. In this context, it helps us focus energies and resources in areas that have the most pressing needs and the most potential for growth.

This study is not a "quick fix" or panacea for churches. It doesn't have—or pretend to have—the final answers for effective Christian education. There may be other factors that are as important as those discovered in the study. Or some of the suggestions from the study and in this book may prove to be ineffective in some congregations and settings. Other innovative approaches also must be explored and tested.

If taken seriously, however, the study's findings call for congregations and denominations to begin restructuring Christian education. Churches that heed the call can expect, in the long run, sustained growth in Christian-education effectiveness. What might this restructuring mean for the church and for specific congregations? In concluding this book, let me suggest some possibilities.

RETHINKING ASSUMPTIONS

As a beginning point, it's time to rethink common assumptions, structures, and formats for Christian education. Until these (and, I'm sure, other) assumptions are faced and addressed, fundamental change will not happen.

Biblical/Theological Literacy—No longer can we assume that people—even adults who grew up in the church—are biblically or theologically literate. No longer can we assume that symbols and traditions that have nourished the church for centuries hold any meaning for today's secularized Christians. This problem concerns more than marginal church members. I recently sat in on a church meeting where leaders were lamenting that children didn't even know the story of Samson. Afterward, a former children's Sunday school teacher admitted that he didn't know it either.

This cultural shift challenges the very core of many Christian-education programs. Most people assume that a children's program is designed to "build a foundation" for a lifetime. But what happens when people don't have that foundation? And, perhaps more to the point, can we assume that a foundation laid in childhood will not crack under the changes and stresses of adulthood?

How People Learn—In a time when most educators recognize the limited usefulness of lectures and one-way communication as vehicles of education, most congregations cling to the approach as if it were a divine gift.

I recently visited a large congregation which was convinced that the cure to its Christian education woes was the hiring of a series of top-notch speakers to lead Sunday morning and Wednesday night sessions. While there certainly is a place for inspiring and provocative lectures, they cannot be the core of an effective Christian-education program that seeks to nourish people's faith.

Unfortunately, the assumption that good education involves transmitting lots of head knowledge grows out of our experience. Relatively few people have experienced truly effective educational processes, particularly as adults. So when push comes to shove, we rely on what we have experienced and what we know. After all, new models are, by definition, unknown and risky.

The Context for Learning—When we use the term *Christian education,* I imagine most people immediately picture a classroom. It probably has a chalkboard (no chalk!), a few chairs, a table or two, a stack of Bibles, and maybe a map of the Holy Land. In essence, we equate Christian education with something that happens in a "Christian education wing" of the church building, at a certain time on Sunday morning (except during the summer, when we have more important things to do).

Though learning can certainly take place in that context, it can happen in many other places as well—around the family dinner table; in a worship service; during an all-church fellowship; over pizza, after a service project; on the picket lines during a protest; during pastoral counseling, or at the bedside of an ill parishioner. Mary Boys puts it this way:

> Whenever men and women have gathered to tell stories and enact rituals in response to the mystery of life, whenever they have searched for truth and sought to do what is good, religious education has been happening. Whether congregated around the fire in a cave, around the dinner table, or in the town square, people have passed on their traditions of faith.[2]

The Role of Leaders and Participants—Whether they're teachers or pastors or Christian-education directors, leaders play a critical role in restructuring Christian education. And for significant change to occur, leaders must do away with common assumptions about their own roles.

As long as leaders are always seen as the experts, church members will not value their own insight and spiritual growth. As long as leaders take full responsibility for all education, members will not see any reason to take responsibility for their own learning. As long as a core of leaders keep skills and knowledge to themselves, a broad base of active, adept laypeople will never be developed.

The Purpose of Christian Education—If you were to ask average church members to tell you the purpose of Christian education in their congregation, what would they say? My hunch is that they'd talk about "teaching Bible stories to children" or "learning about interesting topics."

There appears to be a widespread assumption that Christian education is about new knowledge and children. And until we shift our thinking to understand Christian education as "discovering what it means to be Christian in this time and place," it is unlikely that Christian education will be central to the life of the church.

DISCOVERING NEW MODELS

In the process of examining our assumptions, we also must discover or create new models of learning, teaching, and planning which address key issues. If, for example, few churches model effective teaching methods and processes, what can be done to introduce them into our denominations and congregations? How might we adjust our expectations of teachers, given the realities of their lives? How might we develop Christian education that nourishes both individuals and families?

Recently, I've been suggesting a possibility to congregations. I'm not sure anyone has taken up the idea, but I like it. Suppose congregations were to form "Christian Education Innovations"—study groups of six or eight "big idea" thinkers whose sole responsibility would be to track innovations in education nationally, then work together to discover how to apply new principles and models to their own congregation.

The group process would follow the principles and practices of effective adult education (figuring out what that means might be the first task). Each person would be assigned one or two areas to research. These might include faith development theory; faith formation; cooperative learning; adult education theory; outcome-based education; experiential education and service-learning; youth ministry resources; children's curriculum—any topic that seems potentially relevant to the congregation. Then each person would read books and other material, attend conferences, have interviews with experts in the area, and make site visits to other congregations. All this research could be written up in a paper for group discussion and application to the congregation.

After a year or two, this group (which might meet monthly) would have:

- Documents on various educational trends.
- Brain-stormed lists of ideas for applying the principles to their congregation.
- A church member with particular expertise in, and commitment to, each area of education (which builds the leadership base in the congregation). These people could, in turn, help train teachers in the principles or processes.
- Material to suggest innovations for education that could be used as a model by other congregations.
- A group of people experienced in effective adult education in the church.

Would such a group make a difference? Maybe not. Maybe it would simply be another futile exercise. Maybe there aren't any congregations who see the need for such basic education. Maybe the recommendations and findings would simply be bogged down in committees and we've-never-done-it-this-way-before attitudes.

But the opposite could happen. Study-group members could gain fresh perspectives on their own congregations, as they visit and intentionally observe other congregations. They might make connections between frustrations they've felt in the church and new solutions being experimented with in public schools.

CREATING THE LEARNING CHURCH

I like the title of this book. But I almost called it *The **Learning** Church.* Either title works. What I like about the alternative title is that it highlights the other half of the equation—the outcome of effective Christian education. I also like it because it connects with lots of exciting thinking and work in education and community development.

A recent booklet from the National Community Education Association illustrates my point. Titled *Community Education: Building Learning Communities,* the resource suggests community-based education as a promising solution to the current crisis in public education.[3] The model builds on the idea that education is a lifelong process and that it is at the heart of community life.

In his foreword to that booklet, David Matthews, president of the Charles F. Kettering Foundation, lays the groundwork by summarizing the foundation's research on effective communities: "Effective communities appear to be different, not because of economic or demographic or regional factors, but because they are simply better educated as a community. That is, they are good at educating the whole community in the community's business."[4]

Had it been based on *Effective Christian Education,* that quote would probably be just as accurate if we substituted the word *church* for *community.* Matthews goes on to identify five characteristics of effective communities. I've interpreted the characteristics to show how directly they would translate into creating a teaching (or learning) church.

1. The learning church educates itself as a whole, with all its small groups and interests, about its total mission. "Community education," Matthews believes, "has to provide a picture of the whole, of how the parts fit together. It is not about topics but rather interactions."

2. The learning church doesn't just have the "facts" of faith (theology, biblical studies, ethics, tradition, etc.), but knows what that information means to the lives of the diverse people in the congregation. Further-

more, this knowledge is not just personal knowledge, but a shared knowledge.

3. The learning church doesn't just talk about issues; it talks *through* issues. "It has learned that people don't usually work through problems together who have not talked through them first," Matthews writes.

4. The learning church knows the difference between diverse opinions and the church's collective judgment. Matthews explains it this way in the community context: "Public judgments involve reasoning together and are more reflective than reactive. . . . As a community thinks and works together, it begins to sort out values, work through hard choices, and develop new perspectives." In the process, it discovers shared interests and common ground.

5. The learning church, finally, thinks about leadership differently. It doesn't equate its leaders with its pastors or its staff. It recognizes the gifts of all members for leadership, and it unleashes that leadership power with all its ideas, its commitments, and its relationships. This extra leadership ingredient gives the learning church its edge.

TAKING CHRISTIAN EDUCATION SERIOUSLY

Like Matthews' insights about learning communities, the *Effective Christian Education* study gives a fresh perspective that can take us beyond the inertia of confusion and indecision that seems to have plagued education in mainline churches in recent years. The study turns the kaleidoscope of educational possibilities, helping us see new patterns and new approaches.

Now each congregation must decide how to respond to and act upon the information. Many congregations may choose to ignore the information or let it die from inaction. Other needs seem more pressing or immediate. Other suggestions involve less work. Yet such a response seems short-sighted. Even those who don't agree with the conclusions can learn by wrestling with the study and clarifying their own approaches and agendas.

Other congregations may tinker, adding another program here or adjusting the timing there. This approach seems appealing, since it doesn't involve many risky changes. Everything can stay essentially the way it is. Yet this approach fails to grasp the depth of change that seems essential to address issues raised by the study. A tune-up may help things run more smoothly in the short term, but the long-term impact will be minimal.

Finally, it is my hope that many congregations will take the study seriously and move beyond tinkering to restructuring. This doesn't mean they must use this book (or any book) as the final word or blueprint. Rather, it means examining assumptions, rethinking programs, exploring options, and experimenting with possibilities. It means challenging the study where it doesn't make sense, and, in the process, articulating an approach that *does* make sense.

When churches take this challenge seriously by grappling with the way they nurture faith, then they will be taking Christian education seriously. And they truly will become teaching and learning communities of faith.

Selected Resources

The Adult Learner: A Neglected Species, 3rd rev. ed. Malcolm Knowles (Houston: Gulf Publishing, 1984). Though directed toward human-resource development in businesses, this book surveys the field of adult education from the perspective of the pioneer.

American Mainline Religion: Its Changing Shape and Future. Wade Clark Roof and William McKinney (New Brunswick: Rutgers University Press, 1987). This provocative look at trends in mainline churches sets the context in which Christian education takes place.

Children's Ministry That Works: The Basics and Beyond, ed. Jolene L. Roehlkepartain (Loveland, Col.: Group Books, 1991). This survey of issues in children's education and ministry includes contributions from practitioners across the country. A valuable, current introduction to issues and concerns.

Christian Religious Education: Sharing Our Story and Vision. Thomas H. Groome (San Francisco: Harper & Row, 1980). This seminal book on religious educational content and process focuses on the nature and purpose of religious education, then presents a "shared praxis" model of action and reflection.

Contemporary Approaches to Christian Education, ed. Jack L. Seymour and Donald E. Miller (Nashville: Abingdon Press, 1982). With contributions from Sara P. Little, Charles R. Foster, Allen J. Moore, and Carold A. Wehrheim, this book overviews the practice of Christian education today.

Do It! Active Learning in Youth Ministry. Thom Schultz and Joani Schultz (Loveland, Col.: Group Books, 1987). This practical resource describes how to create experiential learning activities and includes numerous ready-to-use activities.

Effective Christian Education: A National Study of Protestant Congregations—Summary Report on Faith, Loyalty, and Congregational Life. Peter L. Benson and Carolyn H. Eklin (Minneapolis: Search Institute, 1990). This original report gives an overview of the study's findings. Reports with additional information on each denomination in the study are also available.

Empowering Disciples: Adult Education in the Church. William R. Adamson (Winfield, B.C.: Novalis/Wood Lake Books, 1990). Adamson helpfully distills the field of adult education and applies it to the church and its theology.

Exploring Christian Education Effectiveness. Eugene C. Roehlkepartain (Minneapolis: Search Institute, 1990). A practical, concise workbook to guide congregations in assessing their own Christian-education programs. Includes a workshop outline to be used with Christian-education leaders.

Exploring Faith Maturity: A Self-study Guide for Adults. Eugene C. Roehlkepartain and Dorothy L. Williams (Minneapolis: Search Institute, 1990). This guide helps adults explore the many dimensions of a mature faith and reflect on a self-assessment of spiritual understandings. The leader's version includes a manual with six fully planned group study sessions.

Exploring Faith Maturity: A Self-study Guide for Youth. Eugene C. Roehlkepartain and Dorothy L. Williams (Minneapolis: Search Institute, 1990). Similar to the adult version, but geared to the need and learning styles of teenagers.

Five Cries of Parents. Merton P. Strommen and A. Irene Strommen (San Francisco: Harper & Row, 1985). Based on Search Institute research, this book presents concerns of parents and how congregations can address the needs of families.

Five Cries of Youth, rev. ed. Merton P. Strommen (San Francisco: Harper & Row, 1988). Since the publication of the first edition in 1974, this resource has become a foundational resource for the needs and concerns of youth.

44 Ways to Expand the Teaching Ministry of Your Church. Lyle E. Schaller (Nashville: Abingdon Press, 1992). Schaller's practical suggestions run the gamut from scheduling to facilities, to organizing Sunday school, to structuring adult classes.

Harper's Encyclopedia of Religious Education, ed. Iris V. Cully and Kendig Brubaker Cully (San Francisco: Harper & Row, 1990). This indispensible reference book covers more than 600 topics in Christian education.

How Faith Matures. C. Ellis Nelson (Louisville: Westminster/John Knox Press, 1989). Nelson examines sources of faith and the central role of Christian education in faith development.

Mastering the Teaching of Adults. Jerold W. Apps (Malabar, Fla.: Krieger Publishing, 1991). A practical guide to basic skills for teaching adults, including an examination of myths, important teacher characteristics, and content issues.

The Pastor as Religious Educator, ed. Robert L. Browning (Birmingham, Ala.: Religious Education Press, 1989). This collection of expertise by leading thinkers in Christian education examines the theological roots of the pastor's role as educator.

The Power of Christian Education Video Series, produced by James V. Gambone (Minneapolis: Search Institute, 1990). Four videos present key elements of the *Effective Christian Education* study in a visual, attractive format: *Celebrating Possibility,* an inspirational look at congregations that make a difference in people's lives; *Taking Stock: The Shape of Faith Among American Protestants,* describes faith maturity and how to assess where church members are on their faith journey; *Faith Maturity: Where Does It Come From?* explores the crucial life experiences and congregational dynamics that promote mature faith; and *Promoting Faith Maturity: What Congregations Can Do,* suggests ideas for renewing congregational life by promoting effective Christian education.

Profiles of Congregational Life. An in-depth survey service from Search Institute which allows local congregations to survey their members concerning issues of faith maturity, congregational effectiveness, and Christian education. For information, call Search Institute's survey services department, 1-800-888-7828.

Rethinking Christian Education, ed. David S. Schuller (St. Louis: Chalice Press, 1993). Leading thinkers in Christian education expand on the study's findings, based on their own experience and expertise. Contributors include Martin E. Marty, Sara Little, David Ng, Merton P. Strommen, Mary Elizabeth Mullino Moore, Barbara Zigmund, Richard Robert Osmer, and William H. Willimon.

A Teachable Spirit: Recovering the Teaching Office in the Church. Richard Robert Osmer (Louisville: Westminster/John Knox Press, 1990). This historical and theological resource looks at the current state of mainline churches and argues that recovering the teaching office is vital for the future of the church.

Teaching from the Heart: Theology and Educational Method. Mary Elizabeth Mullino Moore (Minneapolis: Fortress Press, 1991). Critiques current educational methods and presents an "organic approach to religious, moral, and theological education."

The Teaching Minister. Clark M. Williamson and Ronald J. Allen (Louisville: Westminster/John Knox Press, 1991). After surveying the history of teaching in the Judeo-Christian tradition, the authors present practical ways pastors can make teaching integral to their ministry and congregational life.

To Set One's Heart: Belief and Teaching in the Church. Sara Little (Atlanta: John Knox Press, 1983). Focusing her thinking around nurturing faith and belief, Little details five models of teaching and how they contribute to faith development.

The Troubled Journey: A Portrait of 6th–12th Grade Youth. Peter L. Benson (Minneapolis: Search Institute, 1990, 1993). Using Search Institute research in public schools, Benson presents a framework for understanding youth in America today. He examines factors that prevent and contribute to at-risk behaviors.

Resources published by Search Institute are available from Search Institute, Thresher Square West, 700 South Third St., Suite 210, Minneapolis, MN 55415. Toll-free: 1-800-888-7828.

List of Worksheets

List of Figures

Appendix

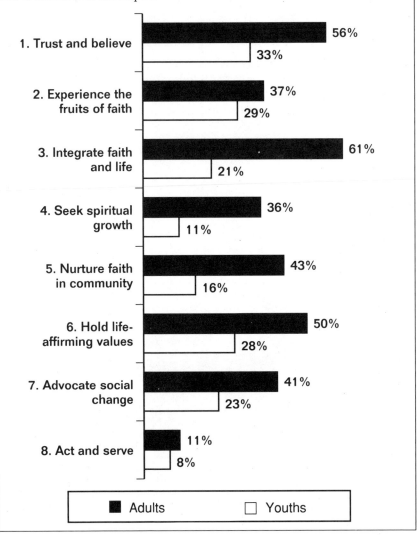

Figure 27
The Shape of Mainline Christians' Faith

Here are the percentages of adults and youths whose average score on the indicators for each mark of faith was 5 or higher, which suggests that this dimension of faith is well-developed.

	Adults	Youths
1. Trust and believe	56%	33%
2. Experience the fruits of faith	37%	29%
3. Integrate faith and life	61%	21%
4. Seek spiritual growth	36%	11%
5. Nurture faith in community	43%	16%
6. Hold life-affirming values	50%	28%
7. Advocate social change	41%	23%
8. Act and serve	11%	8%

■ Adults □ Youths

Figure 28
Denominational Differences in Christian Education Involvement

This chart compares the levels of Christian education involvement among youths and adults in the six denominations in the *Effective Christian Education* study.

Active in Christian Education	**Five Mainline Denominations**						
	Total	CC*	ELCA	PC	UCC	UMC	SBC
Grades K–6	**60%**	61%	67%	69%	66%	56%	48%
Grades 7–9	**52%**	55%	70%	48%	54%	45%	52%
Grades 10–12	**35%**	47%	32%	40%	33%	35%	49%
Adults	**28%**	35%	23%	31%	22%	29%	49%

**CC = Christian Church (Disciples of Christ); ELCA = Evangelical Lutheran Church in America; PC = Presybterian Church (U.S.A.); UCC = United Church of Christ; UMC = United Methodist Church; SBC = Southern Baptist Convention.*

Figure 29
Congregational Emphases:
Perceptions of Adults, Youths, and Pastors

Here are the percentages of adults, youths, and pastors who said each theme is a "strong" or "very strong" emphasis in their congregation (ranked in order by adult responses).

Emphasis in Congregation	Adults	Youths	Pastors
1. Music	75%	64%	58%
2. Supporting members in times of personal crisis	74%	67%	81%
3. Providing members with love, support, and friendship.	69%	79%	75%
4. Providing excellent Christian education for children.	69%	65%	57%
5. Providing meaningful and uplifting worship experiences.	67%	47%	81%
6. Encouraging members to commit their time, talent, and resources to their church.	64%	60%	57%
7. Providing excellent Christian education for adults.	63%	65%	48%
8. Providing excellent Christian education for teenagers.	61%	57%	41%
9. Teaching the Bible.	59%	69%	57%
10. Supporting missionary work.	51%	48%	33%
11. Reaching out to the poor and hungry.	48%	55%	47%
12. Encouraging personal commitment to Jesus.	46%	53%	45%
13. Giving members the strength to face the stress of everyday life.	42%	45%	65%
14. Helping members find meaning and purpose in their lives.	41%	41%	59%
15. Involving members in helping people in your town or city.	40%	41%	38%
16. Speaking out against the sin and evil in the world.	33%	31%	27%
17. Giving members answers to moral questions.	29%	29%	20%
18. Providing members a comforting refuge from all the pain and suffering in the world.	28%	31%	23%
19. Bringing the gospel to people outside the church.	17%	29%	18%
20. Helping members learn about people of different races and ethnic groups.	17%	17%	19%
21. Discussing national and international issues.	12%	16%	13%
22. Getting members to work for social justice and peace.	12%	21%	16%

Figure 30
Do Churches Have a Thinking Climate?

These percentages reflect adults' and teenagers' perceptions about whether their congregation has a thinking climate. The percentages represent those who answered "quite true" or "very true" to each item.

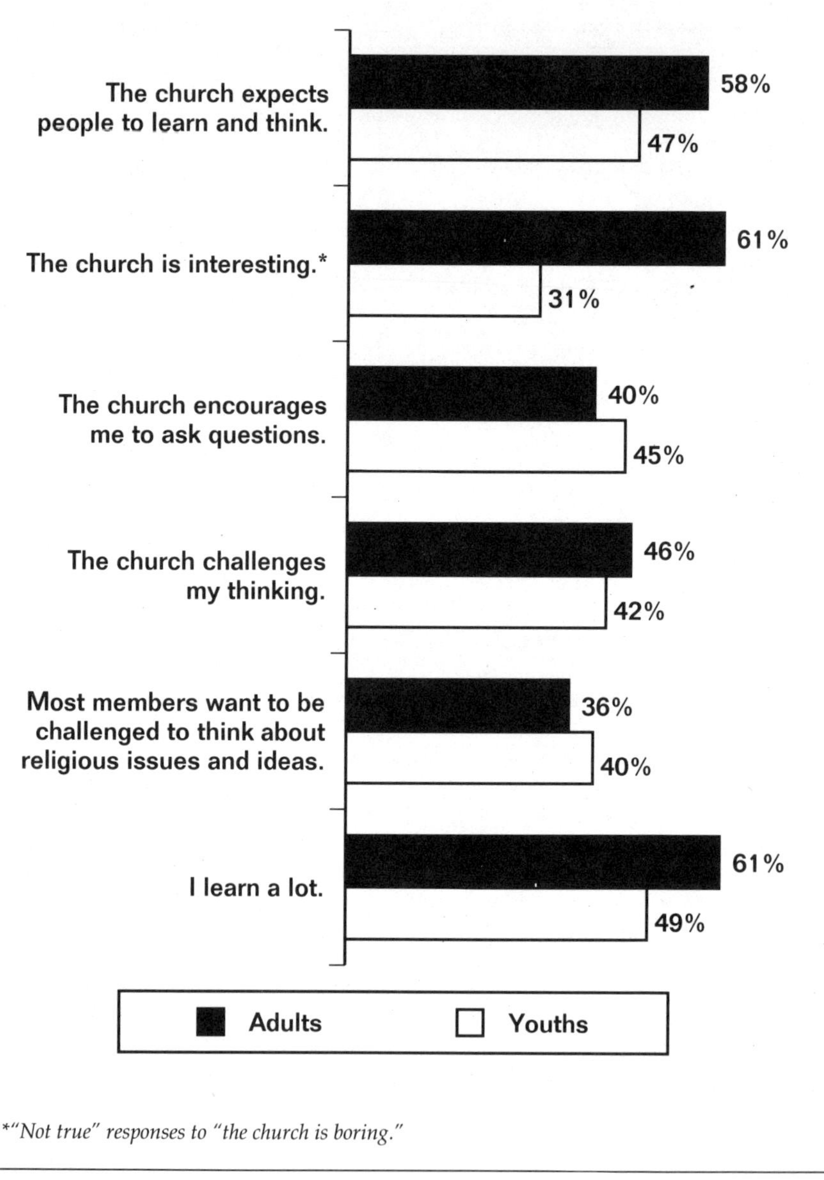

The church expects people to learn and think.
58%
47%
The church is interesting.*
61%
31%
The church encourages me to ask questions.
40%
45%
The church challenges my thinking.
46%
42%
Most members want to be challenged to think about religious issues and ideas.
36%
40%
I learn a lot.
61%
49%
Adults
Youths

*"Not true" responses to "the church is boring."

Figure 31
Curriculum Sources for Different Ages

This chart indicates the types of curriculum congregations use for various ages, based on responses from Christian education coordinators.

	Denomi-national	Another Denomi-nation	Non-De-nomina-tional	Self-Created	Combin-ation*
Kindergarten	60%	11%	11%	0.2%	18%
Grades 1 and 2	62%	9%	10%	0.2%	18%
Grades 3 and 4	62%	10%	10%	0.2%	17%
Grades 5 and 6	60%	10%	10%	1.4%	18%
Grades 7 and 8	50%	9%	10%	4%	25%
Grades 9 to 12	38%	10%	9%	5%	35%
Adult Bible studies	41%	8%	8%	4%	36%
Other adult education	35%	5%	9%	6%	40%

**The most common combination for children: denominational resources and resources from other denominations. The most common combination for youths and adults: denominational resources and nondenominational resources.*

Figure 32
Denominational Differences in Curriculum Choices

This chart compares the percentages of congregations in each denomination that use exclusively their own denomination's resources.

Age Level	CC*	ELCA	PC	UCC	UMC	SBC
Kindergarten	35%	69%	30%	33%	72%	89%
Grades 1 and 2	36%	71%	33%	34%	74%	92%
Grades 3 and 4	36%	72%	27%	35%	76%	95%
Grades 5 and 6	37%	66%	27%	35%	73%	91%
Grades 7 and 8	27%	63%	31%	31%	55%	85%
Grades 9 to 12	32%	45%	18%	24%	44%	86%
Adult Bible study	35%	44%	23%	17%	48%	89%

**CC = Christian Church (Disciples of Christ); ELCA = Evangelical Lutheran Church in America; PC = Presbyterian Church (U.S.A.); UCC = United Church of Christ; UMC = United Methodist Church; and SBC = Southern Baptist Convention.*

Figure 33
Teacher Interests, by Age Level

One way to begin teacher training is to discover teacher interests. Here are the percentages of teachers overall, and for each age level, who said they were "interested" or "very interested" in each topic (arranged by overall interests).

	All Teachers	Adult Teachers	Children's Teachers	Youth Teachers
Learning more about the Bible	81%	79%	82%	85%
Learning more about creative and innovative approaches to Christian education	64%	66%	68%	54%
Better Christian education planning in my church	59%	58%	64%	61%
Learning more about faith development	58%	55%	61%	66%
Getting more help on teaching techniques	53%	54%	56%	50%
Finding better curriculum materials	52%	50%	57%	55%
Learning more about my denomination's theology, tradition, and history	50%	50%	50%	52%
Learning how to evaluate my work as a Christian educator	50%	48%	56%	50%
Learning more about moral education and moral development	49%	47%	57%	47%
Learning more about parent education	48%	51%	54%	33%
More discussion about Christian education with other teachers	45%	45%	48%	41%
More teacher training events	44%	44%	49%	38%

Figure 34
Views of Scripture Inspiration

The *Effective Christian Education* study asked respondents to choose one of the following that best described their view of the Bible:

Interpretation by People of Faith—The Bible was written by persons who were motivated by a deep faith in God and who tried their best to describe and interpret their understanding of God and God's activity in the world.

God Inspired—The Bible is the Word of God. It was inspired by God and recorded by writers who interpreted God's message in the context of their times. It speaks truth on matters of faith and practice, but it may contain some historical and scientific errors.

God Dictated—The Bible is the Word of God. It was dictated by God, word for word, and recorded by writers who were not influenced by their times.

Everything in the Bible is true—historically, scientifically, and in matters of faith and practice.

Book of Wisdom, Legends, and Myths—The Bible records the stories, legends, and myths that people developed to understand the mysteries of life. It contains a great deal of wisdom and insight into the human experience.

A Religious Book—The Bible contains no more truth or wisdom than the religious books of other world religions.

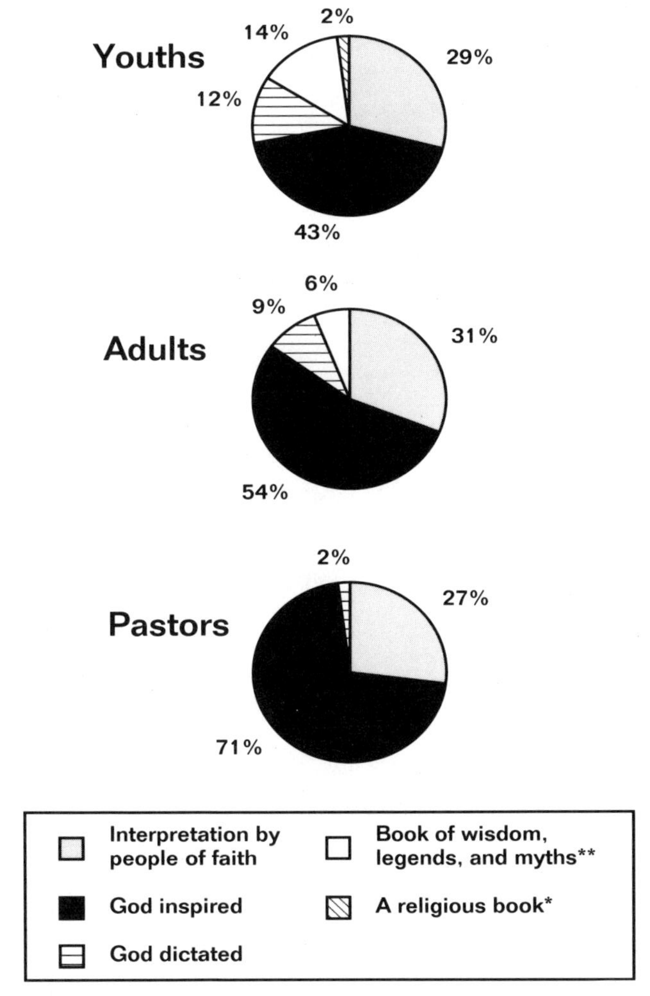

**Rounds to 0% for adults and pastors.*

***Rounds to 0% for pastors.*

Figure 35
Life Events of Active and Inactive Adults

This chart compares the percentages of active and inactive adults who say they have experienced each item in the past two to three years.

Life Experience	Most Active Adults	Inactive Adults
Receiving a lot of love from people in church	89%	35%
Receiving a lot of love from people outside church	73%	67%
A great deal of joy	73%	56%
A serious health problem (loved one)	54%	44%
Death of a loved one	52%	52%
Financial success	47%	39%
A great deal of sadness	36%	44%
Great stress in a job or loss of job	35%	46%
Financial hardship	25%	31%
A career change	24%	16%
A serious health problem (self)	22%	21%
Trouble with raising a child	17%	20%
Family problem with alcohol or other drugs	12%	11%
Legal problems	9%	10%
Marriage	8%	10%
Move to another town or city	8%	7%
Being a victim of crime	6%	8%
Divorce or separation	4%	3%
The birth of a child	6%	16%
Personal problem with alcohol or other drugs	1%	2%

Notes

INTRODUCTION

1. Dennis A. Williams et al., "Can the Schools Be Saved?" *Newsweek* (May 9, 1983), pp. 50-58.

2. Melinda Beck et al., "A Nation Still at Risk," *Newsweek* (May 2, 1988), pp. 54-55.

3. Statistics from the Southern Baptist Convention are not included except where specifically noted; rather, the report focuses on the five mainline denominations. This distinction is important partly because of sampling difficulties in the SBC. For more information, see Peter L. Benson and Carolyn H. Eklin, *Effective Christian Education: A National Study of Protestant Congregations—A Summary Report on Faith, Loyalty, and Congregational Life* (Minneapolis: Search Institute, 1990).

4. Richard Robert Osmer, *A Teachable Spirit: Recovering the Teaching Office in the Church* (Louisville: Westminster/John Knox Press, 1990), p. 5.

5. Benson and Eklin, *Effective Christian Education*, p. 58.

CHAPTER 1: MOVING CHRISTIAN EDUCATION TO CENTER STAGE

1. For a technical overview of the scientific survey process, see Peter L. Benson and Carolyn H. Eklin, *Effective Christian Education: A National Study of Protestant Congregations—A Summary Report on Faith, Loyalty, and Congregational Life* (Minneapolis: Search Institute, 1990), pp. 1-8, 71-79.

2. Ibid., p. 43.

3. Tim Stafford, "This Little Light of Mine: Will Sunday School Survive the 'Me Generation'?" *Christianity Today* (October 8, 1990), pp. 29-32.

4. C. Ellis Nelson, *How Faith Matures* (Louisville: Westminster/John Knox Press, 1989), pp. 182.

5. Ibid., p. 186.

6. Ibid., p. 196.

7. Richard Robert Osmer, *A Teachable Spirit* (Louisville: Westminster/John Knox Press, 1990), p. x.

8. The term *myth* is used in this context to refer to false perceptions, or as the dictionary says, "a notion based more on tradition or convenience than on fact."

9. C. Kirk Hadaway, *What Can We Do About Church Dropouts?* (Nashville: Abingdon Press, 1990), p. 94.

10. Jack L. Seymour and Donald E. Miller, *Contemporary Approaches to Christian Education* (Nashville: Abingdon Press, 1982), p. 147.

11. Malcolm Knowles, *The Adult Learner: A Neglected Species,* 3rd ed. (Houston: Gulf Publishing, 1984), pp. 52-53.

12. Seymour and Miller, *Contemporary Approaches,* p. 157.

13. Donald L. Griggs and Judy McKay Walther, *Christian Education in the Small Church* (Valley Forge: Judson Press, 1988), p. 11.

14. Nelson, *How Faith Matures,* p. 199.

CHAPTER 2. IN SEARCH OF FAITH MATURITY

1. Peter L. Benson and Carolyn H. Eklin, *Effective Christian Education: A National Study of Protestant Congregations—A Summary Report on Faith, Loyalty, and Congregational Life* (Minneapolis: Search Institute, 1990), p. 9.

2. V. Bailey Gillespie, *The Experience of Faith* (Birmingham, Ala.: Religious Education Press, 1988), pp. 56-57. Punctuation clarified.

3. Quoted in Mary C. Boys, *Educating in Faith: Maps & Visions* (San Francisco: Harper & Row, 1989), p. 16.

4. Gordon W. Allport, "The Religious Context of Prejudice," *Journal for the Scientific Study of Religion* (1966) 5:447-57.

5. James W. Fowler, "Faith and the Structure of Meaning," *Faith Development and Fowler,* ed. Craig Dykstra and Sharon Parks (Birmingham, Ala.: Religious Education Press, 1986), p. 15.

6. For a complete discussion of the development of the faith maturity index as well as its scientific reliability, see Peter L. Benson, Michael J. Donahue, and Joseph A. Erickson, "The Conceptualization and Measurement of Faith Maturity," *Research in the Social Scientific Study of Religion,* Vol. 5, ed. Monty L. Lynn and David O. Moberg (Greenwich, Conn.: JAI Press, 1993).

7. Thomas H. Groome, *Christian Religious Education* (San Francisco: Harper & Row, 1989), p. 61.

8. Dietrich Bonhoeffer, *The Cost of Discipleship* (New York: Macmillan, 1963), p. 69.

9. Good News Bible.

10. Suzanne Johnson, *Christian Spiritual Formation in the Church and Classroom* (Nashville: Abingdon Press, 1989), p. 124.

11. *Exploring Faith Maturity,* a series of study guides for youths and adults, build upon this model of faith maturity. Leaders guides are included for group use. Available from Search Institute.

12. David A. Roozen, William McKinney, and Wayne Thompson, "The 'Big Chill' Generation Warms to Worship: A Research Note," *Review of Religious Research* (March 1990), pp. 314-22.

13. Robert Wuthnow, *The Restructuring of American Religion* (Princeton: University Press, 1988), p. 266.

14. About 4.5 percent of the survey respondents were people of color, a figure that roughly matches the percentage of racial/ethnic representation in these denominations (about 3%).

See Wade Clark Roof and William McKinney, *American Mainline Religion: Its Changing Shape and Future* (New Brunswick, N.J.: Rutgers University Press, 1987), pp. 141-42.

We would have preferred not to group all minorities together, given the uniquenesses of each population. But the small numbers of minorities in the sample inhibit further breakdown.

15. According to Gallup polls, 31 percent of all Americans believe the Bible is "the actual word of God and is to be taken literally, word for word," cited in George Gallup, Jr., and Jim Castelli, *The People's Religion: American Faith in the 90's* (New York: Macmillan, 1989), pp. 60-61.

16. See Michael J. Donahue, "Prevalence of New Age Beliefs in Six Protestant Denominations," paper presented at the meeting of the Society for the Scientific Study of Religion, Pittsburgh, November 8, 1991.

17. James W. Fowler, *Becoming Adult, Becoming Christian: Adult Development and Christian Faith* (San Francisco: Harper & Row, 1984), pp. 67-71.

18. Ibid., pp. 57-64.

19. For a more detailed study of at-risk behaviors among youths, and the congregation's potential impact, see Peter L. Benson, *The Troubled Journey: A Portrait of 6th-12th Grade Youth* (Minneapolis: Search Institute, 1990, 1993).

20. Carolyn H. Eklin and Eugene C. Roehlkepartain, "The Faith Factor: What Role Can Churches Play in At-Risk Prevention?" *Source Newsletter* (February 1992).

CHAPTER 3. NURTURING CONGREGATIONAL AND DENOMINATIONAL LOYALTY

1. Richard N. Ostling, "Those Mainline Blues," *Time Magazine* (May 22, 1989), p. 94.

2. J. Edward Carothers, *The Paralysis of Mainstream Protestant Leadership* (Nashville: Abingdon Press, 1990), p. 11.

3. C. Kirk Hadaway, *What Can We Do About Church Dropouts?* (Nashville: Abingdon Press, 1990), chap. 1.

4. Wade Clark Roof and William McKinney, *American Mainline Religion: Its Changing Shape and Future* (New Brunswick, N.J.: Rutgers University Press, 1987), p. 233.

5. Barry A. Kosmin and Seymour P. Lachman, *Research Report: The National Survey of Religious Identification, 1989-90 (Selected Tabulations)*, (New York: The Graduate School and University Center of the City University of New York, 1991), pp. 3-4.

6. Roof and McKinney, *American Mainline Religion*, pp. 40-52.

7. Quoted in Jon R. Stone, "The New Volunteerism and Presbyterian Affiliation," *The Mainstream Protestant "Decline": The Presbyterian Pattern*, ed. Milton J. Coalter, John M. Mulder, and Louis Weeks (Louisville: Westminster/John Knox Press, 1990), p. 142.

8. Quoted in Hadaway, *What Can We Do About Church Dropouts?* p. 24.

CHAPTER 4. PROMOTING FAITH THROUGH CONGREGATIONAL LIFE

1. Quoted in C. Kirk Hadaway, *What Can We Do About Church Dropouts?* (Nashville: Abingdon Press, 1990), p. 58.
2. Daniel G. Bagby, *The Church: The Power to Help and to Hurt* (Nashville: Broadman Press, 1989), p. 123.
3. A helpful manual for creating such an atmosphere is Stephen Kliewer, *How to Live with Diversity in the Local Church* (Washington, D.C.: Alban Institute, 1987).
4. *Active* involvement in church is defined as attending worship weekly or more often, attending a nonworship event 3 or more hours in the last month, *and* volunteering 3 or more hours of service at or through the church in the past month. *Inactive* is defined as never attending worship or only attending a few times a year, or never attended anything other than worship in the past month, and giving no service at or through the church in the past month.
5. Roy M. Oswald and Speed B. Leas, *The Inviting Church: A Study of New Member Assimilation* (Washington, D.C.: Alban Institute, 1987), pp. 51-52.
6. "Forget the Name Tags," *Christianity Today* (December 17, 1990), p. 46.
7. Bagby, *The Church,* p. 119.
8. C. Ellis Nelson, "Congregations' Educational Strategy," *Carriers of Faith: Lessons from Congregational Studies,* ed. Carl S. Dudley, Jackson W. Carroll, and James P. Wind (Louisville: Westminster/John Knox Press, 1991), p. 164.
9. *The Church Today: Insightful Statistics and Commentary* (Glendale, Cal.: Barna Research Group, 1990), pp. 24-25.
10. Kennon L. Callahan, *Twelve Keys to an Effective Church* (San Francisco: Harper & Row, 1983), pp. 24-33.
11. Hadaway, *What Can We Do About Church Dropouts?* p. 41.
12. Duane A. Ewers, *Do You Care?: Compassion in the Sunday School* (Nashville: United Methodist Discipleship Resources, 1988), p. 5.
13. Kenneth C. Haugk, *Christian Caregiving—A Way of Life* (Minneapolis: Augsburg Press, 1984).
14. Peter L. Benson and Carolyn H. Eklin, *Effective Christian Education: A National Study of Protestant Congregation—A Summary Report on Faith, Loyalty, and Congregational Life* (Minneapolis: Search Institute, 1990), p. 66.
15. Suzanne Johnson, *Christian Spiritual Formation in the Church and Classroom* (Nashville: Abingdon Press, 1989), p. 154.
16. Carl S. Dudley and Sally A. Johnson, "Congregational Self-images for Social Ministry," *Carriers of Faith: Lessons From Congregational Studies,* ed. Carl S. Dudley, Jackson W. Carroll, and James P. Wind (Louisville: Westminster/John Knox Press, 1991), pp. 105, 120. (Chapter 10, *The Teaching Church,* explores these images in detail.)

17. Joseph B. Tamney and Stephen D. Johnson, "Religious Diversity and Ecumenical Social Action," *Review of Religious Research* (September 1990), pp. 16-26.
18. Clark M Williamson and Ronald J. Allen, *The Teaching Minister* (Louisville: Westminster/John Knox Press, 1991), p. 106.

CHAPTER 5. HOW CHURCHES SHAPE THEIR EDUCATIONAL MINISTRIES

1. Peter L. Benson and Carolyn H. Eklin, *Effective Christian Education: A National Study of Protestant Congregations—A Summary Report on Faith, Loyalty, and Congregational Life* (Minneapolis: Search Institute, 1990), p. 54.
2. Ibid., p. 54.
3. Here are brief descriptions of these Bible study programs, based on John E. Schwarz, "Twenty Popular Adult Bible Study Programs," *Word and World* (Winter 1990), pp. 60-69:

- *The Bethel Series* was developed by a Lutheran pastor in Wisconsin and surveys the Bible in two years. It includes a 2-week training program for leaders.
- Developed by a United Methodist bishop, *Disciple Bible Study* is a 34-lesson study of the Bible, focusing on discipleship. The course includes some videotaped lectures, as well as a 2-day training for leaders.
- *Search Weekly Bible Studies* is a 5-year course developed by the American Lutheran Church (now ELCA), which covers five biblical themes. The material emphasizes getting adults to read the Bible, reflect on their faith, and reach out to others.
- *The Kerygma Program* was originally developed by a Presbyterian church in Pittsburgh. Its series surveys various biblical themes in 2-hour sessions.
- *Word & Witness* is a 2-year thematic study of the Bible, with heavy concentration on evangelism. It includes 12 days of training for leaders.
- *Trinity Bible Studies* was developed by a United Methodist pastor and includes two 10-lesson classes on the Old and New Testaments. Its three emphases are facts, meaning, and application.
- Developed by an Australian Lutheran pastor, *Crossways!* is a 2-year, book-by-book survey of the Bible and its major themes.

4. Robert Wuthnow, *The Restructuring of American Religion* (Princeton, N.J.: University Press, 1988), p. 126.
5. Ibid., p. 125.
6. Comparisons of active and inactive teenagers found that 74 percent of teenagers who are highly active in church also spend time each week in school clubs. But only 52 percent of inactive teenagers do. Similar differences appear when we look at involvement in music, sports, and nonschool clubs or organizations.

CHAPTER 6. MANAGING AN EFFECTIVE CHRISTIAN EDUCATION PROGRAM

1. Norman R. DePuy, "Responsibility and Authority in the Church," *The Christian Ministry* (March 1987), p. 7.

2. Susanne Johnson, "Administration: Equipping the Saints for Religious Education Ministry," *Religious Education in the Small Membership Church,* ed. Nancy T. Foltz (Birmingham, Ala.: Religious Education Press, 1990), pp. 113-14.

3. DePuy, "Responsibility and Authority, p. 7.

4. William E. Hull, "Ministry by Objectives," *Christian Ministry* (March 1987), p. 19.

5. Ibid.

6. Ibid., pp. 19-20.

7. Jack L. Seymour and Donald E. Miller, *Contemporary Approaches to Christian Education* (Nashville: Abingdon Press, 1982).

8. Sara P. Little, "Religious Instruction," Seymour and Miller, *Contemporary Approaches to Christian Education,* p. 47.

9. Task Force on Education of Young Adolescents, *Turning Points: Preparing American Youth for the 21st Century* (New York: Carnegie Council on Adolescent Development, 1989), pp. 66-67.

10. For a discussion of the role of intergenerational education, see James W. White, *Intergenerational Religious Education* (Birmingham, Ala.: Religious Education Press, 1988).

11. Dennis H. Dirks, "Evaluation," *Harper's Encyclopedia of Religious Education,* ed. Iris V. Cully and Kendig Brubaker Cully (San Francisco: Harper & Row, 1990), p. 233.

12. Search Institute's *Profile of Congregational Life* is an extensive survey to help congregations assess the attitudes, beliefs, perceptions, and religious experiences of their members. Congregations administer the survey, then Search Institute analyzes the results and sends a custom report to the congregation. For information, contact Search Institute's survey services.

A self-administered survey of youth developed by Search Institute is available in Peter L. Benson and Dorothy L. Williams, *Determining Needs in Your Youth Ministry* (Loveland, Col.: Group Books, 1987).

13. Gaylord Noyce, "Administration as Ministry: Taking the Long View," *Christian Ministry* (March 1987), p. 14.

CHAPTER 7. LEADERS WHO MAKE A DIFFERENCE

1. Kennon L. Callahan, *Twelve Keys to an Effective Church* (San Francisco: Harper & Row, 1983), p. 41.

2. Susan Tifft, "Who's Teaching Our Children?" *Time* (November 14, 1988), p. 59.

3. Roy Oswald, with Jackie McMakin, *How to Prevent Lay Leader Burnout* (Washington, D.C.: Alban Institute, 1984), p. 31.

4. One helpful model of training workshops that use innovative teaching techniques, the Volunteer Training Series, is available from Group Books, Box 481, Loveland, CO 80539. Though aimed at youth ministry volunteers, several workshops in these training books have broad application in Christian education.

5. Donald L. Griggs and Judy McKay Walther, *Christian Education in the Small Church* (Valley Forge, Penna.: Judson Press, 1988), pp. 64-65.

6. Oswald, *How to Prevent Lay Leader Burnout*, p. 33.

7. Ibid., pp. 31-32.

8. *What Works: Research About Teaching and Learning* (Washington, D.C.: U.S. Department of Education, 1986), p. 52.

9. William H. Willimon, *Clergy and Laity Burnout* (Nashville: Abingdon Press, 1989), pp. 84-85.

10. Ibid., p. 8.

11. Oswald, *How to Prevent Lay Leader Burnout*, p. 29.

12. Marlene Wilson, *How to Mobilize Church Volunteers* (Minneapolis: Augsburg Publishing, 1983), p. 53.

13. In this study, the Christian education coordinator was identified as that person in the congregation with primary responsibility for Christian education. This person could be either professional staff or a volunteer.

14. Jack L. Seymour and Donald E. Miller, "The Future of Christian Education," *Contemporary Approaches to Christian Education*, ed. Seymour and Miller (Nashville: Abingdon Press, 1982), p. 155.

15. Griggs and Walther, *Christian Education in the Small Church*, p. 45.

16. Quoted in Clark M. Williamson and Ronald J. Allen, *The Teaching Minister* (Louisville: Westminster/John Knox Press, 1991), p. 61.

17. Author's interview with Dr. David S. Schuller, March 27, 1990, in St. Louis, Missouri.

18. Richard Robert Osmer, *A Teachable Spirit: Recovering the Teaching Office in the Church* (Louisville: Westminster/John Knox Press, 1990), p. 205.

19. Janet F. Fishburn, "Leading: Paideia in a New Key," *Congregations: Their Power to Form and Transform*, ed. C. Ellis Nelson (Atlanta: John Knox Press, 1988), p. 203.

20. Daniel Buttry, *Bringing Your Church Back to Life: Beyond Survival Mentality* (Valley Forge, Penna.: Judson Press, 1988), pp. 85-86.

21. *What Works: Research About Teaching and Learning*, p. 50.

22. William R. Adamson, *Empowering Disciples: Adult Education in the Church* (Winfield, B.C.: Novalis/Wood Lake, 1990), p. 25.

23. Seymour and Miller, "Openings to God: Education and Theology in Dialogue," *Theological Approaches to Christian Education*, pp. 9-10.

24. While it would be difficult to measure teachers' faith maturity using the scale developed for the national study, leaders should have a good sense of the faith lives of teachers. Use the survey in chapter 2 as a reminder of the characteristics. It might also be appropriate to use *Exploring Faith Maturity: A Self-study Guide for Adults* (Minneapolis: Search Institute, 1990) as study material for a teacher retreat. It includes a self-assessment for teachers.

25. See Robert K. Greenleaf, *Servant Leadership* (Ramsey, N.J.: Paulist Press, 1978) and Jackson W. Carroll, *As One with Authority: Reflective Leadership in Ministry* (Louisville: Westminster/John Knox Press, 1991).

26. Carroll, *As One with Authority,* p. 100.

27. Ibid., p. 105.

28. Ibid., p. 105.

29. Jackie McMakin, "Vocation: A Key to Energizing Lay Ministries," *How to Prevent Lay Leader Burnout,* ed. Oswald, p. 37.

CHAPTER 8. WHAT SHOULD WE STUDY?

1. Barbara Dolan, "Full House at Willow Creek," *Time* (March 6, 1989), p. 60.

2. Peter L. Benson and Carolyn H. Eklin, *Effective Christian Education: A National Study of Protestant Congregations—Summary Report on Faith, Loyalty, and Congregational Life* (Minneapolis: Search Institute, 1990), p. 54.

3. Since the study sample did not include children, the study does not directly address content areas for younger ages.

4. Merton P. Strommen, *Five Cries of Youth,* rev. ed. (San Francisco: Harper & Row, 1988), pp. 144-45.

5. Jolene L. Roehlkepartain, "Baffled by the Bible," *Jr. High Ministry Magazine* (November-December 1989), p. 12.

6. Dean R. Hoge et al., "Desired Outcomes of Religious Education and Youth Ministry in Six Denominations," *Religious Education Ministry with Youth,* ed. D. Campbell Wyckoff and Don Richter (Birmingham, Ala.: Religious Education Press, 1982), p. 136.

7. Quoted in Dorothy Williams, *There Is a Season: Studies in Human Sexuality for Youth of Christian Churches and Their Parents,* Teacher Manual (Dubuque: Wm. C. Brown, 1985), pp. 7-8.

8. According to a national RespecTeen survey of almost 47,000 young people in public and private schools, conducted by Search Institute, 60 percent of 12th graders are sexually active. Reported in Peter L. Benson, *The Troubled Journey: A Portrait of 6th-12th Grade Youth* (Minneapolis: Search Institute, 1990, 1993), p. 43.

9. Marilyn Elias, "Early Teen Sex May Indicate Drugs, Drinking," *USA Today* (February 6, 1991).

10. Based on percentage of young people who report 11 hours or more study of sexuality issues through the church in their lifetime.

11. Based on percentage of young people who report 11 hours or more study of drugs and alcohol through the church in their lifetime.

12. Many churches have found Search Institute's curriculum *Human Sexuality: Values & Choices* easily adaptable to the church setting, to provide comprehensive, abstinence-based sexuality education to seventh- and eighth-grade students.

13. Robert Coles, *Girl Scouts Survey on the Beliefs and Morals of America's Children* (New York: Girl Scouts of America, 1990), pp. 24-27.

14. Ibid., p. 56.

15. Frederick Buechner, *Wishful Thinking: A Theological ABC* (San Francisco: Harper & Row, 1973), p. 15.
16. Strommen, *Five Cries of Youth,* p. 74.
17. Barbara B. Varenhorst, with Lee Sparks, *Training Teenagers for Peer Ministry* (Loveland, Col.: Group Books, 1988).
18. Walt Marcum, *Sharing Groups in Youth Ministry* (Nashville: Abingdon Press, 1991).
19. Religious News Service, "Gaps Found in Bible Reading," *National Christian Reporter* (January 18, 1991), p. 1.
20. William R. Adamson, *Empowering Disciples: Adult Education in the Church* (Winfield, B.C.: Novalis/Wood Lake, 1990), p. 183.
21. William E. Diehl, *Thank God, It's Monday!* (Philadelphia: Fortress Press, 1982), p. xi.
22. Stephen Hart and David Krueger, "Faith and Work: Challenges for Congregations," *The Christian Century* (July 15-22, 1992), pp. 683-86.
23. Clark M. Williamson and Ronald J. Allen, *The Teaching Minister* (Louisville: Westminster/John Knox Press, 1991), p. 74.
24. C. Ellis Nelson, *How Faith Matures* (Louisville: Westminster/John Knox Press, 1989), p. 204.
25. Stan L. Albrecht and Marie Cornwall, "Life Events and Religious Change," *Review of Religious Research* (September 1989), pp. 23-38.
26. Adamson, *Empowering Disciples,* p. 152.

CHAPTER 9. HOW DO WE STUDY?

1. Peter Swet, "Who's That Funny Guy with the Wrench?" *Parade Magazine* (August 26, 1990), pp. 4-5.
2. William R. Adamson, *Empowering Disciples: Adult Education in the Church* (Winfield, B.C.: Novalis/Wood Lake, 1990), p. 9.
3. Ibid., pp. 44-45.
4. Peter L. Benson and Carolyn H. Eklin, *Effective Christian Education: A National Study of Protestant Congregations—A Summary Report on Faith, Loyalty, and Congregational Life* (Minneapolis: Search Institute, 1990), p. 54.
5. Summarized in Malcolm Knowles, *The Adult Learner: A Neglected Species,* 3rd ed. (Houston: Gulf Publishing, 1984), pp. 86-87.
6. Ibid., pp. 189-91.
7. Thom Schultz and Joani Schultz, *Do It! Active Learning in Youth Ministry* (Loveland, Col.: Group Books, 1987), p. 13.
8. Adamson, *Empowering Disciples,* p. 41.
9. Quoted in Knowles, *Adult Learner,* p. 88.
10. "A Nation at Risk: Another View," a joint statement of the National Association for Experiential Education, the Council for the Advancement of Experiential Learning, and the National Society for Internships and Experiential Education.

Reprinted in *Growing Hope: A Sourcebook on Integrating Youth Service into the School Curriculum,* Pilot Edition (Minneapolis: National Youth Leadership Council, 1989), section 1, pp. 2-3.

11. Schultz and Schultz, *Do It!* p. 10.

12. Jane Kendall, "From Youth Service to Service Learning," excerpted in *Growing Hope,* section 1, p. 19.

13. Adapted from Schultz and Schultz, *Do It!* pp. 41-46.

14. Eugene C. Roehlkepartain, *Youth Ministry in City Churches* (Loveland, Col.: Group Books, 1989), pp. 143-44.

15. Dean E. Feldmeyer, "Building a 'Storm Home' for Youth Ministry," *The Christian Ministry* (July 1987), p. 8.

16. Denny Rydberg, *Building Community in Youth Groups* (Loveland, Col.: Group Books, 1985), pp. 18-21.

17. Roland D. Martinson, *Effective Youth Ministry: A Congregational Approach* (Minneapolis: Augsburg Press, 1988), p. 102.

18. Anthony Campolo, *Ideas for Social Action* (El Cajon, Cal.: Youth Specialties, 1983), p. 10.

19. Knowles, *Adult Learner,* p. 14.

20. Ibid., pp. 76-78.

21. Thomas H. Groome, *Christian Religious Education: Sharing Our Story and Vision* (San Francisco: Harper & Row, 1980), p. 188.

22. Adamson, *Empowering Disciples,* p. 39.

23. *Faith Development and Your Ministry* (Princeton: Princeton Religious Research Center, n.d.), p. 60.

24. Knowles, *Adult Learner,* pp. 84-85.

25. Adamson, *Empowering Disciples,* p. 152.

26. Stephen Kliewer, *How to Live with Diversity in the Local Church* (Washington, D.C.: Alban Institute, 1987), p. 37.

27. Quoted in Knowles, *Adult Learner,* p. 90.

CHAPTER 10. FAITH IN ACTION

1. Donald G. Emler, *Revisioning the DRE* (Birmingham, Ala.: Religious Education Press, 1989), p. 59.

2. Focusing this chapter exclusively on the horizontal dimension of faith is not intended to indicate this dimension's priority over the vertical dimension. Rather, it seeks to correct the imbalance in the reality that the vertical dimension already tends to be more strongly emphasized in congregations.

3. Patricia Washburn and Robert Gribbon, *Peacemaking Without Division: Moving Beyond Congregational Apathy and Anger* (Washington, D.C.: Alban Institute, 1986), pp. 3-8.

4. Ibid., p. 7.

5. Ibid.

6. Also see Eugene C. Roehlkepartain, *Building Bridges: Teens in Community Service* (Minneapolis: Lutheran Brotherhood, 1991). Available free of charge by calling 1-800-888-3820.

7. Commission on Work, Family and Citizenship, *The Forgotten Half: Pathways to Success for America's Youth and Young Families*, Final Report (Washington, D.C.: William T. Grant Foundation, 1988), p. 79.

8. Dan Conrad and Diane Hedin, *High School Community Service: A Review of Research and Programs* (Madison, Wis.: National Center on Effective Secondary Schools, 1989), p. 27.

9. Jane C. Kendall and Associates, *Combining Service and Learning: A Resource Book for Community and Public Service, Vol. I* (Raleigh, N.C.: National Society for Internships and Experiential Education, 1990). For more information, contact the organization at 3509 Haworth Drive, Suite 207, Raleigh, NC 27609; Ph. 919-787-3263. For another foundational guide, see Dan Conrad and Diane Hedin, *Youth Service: A Guidebook for Developing and Operating Effective Programs* (Washington, D.C.: Independent Sector, 1987).

10. Marlene Wilson, *How to Mobilize Church Volunteers* (Minneapolis: Augsburg Press, 1983), p. 107.

11. Carl S. Dudley, "From Typical Church to Social Ministry: A Study of the Elements Which Mobilize Congregations," *Review of Religious Research* (March 1991), pp. 195-212. Dudley also presents his findings with Sally A. Johnson in *Carriers of Faith: Lessons from Congregational Studies*, ed. Carl S. Dudley, Jackson W. Carroll, and James P. Wind (Westminster/John Knox Press, 1991), pp. 104-21.

12. Dudley and Johnson, *Carriers of Faith*, p. 112.

13. Ibid., p. 110.

14. Ibid., p. 113.

15. Ibid., p. 120.

CHAPTER 11. NURTURING FAITH IN FAMILIES

1. Eugene C. Roehlkepartain, ed., *The Youth Ministry Resource Book* (Loveland, Col.: Group Books, 1987), p. 25.

2. Richard P. Olson and Joe H. Leonard, Jr., *Ministry with Families in Flux: The Church and Changing Patterns of Life* (Louisville: Westminster/John Knox Press, 1990), p. 9.

3. Janet Huber Lowry, "Families in Church and Society: Sociological Perspectives," *Faith and Families*, ed. Lindell Sawyers (Philadelphia: Geneva Press, 1986), p. 43.

4. Olin Robison, "Speaking the Truth to Our Children," *Christian Century* (December 3, 1986), p. 193.

5. Peter L. Benson, *The Troubled Journey: A Portrait of 6th–12th Grade Youth* (Minneapolis: Search Institute, 1990, 1993), p. 92.

6. John Bradshaw, *Bradshaw on the Family: A Revolutionary Way of Self-discovery* (Deerfield Beach, Fla.: Health Communications, 1988), p. 26.

7. Merton P. Strommen and A. Irene Strommen, *Five Cries of Parents* (San Francisco: Harper & Row, 1985), p. 130.

8. Ibid., pp. 133-34.

9. Roehlkepartain, *Youth Ministry Resource Book*, p. 32.

10. Strommen and Strommen, *Five Cries of Parents*, p. 134.

11. "Family Meals: On the Verge of Extinction," *Parents of Teenagers* (February-March 1991), p. 27.

12. Jim Larson, *A Church Guide for Strengthening Families: Strategies, Models, Programs, and Resources* (Minneapolis: Augsburg Press, 1984), pp. 17-18.

13. George Gallup, Jr., and Jim Castelli, *The People's Religion: American Faith in the 90's* (New York: Macmillan, 1989), p. 147.

14. Archbishop Thomas C. Kelly, O.P., and the Archdiocesan Planning Commission, *Teaching and Sharing Our Faith: Lifelong Formation and Education in the Archdiocese of Louisville* (Louisville: Archdiocese of Louisville, 1990), p. 12.

15. Carol Rose Ikeler, "Family Worship," *Harper's Encyclopedia of Religious Education*, ed. Iris V. Cully and Kendig Brubaker Cully (San Francisco: Harper & Row, 1990), pp. 705-6.

16. Trevor's complete story is told in Frank and Janet Ferrell, *Trevor's Place: The Story of the Boy Who Brings Hope to the Homeless*, rev. ed. (San Francisco: Harper & Row, 1990).

17. James McGinnis and Kathleen McGinnis, "The Social Mission of the Family," *Faith and Families*, ed. Sawyers, p. 101.

18. Kathleen McGinnis and James McGinnis, *Parenting for Peace and Justice: Ten Years Later* (Maryknoll, N.Y.: Orbis Books, 1990), pp. 97-111.

19. Olson and Leonard, *Ministry with Families in Flux*, pp. 179-180.

20. Joe Leonard, Jr., *Planning Family Ministry: A Guide for a Teaching Church* (Valley Forge, Penna.: Judson Press, 1982), p. 51.

CHAPTER 12. WHERE HAVE ALL THE PEOPLE GONE?

1. Roland D. Martinson, *Effective Youth Ministry: A Congregational Approach* (Minneapolis: Augsburg Press, 1988), p. 99.

2. Ibid., p. 97.

3. C. Kirk Hadaway, *Church Growth Principles: Separating Fact from Fiction* (Nashville: Broadman Press, 1991), p. 128.

4. Kenneth L. Woodward, "A Time to Seek," *Newsweek* (December 17, 1990), p. 52.

5. Ibid., p. 51.

6. *The Unchurched American: Ten Years Later*, ed. George Gallup, Jr. (Princeton, N.J.: Princeton Religion Research Center, 1988), p. 61.

AFTERWORD: CREATING A NEW FUTURE

1. John H. Leith, *From Generation to Generation* (Louisville: Westminster/John Knox Press, 1990), p. 19.

2. May Boys, *Educating in Faith: Maps and Visions* (New York: Harper & Row, 1989), p. 3.

3. Larry E. Decker and Associates, *Community Education: Building Learning Communities*, rev. ed. (Alexandria, Va.: National Community Education Association, 1992).

4. Decker, *Community Education*, p. 3.